Leeds Trinity University

LIBRARY

This book is due for return on or before the last date stamped below

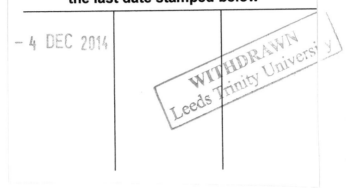

MANCHESTER
1824

Manchester University Pr~

D0542243

Pockets of resistance

British news media,
war and theory in the
2003 invasion of Iraq

Piers Robinson, Peter Goddard,
Katy Parry and Craig Murray
with Philip M. Taylor

Manchester University Press

Manchester and New York

distributed in the United States exclusively by Palgrave Macmillan

Published by Manchester University Press
Oxford Road, Manchester M13 9NR, UK
and Room 400, 175 Fifth Avenue, New York, NY 10010, USA
www.manchesteruniversitypress.co.uk

070·44995670443
ROB

Distributed in the United States exclusively by
Palgrave Macmillan, 175 Fifth Avenue, New York,
NY 10010, USA

Distributed in Canada exclusively by
UBC Press, University of British Columbia, 2029 West Mall,
Vancouver, BC, Canada V6T 1Z2

British Library Cataloguing-in-Publication Data
A catalogue record for this book is available from the British Library

Library of Congress Cataloging-in-Publication Data applied for

ISBN 978 0 7190 8445 4 paperback
ISBN 978 0 7190 8158 3 hardback

First published 2010

Typeset in Minion
by Servis Filmsetting Ltd, Stockport, Cheshire
Printed in Great Britain
by CPI Antony Rowe, Chippenham, Wiltshire

Contents

List of tables and figures

Tables

Figures

Preface and acknowledgements

It is has often been noted that news reporting of war tends to introduce new terminology to the language. Such terms generally originate from briefings and other government and military media-management activities attended by journalists. While watching and reading some of the extensive British news coverage given to the 2003 invasion of Iraq, one of the new phrases that we noticed was 'pockets of resistance'. Journalists would report that significant Iraqi positions had been taken by coalition forces but that 'pockets of resistance' remained, often making it too dangerous to travel there. We found the implications of this term, and the fact that it had passed into news coverage largely without challenge, to be revealing: it seemed to allow the coalition to claim that targeted locations had fallen before Iraqi resistance had actually been overcome. This was but one of many aspects of the news reporting of the invasion that raised questions for us and inspired us to want to enquire in detail into how the war was reported. This book is the end result of that enquiry.

This book derives from an 18-month-long project funded by the Economic and Social Research Council (ESRC): 'Media Wars: News Media Performance and Media Management during the 2003 Iraq War' (RES-000–23–0551). The principal applicant was Piers Robinson, co-applicants Peter Goddard, Robin Brown, Philip M. Taylor; the principal research assistant was Katy Parry, and Craig Murray and Cristina Archetti were also research assistants. The media analysis was conducted at the School of Politics and Communication Studies, University of Liverpool (Piers Robinson, Peter Goddard, Katy Parry, Craig Murray) while the media-management analysis was conducted at the Institute of Communications Studies, University of Leeds (Robin Brown, Philip M. Taylor, Cristina Archetti).

Although the production of this book has been a collaborative effort, Piers Robinson was the primary writer, responsible for the development of the theoretical material and oversight of the project, Peter Goddard contributed analysis of UK press performance, including the case study of Ali Abbas, and provided oversight of the writing and drafting, Katy Parry contributed analysis of visuals, while Craig Murray took the initial lead on the case study analysis of the UK anti-war movement. As part of the Leeds University-based team analysing media management, Philip M. Taylor contributed analysis of coalition media-management operations.

In addition, for their love and support, we would like to thank our families: Stefanie Haueis, Clara Haueis-Robinson and Marie Haueis-Robinson, Martha Goddard and Ben Goddard, Paul Foster, Arna Vikanes Sørheim. For intellectual feedback and encouragement, we wish to thank Stefanie Haueis, Scott Althaus, Rodney Benson, John Corner, Neil Gavin, Daniel Hallin, Eric Herring, Phil Seib, Howard Tumber, Gadi Wolfsfeld. For taking time out of their busy schedules to talk to us about their experiences, we thank Richard Beeston, Tim Butcher, Patrick Cockburn, James Meek, Bill Neely, Tom Newton Dunn, Ed Pilkington, Richard Sambrook, Jon Snow, Angus Taverner, Alex Thomson. Earlier versions of some of the material in this book have been published as research articles (Robinson et al., 2009; Robinson, Goddard and Parry, 2009; Goddard, Robinson and Parry, 2008; Murray et al., 2008, Robinson et al., 2005) and for this we would like to thank the following journals: *Journal of Communication, American Behavioral Scientist, Media, War and Conflict, European Journal of Communication* and *Media, Culture and Society.*

1

Introduction

Overview

News media are central to the phenomenon of war. Many commentators argue that this is even more so today, given the 'globalised' environment of 24-hour news channels, real-time reporting and the Internet that surrounds us. Indeed, descriptions of changes to the dynamics of contemporary conflict and its mediation abound, from 'virtual war' (Ignatieff, 2000) through to 'postmodern war' (Hammond, 2007b). Nevertheless, wars – from the Crimean to the Iraq War – have regularly attracted substantial levels of news media attention. Moreover, as Philip Knightley records so persuasively in *The First Casualty* (2003), a familiar set of issues concerning news media and war can be traced back through history. Government and military censorship, journalists tempted to appeal to the patriotism of their readers, reporters 'embedded' with troops (including in the First World War) and news values that promote a focus on heroism and drama are all recurrent features of war reporting. Underlying the relationship between news media and war are simple, if rarely stated, truths.

The first is that war concerns matters of life and death in the most immediate sense, involving combatants and their families, civilians caught in the crossfire and the array of actors that have now increasingly come to be involved in contemporary warfare, including aid workers and journalists themselves. Second, the decision to go to war is the most serious and high-level one that any government can take because providing security to its citizens and protecting the national interest are seen as primary functions of the state. But, at least within democratic states, the general expectation is that governments must possess a persuasive rationale for any decision to embark on war and obtain, by democratic means, the consent of the population. With this expectation in mind, the news media become a central site within which ideas about the issue of war are discussed, and a vital tool to ensure that there is full, free and open debate both about the decision to go to war and the continuing conduct and rationale for military operations once it is underway. War is also a severe test of such democratic expectations, in part because government and military demands for support often clash with the roles expected of a free and independent news media.

In fact, as shown in Chapter 2, our existing understanding of the relationship between news media and government in wartime remains heavily influenced by claims that, particularly after the commencement of military action, news media become subservient to government and serve to mobilise support for war. From this perspective, news media rarely live up to the democratic ideals previously described. For many scholars of wartime media–state relations, a combination of mutually reinforcing constraints prevents news media independence during war. Over-reliance on official sources, the pull of patriotism, the influence of sophisticated state-led media-management operations, and ideological constraints – anti-communism during the cold war, for example – are all invoked in order to explain patterns of news media deference to government. Implicit throughout much of this critical literature is a normative assumption that news media *should* be doing more in order to maintain independence and to hold government and military to account. This perspective, however, is not shared by all. For some, news media are beasts to be tamed during war which, if left unchecked, can cause public demoralisation and military failure. President Nixon (1978: 350) gave the following assessment of US coverage of the Vietnam War:

> The Vietnam War was complicated by factors that never before occurred in America's conduct of war . . . More than ever before, television showed the terrible human suffering and sacrifice of war. Whatever the intention behind such relentless and literal reporting of war, the result was a serious demoralization of the home front, raising the question whether America would ever again be able to fight an enemy abroad with unity and strength of purpose at home.

What is implied by such arguments, although rarely stated, is a normative assumption, arguably at odds with the democratic ideal mentioned above, that news media should support government policy during war and help to mobilise public support for military action.

Between these contrasting descriptions of wartime media coverage, and their associated normative stances, lies a good deal of academic uncertainty. For some, changing geo-political landscapes, including the passing of the cold war, and developments in communication technology, have decreased the extent of news media deference in war and enabled greater independence. For others (e.g. Wolfsfeld et al., 2008: 401), levels of news media independence during war vary across circumstances and time, with media at times rallying to the support of government war objectives and at other times adopting a more critical stance.

One cause of this uncertainty lies in the absence of systematic, reliable and codified empirical research. Across the field of scholarship, many claims abound as to the nature of contemporary news media coverage of war. Taking one example, Tumber and Webster's (2006) *Journalists Under Fire* sets out a common set of arguments about wartime media. These include suggestions that the

> very presence of so many and of such disparate types of journalism drawn to war situations, the sheer volume of reportage, and the unmanageable character of so many aspects of war, ensure that undesirable stories will somehow reach the audience. (Tumber and Webster, 2006: 18)

and that

> reports and images that cause headaches for perception managers are easy to find . . . It can be a photograph of a distressed child, reports of discontent amongst combatants, the killings of an innocent bystander by our side or tales of abuse of prisoners by their guards . . . Such bad news stories can readily amplify into fears of 'another Vietnam', calls to 'get the boys home', and angst about 'what are we fighting for'. (Tumber and Webster 2006: 36)

These claims are undoubtedly true, but the important question is, to what extent? Unless systematic and detailed content analysis of actual news media coverage is carried out which, for example, documents the amount of coverage devoted to casualties as well as the form that it takes, it is not possible to be sure how accurate or balanced many of the claims about news media and war actually are. Systematic, detailed, and indeed time-consuming, empirical research is necessary if our understanding of news media and war is to be reliably and accurately informed. Meanwhile, there continues to be a lack of clarity over the way in which media *should* report war and what that coverage would actually look like in practice. Finally, associated with this academic uncertainty are a variety of methodological issues concerning how researchers should go about measuring news media coverage in order to provide accurate assessments of news media performance during war.

It is in this context of contrasting claims, normative disagreements and empirical uncertainty that this book analyses British news media coverage of the 2003 invasion of Iraq. Central to our analysis is a systematic and detailed content and framing analysis of mainstream TV news and newspaper coverage of the 2003 invasion, supported by detailed case studies, interviews with relevant journalists and reviews of key primary and secondary sources. Our work here is driven by two principal objectives and two secondary ones. The first is to theorise, define and operationalise an analytical framework which can provide for a systematic and rigorous analysis of wartime media coverage. As we demonstrate in Chapter 2, some of the key literature that focuses on news media and war is under-theorised and, at times, employs inadequate methodologies. This problem is also identified by Denis McQuail with respect to the entire field of media and war studies: 'Western "communication science" does not offer any clear framework for collecting and interpreting observations and information about contemporary war situations, only a disparate set of issues and formulations, in varying states of development and supported only in varying degrees by effective methodologies' (McQuail, 2006: 114). Through our analytical framework, which consolidates and refines existing theories, models and hypotheses from across the field of political communication, we aim to overcome these limitations. The framework sets out three models of wartime media performance: the *elite-driven model*, in which news media coverage is hypothesised to be *supportive* of government war aims; the *independent* model, where news media remain balanced towards events and produce *negotiated* coverage; and the *oppositional model* whereby news media offer a profound challenge to the legitimacy and conduct of a conflict and generate *oppositional* coverage. We explain these models further in Chapter 3, describing the form and content of news media coverage associated with each of them and detailing the explanatory factors invoked by earlier scholars to account for them. Finally, drawing on realist, liberal and critical perspectives from International Relations scholarship, we identify the normative assumptions that underpin each model of media performance. Overall, we provide a comprehensive and integrated framework for the analysis of news media coverage of war which we hope will be of interest and value to other scholars.

Our second principal objective is to apply this framework to the case of British media coverage of the 2003 invasion of Iraq. In broad terms, our framework enables us to test the validity of the three models (elite-driven, independent and oppositional) by examining the content of news media during this conflict. In doing so, we are able to provide a detailed assessment of the extent to which different news media outlets were able to maintain independence and autonomy during the war. For example, our research allows us to demonstrate the extent to which news media either acquiesced when confronted with government attempts to influence them or adopted an oppositional, even anti-war, stance, as many politicians and commentators claimed. Besides identifying overall trends in coverage, we are also able to describe how it varied over time and between different news media outlets. Accordingly, we are able to offer aggregate-level findings for news media performance in relation to the elite-driven, independent and oppositional models, as well as a nuanced understanding of where and when different modes of news media performance came in to play. As such, our analysis provides a sophisticated and detailed analysis of news media coverage of war, which also offers a comprehensive and authoritative assessment of how UK journalists covered the most controversial war in recent British history. Moreover, by providing a definitive assessment of news media performance during the invasion of Iraq, our work contributes directly to public and political debates about the way in which this war was reported.

In addition to these principal objectives there are two others. First, we are able to use our analytical framework, detailing the key explanatory factors associated with each model of news media performance, to assess the relative importance of factors regularly invoked in order to explain elite-driven, independent and oppositional reporting. In particular, we draw on our data in order to assess the importance of ideology, uncontrolled events, patriotism, use of official sources by journalists, professional autonomy and news media system characteristics in shaping news media coverage of the war. Second, in concluding this book, we relate our findings back to the normative positions, integral to our analytical framework, which provide competing justifications for different modes of news media performance in war. This final section, which is based on our interviews with journalists, considers the difficulties facing news media in juggling liberal democratic expectations for independent coverage with military and government expectations for a supportive news media. Overall, and in tandem with our findings which highlight how some news reports were remarkably successful at achieving balance and autonomy, we hope to provide insights into the conditions under which war journalism can achieve, as McQuail (2006: 117) puts it, 'higher standards than are generally aimed for or achieved at present'.

The 2003 invasion of Iraq

The central focus of this book is British news media coverage of the 2003 invasion of Iraq. The invasion was one of the most high profile military actions that the United Kingdom has embarked upon in the last 60 years, with British forces directly involved in the operation to invade Iraq and overthrow Saddam Hussein's regime. It represents a fascinating case, involving the most contentious foreign policy decision taken by a British government at least since the Suez crisis in 1956. Associated with the controversial nature of the Iraq War were unprecedented levels of public and political dissent and the continuance, by some newspapers, of an anti-war stance even when major combat operations were underway.

At least initially, the Iraq War was presented as one of national interest. Prior to the invasion, the British government argued that Saddam Hussein had maintained a programme to create and stockpile weapons of mass destruction (WMD), which posed a 'current and serious threat to the UK national interest' (Prime Minister's Office, 2002). As such, the war can be classified among the broader set of cases where Britain has deployed troops in major combat operations on matters of national interest. Earlier examples include the Gulf War (1991), the Falklands War (1982), the Suez crisis (1956) and the Korean War (1950–53). Such cases can be distinguished from interventions during humanitarian crises, such as Operation Allied Force in Kosovo (1999), which rarely involved the deployment of troops in major combat roles and where human rights issues, rather than matters of national interest, have been argued to be of chief concern. These so-called humanitarian wars raise different questions for media–state relations, which have generally concerned the effect that news media coverage of suffering people has in encouraging Western governments to intervene during these crises (Robinson, 2002). The type of conflicts to which the Iraq War belongs are 'limited wars' (Carruthers, 2000: 108), at least from the perspective of Britain, in that they involve the mobilisation of armed forces for relatively short periods of time without the nation being placed on a war footing. They also represent wars of choice. These cases can be distinguished from 'total wars' (Carruthers, 2000: 54) such as the Second World War, which involved a direct threat to national survival and, consequently, little expectation of an independent news media.

We believe the invasion phase to be a crucial period to analyse because it represents a moment of unprecedented media attention, with blanket coverage and massive resources being devoted by both government and news media. Furthermore, with extraordinary levels of elite and popular dissent occurring at a time when British forces were engaged in major combat operations, the invasion phase was a critical period for government attempts to influence news media output and an important test of the news media's ability to maintain independence. Understanding how government and news media interacted at this crucial moment provides a vital insight into the dynamics of wartime media–state relations. Consequently, we do not provide a sustained analysis here of how British news media handled the run-up to the conflict when there were extensive discussions over whether war was justified. Although this period is certainly worthy of investigation, our primary concern is with the way in which news media cover war once it is underway. However, we do extend our analysis to assess news media performance immediately prior to the invasion. In doing so we are able to examine how coverage changed between the pre-war debate about whether to go to war and the start of the armed action.

Similarly, our analysis phase ends shortly after Baghdad fell to US troops and resistance from Saddam Hussein's regime ceased. Following the invasion period, the nature of British military involvement shifted from a major war-fighting role to a law-and-order policing task limited to the south of Iraq which was, for some considerable time, relatively stable. During this time, most of the political and media debate in Britain concerned the growing low-intensity conflict within US-controlled central Iraq, suicide bombings in and around Baghdad, the prisoner abuse scandals at Abu Ghraib, the failure to find WMD, and the legal case for war. Although news media coverage of this period would make an intriguing subject for analysis, it cannot readily be characterised as a case in which British forces were directly involved in substantive war-fighting operations. However, our analysis does extend for a week beyond the fall of Baghdad, allowing us to provide insights into how the focus of coverage rapidly changed from battlefield operations to questions of law and 'disorder' in Iraq – the beginning of a pattern of coverage which is likely to have continued, more or less, throughout the remainder of the UK's involvement in Iraq. In addition, when we make general claims about news media performance, based on our findings, we ensure that the fact that we focused on the high-intensity war fighting period is carefully taken into account. We also take time in the conclusion to set out key research questions that need to be addressed when considering news media performance during the post-invasion and occupation phase. Of course, British news media coverage of war is the primary research focus of our study and, in this respect, the events of the period that it covers are comparable with the cases of major British military operations that we identified earlier (the 1991 Gulf War, the Falklands War, the Suez crisis and the Korean War).

UK news media

Our study focuses on coverage of the invasion in television news and the national press in Britain. We survey the principal news programmes of four key television broadcasters – BBC, ITV, Channel 4 and Sky – and news coverage in seven national daily newspapers, together with their Sunday equivalents – *Sun*/*News of the World*, *Daily* and *Sunday Mirror*, *Daily Mail*/*Mail on Sunday*, *Independent*/*Independent on Sunday*, *Guardian*/*Observer*, *Daily* and *Sunday Telegraph*, *Times* and *Sunday Times*. During the period of study – early 2003 – these traditional media remained dominant in Britain compared to the relatively new, yet rapidly growing, online news media. Television was a news source for 91 per cent and newspapers for 73 per cent, but only 15 per cent used the Internet for news according to 2002 research (Hargreaves and Thomas, 2002). The same survey also showed that television was the most trusted news source; at least 80 per cent trusted news on British terrestrial channels, with BBC News the most trusted at 92 per cent.

So, taken together, these news media outlets constitute the major component of the UK public sphere, serving as key information sources for the public. This wide cross-section of UK news media enables us to provide a comprehensive analysis of the British public sphere in a time of war. Our analysis of television news coverage also allows us to assess how successfully journalists and editors fulfilled their regulatory obligations to maintain balance and impartiality. For the press, more opinionated and partisan than television news, our analysis of coverage provides a unique opportunity to compare the range and tenor of reporting between different titles, including those that took the unprecedented decision to oppose the war even after British troops had gone into action. These anti-war titles offer a unique opportunity to test how far a newspaper is able to challenge government policy and military objectives under the conditions of war.

Patriotism, nationalism and terminology

Throughout this book, matters of nationality, patriotism and national identity frequently occur. Because of this, it is important briefly to set out our understanding of these terms. Patriotism is commonly understood to refer to a sentiment that involves an individual's feeling of love and affinity for his or her country. While it is often seen as a more benign phenomenon than nationalism, which carries connotations of extremism and active dislike of other nations, both patriotism and nationalism are a consequence of national identity. In this study, we adopt Billig's (1997) perspective, which sees the two phenomena as, broadly speaking, similar in that both are socially constructed (Anderson, 1991) and both involve individuals feeling a sense of belonging and loyalty to their nation. On a related matter, we regularly use terms such as nation, country, patriotism and war. In doing so, we do not assume that such terms relate to any kind of objective or necessary reality. We understand all as socially constructed phenomena: for example, the nation is an 'imagined community' (see Anderson, 1991; Gellner, 1983) and patriotism is constructed through various processes that bring an individual to feel loyalty to his or her nation; it is not innate or natural as claimed by some (e.g. Smith, 1986). Following on from this, we assume also that patriotism/nationalism is constructed, in large part, through complex processes emerging from both elite groups and the institutions of the state (Barabantseva, 2010).

Objectivity, bias, framing and audience reception

Political communication scholarship has long been sensitive to the difficulties surrounding terms such as *objectivity* and *bias*. The use of such terms often triggers accusations of modernist conceptions of the truth being available and identifiable. Indeed, and reflecting the influence of post-modern thinking, most scholarship has preferred to use terms such as framing, when discussing trends in news media coverage. The concept of framing encourages us to understand that there may well be competing truths and perspectives and that the task of media scholars should be to identify these, and in doing so reveal the influence of power on news media representations (see Chapter 3). In this study, we presume that one can evaluate the extent to which news media represent competing views or side with one view over another but without assuming that there is one, objective, truth against which to measure news media coverage. So, when we use terms such as 'neutral', 'balanced', or sometimes 'objective', we do this for the sake of succinctness and the reader should not infer that we have some outdated belief in objectivity and truth. Also, this study is concerned with the relationship of news media to what can be described as official narratives and claims. Our goal is to measure the extent to which news media supported, stood apart from, or actively challenged government and military officials. In doing so, we make no claims about the resulting influence of coverage on audiences.

Outline of chapters

In Chapter 2, we provide a detailed and critical review of key studies that have analysed news media coverage of war. Largely empirical, rather than theory driven, these studies provide useful insights into both the content and form of wartime media coverage and suggest various explanations for their observations. Particular emphasis is placed on identifying the limits of existing studies and clarifying the differing explanatory and descriptive claims made throughout this literature. The chapter also introduces broad debates that have emerged since the late 1980s regarding the impact of ideology, new technology and media management. In Chapter 3, we turn to the development of our analytical framework, which is designed to provide a systematic and theoretically grounded basis for our analysis of news media coverage. In doing so, we draw upon the wide range of models and hypotheses from across the field of political communication and, combining them with some of the key issues and insights identified in Chapter 2, set out three models of news media performance: the elite-driven, independent and oppositional models. Chapter 4 is designed to place our research in context by describing the character of the press and broadcasting in Britain, and outlining the major news events surrounding the Iraq invasion.

Chapters 5 and 6 present the results of our empirical research. In Chapter 5, we examine the extent to which news media conformed to the predictions of the elite-driven model, drawing upon our content and framing analysis of news media coverage of the war, including how it was represented visually. To supplement this account, we also provide examples of coverage, together with material from our interviews with journalists. In addition, we evaluate the evidence that emerges for the key explanatory factors associated with the elite-driven model. The independent and oppositional models are the focus of Chapter 6, and here we document the circumstances under which British media offered negotiated and oppositional reporting of the war, again illustrating our account with extracts from news coverage and insights from journalists. Drawing on time series data, we also pay attention to changes in the character of coverage as the pre-war debate gave way to the invasion itself and, later, as the fall of Baghdad heralded a shift away from the reporting of major military operations. This time series analysis allows us to discuss the extent to which news media performance differs significantly between war and non-war periods. As in Chapter 5, we also account for our findings in relation to the explanatory factors associated with the independent and oppositional models.

Chapter 7 delves further into our analysis of news media coverage to provide three case studies which, in different ways, illuminate each model of news media performance in wartime and serve to strengthen some of the key findings emerging from our study. We examine a case in which news media were heavily supportive of the coalition (the case of Jessica Lynch), one where a more independent and critical line was taken (the case of Ali Abbas, who was maimed in a coalition airstrike) and one in which the news media's attitude to outright opponents of the war could be assessed (the case of the anti-war movement).

We conclude our study, in Chapter 8, with a synthesis of the results of our empirical analysis and discuss their implications for a theoretical understanding of wartime media–state relations. Within this process, we pay close attention to the applicability of the elite-driven, independent and oppositional models and consider the implications of our findings in relation to broader debates about the impact of new technologies, changing geo-political contexts, contemporary approaches to media-management, as well as theoretical debates. In the closing pages, we move beyond descriptive, explanatory and theoretical issues to reflect on the normative question of how news media *should* report war. Here we discuss the pressures faced by journalists, especially those deriving from an instinctive affiliation with the forces of their own side and from the higher professional ideals associated with detached or objective reporting. We also identify the conditions under which greater media autonomy is possible.

2

Mobilising for battle: The news media and war from Vietnam to Iraq

This chapter examines the study of news media and war, moving on to review key works that have analysed, in a systematic fashion, the content and framing[1] of wartime news media coverage. Beginning with Vietnam, these systematic studies include work on the 1982 Falklands conflict, the 1992 Gulf War, and three studies of the 2003 Iraq War. We pay close attention to the descriptive claims these studies make, to the explanations offered for the coverage that they observe, and to the strengths and weaknesses of the various methodologies employed. We highlight, in particular, different ways of explaining observed patterns of news media performance. In the latter part of the chapter, we outline recent debates concerning the impact on media–state relations of the passing of the cold war, the introduction of new communications technology and intensified government media-management activities. The analysis of media management includes an overview of coalition media operations during the 2003 Iraq War. We conclude by setting out the case for a theoretically grounded, normatively engaged and methodologically rigorous approach to studying news media and war.

The study of news media and war

The topic of news media and war has inspired a voluminous literature, which spans the fields of 'media and communications, political science, sociology, history [and], psychology' (Hoskins et al., 2008).[2] One strand of this literature has focused on providing wide-ranging but rich historical analyses of the relationship between war, news media and the state (e.g. Badsey, 2010; Knightley, 2003; Taylor, 1997). Other scholars have explored government media-management strategies, offering research ranging from qualitative analyses through to systematic social scientific exploration (e.g. Cortell et al., 2009; Miller, 2004; Thrall, 2000; Young and Jesser, 1997). Another vein of work focuses on the experiences of those involved in the reporting of war (e.g. Katovsky and Carlson, 2003; Moorcroft and Taylor, 2008; Morrison and Tumber, 1988; Tumber and Webster, 2006), while a related literature has emerged assessing news coverage of humanitarian crises and their associated civil wars (e.g. Allen and Seaton, 1999; Chouliaraki, 2006; Minear et al., 1996; Moeller, 1999; Robinson, 2002; Shaw, 1996).

Moving closer to the focus of this study, a considerable body of work – monographs, research articles and edited collections – examines the role and output of news media during major armed conflicts. Although some of this corpus is theoretically orientated, much of it involves the largely unsystematic analysis of the content and form of media coverage of war (Allan and Zelizer, 2004; Cottle, 2006; Der Derian, 2009; Friel and Falk, 2007; Hammond, 2007a and b; Hoskins, 2004; Miller, 2004; Seib, 2004; Thussu and Freedman, 2003).

Other studies have concentrated on online news reporting (e.g. Allan, 2004; Dimitrova et al., 2005; Dimitrova and Neznanski, 2006; Matheson and Allan, 2009; Schwalbe, 2006; Wall, 2005) and on the way in which war is represented visually by news media. While visuals have tended to receive minimal appreciation, and secondary scrutiny at most in much political communication research (Hansen et al., 1998), the recent conflicts in Afghanistan and Iraq have coincided with a surge of interest in 'visual culture' (Mitchell, 1994; 2002). Specifically, there is a growing recognition of the legitimising or destabilising functions of media images during conflict (see Andersen, 2006; Michalski and Gow, 2007; Mirzoeff, 2005). Quantitative studies of visual content have flourished in recent years, particularly with regard to US news media coverage of the Iraq conflict (Griffin, 2004; King and Lester, 2005; Schwalbe, 2008; Silcock et al., 2008), and a small number of studies have involved UK news media in single-issue or comparative research (Fahmy, 2007; Fahmy and Kim, 2008; Wells, 2007). Finally, a large body of literature has emerged examining news media and the 'war on terror' or terrorism in general. We prefer to keep this work distinct from the war and news media literature discussed here. Terrorism is a form of activity that is very different from traditional war. Moreover, conflating terrorism with the topic of war risks reinforcing widely contested and problematic arguments that combating terrorism should be considered a form of war.

The literature review provided in the following pages is concentrated on the surprisingly small number of studies that are based on detailed systematic content and framing analysis of news media coverage of war. By 'systematic content and framing analysis', we mean research that employs a structured, codified and transparent approach to analysing news media coverage, and which aims to achieve high levels of reliability and validity.[3] This social scientific approach enables general claims to be made about the content of news media coverage, minimises problems associated with researcher bias and provides data strong enough for theory development and testing (although nearly all of the work reviewed here has been concerned primarily with empirical analysis rather than theory). In selecting systematic studies for review we have drawn on the most notable and significant studies of this kind. Our goal is to identify the strengths and weaknesses of the existing literature and to establish the current state of knowledge in this area. In doing so, our overall objective is to direct our content and framing analysis of news media and war towards a more precise, grounded and richer analysis.

There is also a broader theoretical and specifically social scientific literature that theorises the relationship between news media and the state in general terms (e.g. Baum, 2004; Baum and Potter, 2008; Bennett, 1990; Cook, 1998; Entman, 2004; Herman and Chomsky, 1988; Lawrence, 2000; Mermin, 1999; Robinson, 2002; Sparrow, 1999; Wolfsfeld, 1997). Much of this literature, set primarily in the US context, does at times analyse cases of wartime news media coverage. But such analysis, often using comparatively straightforward indicators of news media content, generally serves as a means to test theoretical propositions: detailed content and framing analysis is not the primary objective of this research. As such, this literature does not form part of the focused review conducted in the pages that follow. This theoretical literature on media–state relations, however, is discussed and drawn heavily upon in Chapter 3 where we set out the analytical framework for this study: In this chapter, we combine the insights gleaned from our review of content and framing analyses of news media and war with theories of media-state relations in order to construct an analytical framework suitable for the study of news media and war. Indeed, the marrying of detailed content and framing analysis of wartime news media coverage with the broader theoretical literature on media–state relations is a major part of the contribution that this study seeks to make. For now, however, we turn our attention to the key content and framing analyses of wartime news media coverage.

Vietnam

Existing studies of news media and war provide a relatively consistent assessment of the attitude of wartime news media coverage. As Susan Carruthers (2000: 271–2) argues, the media have traditionally 'served the military rather well' despite controversies over news media bias that have often been quite heated. As such, the prevailing academic orthodoxy sees news media as lacking independence when covering war, producing instead coverage that favours their own side and privileges the viewpoints of their own governments. The intellectual origins of this orthodoxy can be traced back to Daniel Hallin's (1986) study *The Uncensored War*.[4] The controversy addressed by Hallin's work concerned the claim that negative and oppositional news media coverage of the Vietnam War had sapped public and political support for the war and contributed, ultimately, to US defeat. This perceived phenomenon has become known as the Vietnam Syndrome, representing the belief held widely among policy-makers and the military that, in democracies, public aversion to casualties and news media coverage of the graphic realities of war serve to undermine public support for war.

The strength of Hallin's content analysis lies in its systematic and codified approach, detailing subject matter (e.g. battle successes and battle failures, civilian casualties, anti-war protest) and sources used by US news media, and assessing the tone of news stories. His study draws on a sample of 779 television broadcasts from between 1965 and 1973, as well as *New York Times* coverage of the war. It is sensitive to different types of criticism found in news media coverage and distinguishes between, and accounts for, both 'procedural' and 'substantive' forms. Here, procedural criticism is understood to concern debate over the implementation of a policy, such as the tactics employed during a war; substantive criticism, in contrast, relates to the underlying rationale of a policy, such as the justification for a particular war.[5]

In general terms, Hallin's (1986) analysis persuasively challenges both the reality of the Vietnam Syndrome and claims of an oppositional news media during the Vietnam War – a finding that is widely accepted among academics but less so within military and political circles. More specifically, he finds that US news media coverage of the war was broadly supportive of it, at least until 1968. During this phase, according to Hallin, media operated within a 'sphere of consensus', mirroring the extent of elite debate, and coverage reflected well on US forces. He notes how the central story for journalists covering Vietnam was of 'American Boys in action' (1986: 129) and that coverage tended to represent the US as 'holding the military initiative', with assessments of military progress prior to 1968 emphasising US success (1986: 146). In 1968, however, communist forces launched the Tet Offensive, which involved an uprising throughout South Vietnam. At this point, according to Hallin, critical reporting did start to emerge in mainstream US news media. However, this was not so much because journalists were starting to oppose the war, but because elements within the Johnson administration itself had started to argue publicly over the course of the war. By now, the US political establishment had become divided between 'hawks', who believed victory needed to be achieved whatever the cost, and 'doves', who argued that the price of victory in Vietnam was not worth paying. Hence, rather than journalists themselves adopting an oppositional stance, the growth in critical coverage was actually the result of reporting that mirrored the debate within the US foreign policy establishment. The scope of reporting had by now extended to embrace a 'sphere of legitimate controversy', involving procedural news media criticism pertaining primarily to whether or not the US was winning the war in South East Asia. Importantly, however, US news coverage never moved beyond this point into a 'sphere of deviance' whereby fundamental or substantive-level criticisms of the legitimacy of US action in Vietnam were made. For example, some US citizens had come to view the war in Vietnam as both immoral and an act of aggression, but Hallin (1986: 207–8) notes that 'during the Vietnam War issues of this sort were simply not on the news agenda. Never, for example, did I hear an American utter the word *imperialism* on television.' Instead, 'what journalists did was to defend the honorableness of American motives' (Hallin, 1986: 207–8; original italics).

Hallin accounts for his findings by reference to two factors. In the first place, he identifies the ideology of anti-communism as a primary factor in ensuring that 'journalists and government policymakers were united' over the fundamentals of the US strategy aimed at containing communism (Hallin, 1986: 24). The second factor is the dependence of journalists upon official sources, which he attributes to a specific interpretation of what constituted 'objective' journalism. According to Hallin (1986: 63–70), the 'ideological system' and 'myth' of objective journalism developed as a way of legitimising the news media in the face of ever-increasing concentration of ownership in the media industry. When the number of newspapers was large, partisan and adversarial news could be justified because of the plurality of viewpoints expressed in a supposed free market of ideas. With an increasingly concentrated media industry, the number of independent newspapers declined in each market and so did the plurality of viewpoints expressed.[6] In order to defend themselves against charges of political bias, journalists adopted the concept of objective journalism whereby:

> the journalist's basic task is to 'present facts', to tell what happened, not to pass judgement on it. Opinion should be clearly separated from the presentation of news . . . News coverage of any political controversy should be impartial, representing without favour the positions of all the contending parties. (Hallin, 1986: 24)

According to Hallin, the unintended consequence of 'objective' journalism was that, as journalists were meant simply to gather the political 'facts' from which to construct the news, those with political authority 'were guaranteed access to all the major media – and protected against "irresponsible" attack – by virtue of their position, not their particular party or politics' (Hallin, 1986: 70). The result was a tightening of the link between journalists and the state, and increased power for government officials to influence the news both through agenda setting and the framing of issues. 'Objective' journalism had, according to Hallin, led to the loss of a critical edge on the part of journalists.

The Falklands War

Subsequent content analysis-based studies of news media and war largely support Hallin's findings, although there is considerable variation in both the depth of later research and the explanatory factors invoked in order to explain news media performance. The Glasgow University Media Group's (GUMG)

(1985) analysis of how British television news performed during the 1982 Falklands War, when British forces recovered the Falkland Islands following their invasion by Argentina, paints a picture of news media subservience both to government war objectives and to the perceived national interest. GUMG does not provide a comprehensive analysis of coverage during this conflict, however, and its claims are based primarily on two case studies. The first is a comparative analysis of coverage of the sinking of the Argentine cruiser *General Belgrano* and of the destruction of the British destroyer HMS *Sheffield*. The second is an analysis of coverage of British airstrikes on Argentine positions at Port Stanley airfield.

According to their analysis, three factors conjoined to restrict 'open news and free information' (GUMG, 1985: 8) during the war: The first related to censorship and control by the British Ministry of Defence, which led to only a handful of journalists being allowed to travel to the Falklands, all of whom were reliant on military communications to file reports. The second concerned the dynamics of the British lobby system whereby a select body of journalists receive regular briefings from government on the understanding that they are not attributable and that such privileges will be withdrawn from any that abuse them.[7] The third factor was a pattern of self-censorship by journalists and editors who were reluctant to run counter to the patriotism of the public (1985: 8). Interestingly, with respect to public opinion, GUMG point out that broadcasters justified their compliant stance by reference to claims of widespread public support for the war: 'ITN used its assumption of "majority support for Task Force action" to justify its intended policy of giving a "nightly offering of interesting, positive and heart-warming stories of achievement and collaboration born out of a sense of national purpose"' (1985: 173–4).

As a consequence of these factors, argues GUMG (1985: 172–3), UK television news coverage of diplomatic efforts to avoid the war presented their failure as the result of Argentine intransigence in the face of urgent British attempts to seek a diplomatic solution. Based on their detailed analysis of the two events during the war itself, GUMG argues that coverage displayed a systematic bias toward the official British perspective on events. For example, a comparison of the coverage of the Argentine *General Belgrano* with that of the British HMS *Sheffield* demonstrates that the sinking of the *Belgrano* was framed so as to emphasise the rescue of survivors (1985: 31) whereas the destruction of the *Sheffield* was framed so as to 'stress the [number of] casualties' (1985: 41). This divergent framing of two similar events, according to GUMG, served to neutralise public shock at the large loss of life on the *Belgrano* and to rally support for the government's tough line on the Argentine invasion by emphasising British casualties from the *Sheffield*. With respect to the 'home front', GUMG find that 'Task Force families – the women in particular – were mainly presented as models of support for the war but were largely denied the possibility of expressing their own opinions and doubts' (1985: 94).

The 1991 Gulf War

The 1991 Gulf War, with its real-time coverage, images of smart bombs hitting their targets and flashy set-piece press briefings, represented the arrival of a new era in wartime news media reporting. With respect to this conflict, Bennett and Paletz's edited collection *Taken by Storm* (1994) provides a diverse range of articles examining different facets of US media–state relations during the crisis, including analysis of the run-up to the war and of the conflict phase itself. Although it is one of the most widely cited accounts of media and war, none of the studies reported in this collection achieve the depth of analysis reached in Hallin's (1986) work on Vietnam. Out of twelve chapters, only two have a basis in systematic content analysis of US news media coverage of the war itself: Iyengar and Simon (1994: 167–85) analyse a sample of ABC coverage in order to assess the relative balance of thematic and episodic news,[8] while Brody (1994: 210–27) offers no primary analysis of news coverage but draws instead on *Executive Trend Watch*'s National Media Index and Vanderbilt University's 'Television News Index and Abstracts'. *Taken by Storm* does, however, portray a picture of American news media as largely compliant with the viewpoints of the US government. Bennett and Paletz (1994: 284) attribute these broad findings to 'dependence on military sources', adding that 'insufficient dedication to the freedom of the press, fear of provoking government outrage, shared frames of reference with governing elites, and the pursuit of sales and ratings are among the factors that help explain the acquiescence to government curbs'.

In contrast, David Morrison's *Television and the Gulf War* (1992) offers a more detailed analysis, focusing on how British television news covered the war.[9] His content analysis yields a range of quantitative manifest-level data, including the amount of time devoted to coverage of the war, the subject matter of news reports, the gender of news presenters and the frequency with which different presenters appeared, the sources drawn upon by journalists, the visuals used, and the origins of restriction and censorship (Morrison, 1992: 68–74). He finds that news reports were dominated by coverage of the progress of battle, speculation over the ground campaign, concern over air and scud attacks, troop movements, attack strategies and weaponry (1992: 67).

Conversely, information about the initial Iraqi invasion of Kuwait in August 1990 and the historical context for the conflict received scant attention from British television news, while few images of death reached the evening broadcasts (Morrison, 1992: 68). Morrison also attempts, in a more limited fashion, to assess whether coverage was biased either in favour of or against the official perspective towards the war. Usefully, he analyses the relative frequency with which different 'reasons for hostilities' (1992: 77) were aired and finds that official narratives regarding the liberation of Kuwait predominated over alternative claims – regarding oil, for example. In addition, he quantifies the number of critical and supportive comments made by politicians about the war (1992: 79), as well as the number of times positive and negative qualities were associated with key leaders (1992: 82–3). Here, he finds that relatively few criticisms of the war were aired and that Saddam Hussein received the largest quantity of negative commentary from journalists.

However, this more evaluative aspect of the analysis is quite brief and, unlike Hallin's (1986) work, does not provide a more thorough assessment of the extent to which TV coverage conformed to, or deviated from, the official position on the war. Importantly, Morrison analyses neither the tone nor the framing of news reports and cannot, therefore, offer an overall assessment of whether coverage supported the coalition forces or adopted an oppositional stance. Furthermore, in measuring critical comments from politicians, he does not distinguish between procedural and substantive criticism. The analysis is also limited by its focus on TV news (there is no comparable assessment of national newspapers) and by the absence of any clear attempt to consider possible explanations for the findings.

In summary, then, the studies reviewed so far tend to highlight the conformity between news media and government in wartime. However, no other study approaches Hallin's analysis in providing a comprehensive and in-depth examination of American or British coverage. The later studies have provided relatively incomplete snapshots of wartime coverage (Bennett and Paletz, 1994; GUMG, 1985) or have focused on quantitative manifest-level content analysis at the expense of a more detailed and qualitative assessment of the tone and framing of news reports (Morrison, 1992). As explanations of wartime media performance, a variety of factors are put forward: Only Hallin cites cold war ideology, while Bennett and Paletz, GUMG and Hallin all argue for the importance the news media's reliance upon official sources. In addition, GUMG and Bennett and Paletz identify the importance of patriotism.

The 2003 invasion of Iraq

A number of published studies provide detailed and systematic content and framing analyses of news media coverage of the Iraq War. For example, Entman et al. (2009) analyse casualty-related coverage for the period 2003–7 and there is a growing literature examining coverage associated with embedded reporters (Haigh et al., 2006; Lindner, 2009; Pfau et al., 2004). These studies consider specific aspects of coverage, rather than assessing the overall contours and features of news reporting; the results are discussed at later stages in this book. In addition, Dimitrova and Strömbäck (2005) have produced a comparison of subject matter and tone between US and Swedish coverage of the invasion; Robertson (2004) offers a careful analysis of Scottish newspaper coverage of the period prior to the invasion; and Kolmer and Semetko (2009) provide a systematic comparison of news media reporting of the invasion across six national/regional contexts. These are excellent analyses and we draw on their findings in the concluding chapter, but none of them provide thorough, in-depth assessments of wartime coverage or a detailed focus on its form and content as our study – and the studies reviewed in the following pages – attempts to do. It is to these studies that we now turn our attention.

There have been three major studies of news coverage of the 2003 Iraq War – one examining coverage in the USA, and two in the UK. The first is by Aday, Livingston and Hebert (2005), the second forms part of Tumber and Palmer's book *Media at War* (2004), and the third is the study conducted at the Cardiff School of Journalism by Lewis et al. (2006). Of these, only the US-based study includes inter-coder reliability testing of results, and only Lewis et al. devote substantive attention to explaining the overall contours of the coverage that they describe.[10] However, each study is sophisticated and informative, indicating the kind of high quality and rigorous research that is now carried out into news media coverage of war.

The Aday, Livingston and Hebert (2005) study analyses ABC, NBC, CBS, CNN and Fox (FNC) coverage of the invasion, as well as that of Al Jazeera in order to provide an international comparison. As with Hallin (1986), their approach involves identifying the subject matter of news reports – in order to provide a 'macro-portrait' (Aday, Livingston and Hebert, 2005: 3) of how US television covered the invasion – as well as measuring the tone of individual news stories. Their overall aim is to assess the degree of objectivity achieved by different news outlets, so they classify news reports as neutral, critical or supportive towards the invasion. They operationalise 'objective' (neutral) coverage as involving the absence of clearly evaluative and value-laden reporting by journalists. Essentially, based on the examples that they provide, Aday, Livingston and Hebert's (2005: 9–10) classification schema involves assessing the language employed by journalists in their reports. So a report describing American forces as 'courageous' would be coded as supportive while one referring to them 'slaughtering' civilians would be coded as critical (Aday, Livingston and Hebert, 2005: 10). Their research method and operationalisation of objective reporting leads to contrasting arguments concerning the way US news media portrayed the invasion of Iraq. Based on the subject matter of news reports, Aday, Livingston and Hebert (2005: 11–12) find that coverage was dominated by the subject of battle, that domestic dissent and international diplomacy were largely absent and that little attention was paid to casualties. Conversely, their analysis of story tone indicates that: 'the vast majority of coverage . . . achieved a neutral tone' (Aday, Livingston and Hebert, 2005:

12). Only Fox News (FNC) failed to fit this model. Otherwise, the proportion of 'neutral' stories found ranged from 89 per cent (Al Jazeera) to 96 per cent of coverage (ABC and CBS) (Aday, Livingston and Hebert, 2005: 12). Overall, they conclude that:

> the overwhelming number of stories aired during the war on American networks and on Al Jazeera – with the exception of FNC – were neutral at the story level but that the general picture of the war presented by the news focused primarily on its whiz-bang aspects at the expense of other important story lines. (Aday, Livingston and Hebert, 2005: 14)

So, on the one hand, Aday and his team identify a degree of bias in the subject matter of news reports which helped to create a picture that was relatively 'comfortable' from a coalition perspective. As such, their findings are in step with academic orthodoxy that highlights the lack of news media neutrality in war. But in contrast to these studies, their measurement of the tone of reports indicates that most of the coverage was objective, suggesting a shift toward greater news media autonomy, at least with respect to the 2003 invasion of Iraq.

A problem with this study is its definition and operationalisation of 'objectivity' in terms of straight versus evaluative reporting by journalists. This portrayal of objectivity rests on a distinction between the language and tone used by reporters (which can either be critical, supportive or neutral) and the subjects of news stories which, according to their definition, are unrelated to the issue of objectivity. As long as a journalist avoids overtly partisan or emotive language, a report is understood to be objective according to the classification provided by Aday and his team.

This distinction, however, is open to question. A journalist might avoid a critical and evaluative tone when covering a story about coalition humanitarian operations but still produce a report that reflects a coalition perspective. For example, during the 2003 Iraq War, the coalition actively sought to encourage coverage of humanitarian operations relating to the port town of Umm Qsar and attempts by British forces to dock the Sir Galahad relief ship.[11] Even if a journalist reported these events 'straight', this, at the very least, reflects the humanitarian frame promoted by the coalition. So although it identifies how often journalists deployed a biased tone, the Aday, Livingston and Hebert (2005) study does not address the extent to which news reports either reflected or challenged official perspectives on the war. In order to do this, more sensitive measures, able to detect subtle forms of bias and framing, would have been required.

Tumber and Palmer's *Media at War* (2004) provides an analysis of British television and press coverage of the war, as well as analysing a sample of pre-war newspaper coverage and a snapshot of post-war coverage.[12] They develop four indicators by which to measure the relative objectivity of British news outlets. First, they assess the extent to which the subject matter of news reports focused on either the conduct of the war or, alternatively, its 'long-term political purposes' (Tumber and Palmer, 2004: 100). Here, they find that television news concentrated overwhelmingly on the conduct or progress of the military campaign but that newspapers maintained a significant degree of attention to the long-term political purpose of the war (2004: 101–2). Second, they identify the different sources used by journalists and find that coalition sources dominated across all of the news outlets (2004: 103). Third, they quantify the number of positive and negative 'mentions of the activities of the coalition partners' (2004: 99) and find, significantly, that there was more negative commentary with regard to the progress of the war than positive. For example, only 35 per cent of BBC reports offered good news for the coalition with 60 per cent reporting bad news; similarly, 43 per cent of ITV reports contained good news and 53 per cent bad news (2004: 104–6). Finally, they measure the tone of reporting in order to assess whether journalists were applying an objective, a sceptical or a heroic tone. Here, consistent with Aday, Livingston and Hebert (2005), they find that television news was overwhelmingly objective in tone (Tumber and Palmer, 2004: 106). However, when examining the press, their analysis shows that 'the right-wing press is less likely to be sceptical [towards the coalition] than the left-wing titles, and more likely to adopt a positive, supportive tone of voice' (2004: 105–6).

Overall, the data presented by Tumber and Palmer suggests that, whereas British news media relied heavily on coalition sources and, on television at least, reported with a largely objective tone, coverage was largely negative from a coalition perspective. This contrasts with the Aday, Livingston and Hebert (2005) study, which found that US coverage was largely objective and, unusually given the findings of previous studies (Bennett and Paletz, 1994; GUMG, 1985; Hallin, 1986), indicates that coverage of the 2003 Iraq War was surprisingly critical. Although this is clearly an important finding, the extent to which it can be interpreted as a definitive assessment of news media performance during the war is more limited. The measure is based on the frequency of positive and negative mentions of coalition activities, but no information is provided as to how news reports were actually analysed by coders, and the criteria by which a report was coded as either positive or negative (from the perspective of the coalition) is left opaque.[13]

Furthermore, their measure does not distinguish between procedural and substantive criticism. As such, Tumber and Palmer are unclear as to whether the high quantity of negative commentary concerned procedural issues such as tactics and the progress of the military campaign, or was directed towards the legitimacy of the war itself. Finally, Tumber and Palmer are wary of using their findings to address the question of the overall objectivity of the British news media during the war. Instead, they adopt the position that as their study is 'based on inter-channel comparisons, not upon some independent, external benchmark . . . all judgements about objectivity are comparative, not absolute' (2004: 97). As such, they sidestep the question of overall news media objectivity during the war in favour of a discussion regarding the relative objectivity of news media outlets.

The Cardiff study (2006), led by Justin Lewis, is more direct in its criticism of news media performance during the Iraq War. Their study analyses British television news coverage of the war[14] and involves the measurement of several elements in news reports. They examine the authorship of news reports and find that most (48 per cent) originated from studio anchors, with embeds responsible for 9 per cent of all reports (Lewis et al., 2006: 116). They also quantify the different sources used by television news, finding that coalition sources represented 46 per cent of all onscreen sources, although official Iraqi sources made up a significant 30 per cent of sources (2006: 120). Finally, in order to assess bias, they examine 'two long-running stories that were central to the government's case for war: claims about Iraqi possession of weapons of mass destruction (WMD); and the attitude and welfare of the Iraqi people themselves' (2006: 121).

With regard to WMD, they count the number of references in news media reports that 'asserted or implied the *possible or likely* presence of chemical and biological weapons, and those references that *cast doubt* on Iraqi WMD capability' (2006: 121; original emphasis). Here, they find that broadcasters were eight times more likely to suggest the presence of WMD than to cast doubt on their existence. With regard to the Iraqi people, Lewis et al. coded reports in order to assess whether they portrayed Iraqis as 'welcoming the troops as a liberating force (and thereby supporting the government's case)', or showed them as 'less enthusiastic or even antagonistic' (2006: 123). Finding that reports showing Iraqis as welcoming outnumbered those showing the opposite by two to one, Lewis and his team deduce that there was 'a subtle but clear bias toward [these] two central pro-war assumptions' (2006: 126). Explaining their findings, the team conclude that the use of embedded sources and a desire for dramatic coverage were both important factors in drawing news outlets towards a focus on the progress of war, at the expense of a detached and more questioning stance (2006: 188–97).

As with the Tumber and Palmer (2004) study, the approach taken by Lewis and his colleagues faces several limitations: First, their analysis of the bias issue is limited to an investigation only of the WMD and Iraqi people stories. Although, in contrast to Tumber and Palmer, they find evidence of a pro-coalition bias here, there is no attempt to differentiate between procedural and substantive-level issues. Second, their analysis does not attempt to assess the overall tone or framing of news reports; as a consequence they cannot offer an overall assessment of bias and objectivity. This is a limitation that Lewis et al. (2006: 126) acknowledge themselves, explaining that: 'the data presented here ignores some of the more detailed content of the coverage . . . [and] offer[s] only a glimpse into broader questions about the nature and tone of the narrative of war coverage'.

Overall, the three studies offer useful insights into specific aspects of coverage: Aday, Livingston and Hebert (2005) provide a convincing analysis of where and when US journalists departed from a straight or neutral tone; Tumber and Palmer (2004) illuminate the proportion of critical commentary emanating from British journalists regarding the military progress of the war; Lewis et al. (2006) convincingly reveal a subtle bias in favour of the coalition viewpoint in news reporting about WMD and Iraqi sentiments towards the invasion. However, none of the studies are able to provide a more comprehensive assessment of news media bias and objectivity. The Aday, Livingston and Hebert study is limited in this respect by an operationalisation of objectivity that rests on a questionable distinction between language/tone and the subject matter of news reports. Neither of the British studies distinguishes procedural from substantive criticism, nor are they able to provide a fuller analysis of news media objectivity and bias during the invasion. None of the studies attempts to measure more subtle forms of bias via framing analysis. Finally, it is also worth noting that the three studies, where they do offer insights into questions of objectivity and bias, offer strikingly different assessments. Aday, Livingston and Hebert (2005: 14) suggest that coverage was largely objective, Tumber and Palmer (2004) uncover a good deal more criticism than support for the military campaign while, in contrast, Lewis et al. (2006) find evidence of pro-coalition bias.

Summary

To sum up our review of the field, we have shown that the major systematic content and framing analyses have traditionally indicated a pattern of news media deference to government in wartime, although the recent Iraq War research paints a more ambiguous picture. At the time of writing, Hallin's work on US news media coverage of Vietnam remains the most thorough, in-depth and comprehensive account of news media and war to date, but is a study conducted a quarter of a century ago of a war that was fought years earlier than that. In comparison, the studies by the Glasgow University Media Group (1985), Morrison (1992) and Bennett and Paletz (1994) offer incomplete and fragmented accounts of wartime news media coverage. The three studies of the 2003 Iraq War (Aday, Livingston and Hebert, 2005; Lewis et al., 2006; Tumber and Palmer, 2004) offer high quality, sustained and detailed accounts of wartime coverage but, for the various reasons set out earlier, none provides a comprehensive assessment of news media performance. Furthermore, the three studies make divergent claims concerning news media bias. Explanations for wartime coverage are also disjointed. Some studies (Aday Livingston and Hebert, 2005; Morrison, 1992; Tumber and Palmer, 2004) provide little by way of explanation. For those that do, reliance on official sources is invoked in many of the studies (Bennett and Paletz, 1994; GUMG, 1985; Hallin, 1986; Lewis et al., 2006), while cold war ideology (Hallin, 1986) and patriotism (Bennett and Paletz, 1994; GUMG, 1985) feature as possible alternative or complementary causal mechanisms. So, even based only on the studies reviewed here, it is reasonable to conclude that there is a good deal of empirical uncertainty regarding news coverage of the 2003 Iraq War and of war more generally.

In addition, this literature largely overlooks the theoretical and normative concerns that underlie the study of news media and war. Besides Hallin's (1986) study of Vietnam, the major content and framing analyses reviewed here (Aday, Livingston and Hebert, 2005; Bennett and Paletz, 1994; GUMG, 1985; Lewis et al., 2006; Morrison, 1992; Tumber and Palmer, 2004) provide little that engages explicitly with theoretical matters, operating primarily as empirical studies. As shown in Chapter 3, there is an abundance of models and theories from across the field of political communication which can be drawn upon in order to provide a solid analytical foundation for the study of news media and war, so one of our central tasks will be to set out just such a theoretical/analytical foundation.

With respect to normative issues, these studies are surprising for the absence of explicit debate and insight as to the role that journalists *should* perform in the context of war. At the very least, the lack of such debate threatens to cause confusion as to how we should analyse and interpret wartime news media performance. For example, in his review of the field, Jerry Palmer notes that studies critical of news media performance during war often assume that news media should apply the democratic norms of 'oversight and accountability' (Palmer, 2005: 380) even when confronted with issues of national security and war. However, this critical position is at odds with that which asserts that media 'ought to be subordinate to government purposes, as a matter of duty' (Palmer 2005: 379). Similarly, in reviewing recent work by Bennett et al. (2007), which is strongly critical of US news media for failing to provide proper oversight of the Bush administration both before and after the invasion of Iraq, Gadi Wolfsfeld comments:

> If the two major parties in the United States are pretty much in agreement on an issue, is it realistic to expect the media to provide the alternative view? . . . Although we certainly should reject jingoism, it seems impractical – *and even problematic* – to demand that editors and reporters lead the charge against any war that enjoys a high level of political consensus [emphasis added]. (Wolfsfeld, 2008: 198)

Here, discussion of what is practical or reasonable to expect of news media in wartime is confused further by lack of attention to what news media should have been doing. For Bennett et al. (2007), US news media should have been pro-active in challenging the Washington political establishment; for Wolfsfeld (2008), it would have been problematic for journalists to go against the prevailing political consensus. Furthermore, these two normative positions seem to omit a middle ground position wherein news media neither support governments in war slavishly nor merely oppose for the sake of opposition. For example, US journalists might see it as their role to ensure that a variety of official and 'non-official' (or non-US) viewpoints are given an adequate airing. Alternatively, if news media do offer 'support' to a particular war, they can still hold governments to account over how that war is prosecuted – by ensuring that the issue of civilian casualties forms a significant component of coverage, for example. Due to the absence of focused normative debate, we will spend part of the next chapter outlining key normative positions regarding 'appropriate' roles for news media in wartime. Our goal here is not to resolve these debates over the appropriate role for news media during war. Rather, we wish to offer a way of structuring discussions about news media performance which gives transparency to assumptions about what news media coverage *should* look like, and to the rationalisation for different modes of news media performance.

Current debates

Besides the limitations we have identified in the studies reviewed so far, even greater uncertainty over wartime media–state relations, and the media–foreign policy nexus in general, derives from a much broader set of dynamics. Recent years have seen the emergence of debates concerning the consequences for journalism of shifting ideological imperatives, developments in communications technology and enhanced media-management strategies on the part of governments. Here, many academics and commentators argue that the ending of the cold war and the expansion of communications technology have extended the scope for a more independent and critical news media. Conversely, some argue that strengthened media-management operations have ensured a continued advantage for governments pursuing war. Whatever the effects may be, such debates inevitably challenge academic orthodoxies regarding the subservience of news media to government.

The end of the cold war and the death of ideology

For some academics, the passing of the cold war has reduced the impact of ideology, redefining media–state relations and enabling journalists to become more independent of their respective foreign policy elites. For example, commentators including Entman (2000), Hoge (1994) and Mandelbaum (1994) have argued that the new humanitarian interventions in territories such as Northern Iraq (1991) and Somalia (1992–93) were driven by news media coverage (the so-called CNN effect) operating in the geo-political vacuum created by the collapse of the cold war anti-communist consensus. While most researchers agree that initial claims concerning the CNN effect overstated its importance (e.g. Gowing, 1994; Robinson, 2002), it remains tempting to believe that we live in very different and more open times than was the case during the cold war. As Entman argues:

> [J]ournalistic motivations embodied in independent, watch-dog self-images and ideals, often encourage a move toward questioning government authority more than was the habit during the cold war. Indeed, even during popular and seemingly successful wars, the media now pounce upon any signs of failure or 'quagmire' and in doing so apply their own evaluative criteria as much as indexing elite opposition. (Entman, 2003: 423)

Similarly, but with respect to a British context, Tumber and Webster argue that the ideology of patriotism nowadays holds less purchase on both the public and journalists:

> [I]n most advanced societies outside of the United States, heroic nationalism holds less of an appeal. There is a heightened awareness of the artificiality of national frontiers, there is consciousness that other cultures are equally rich . . . in countries like Britain, nationalism is on the ebb. (Tumber and Webster, 2006: 163)

Of course, even if the passing of the cold war has made a difference to media–state relations, new meta-narratives may have emerged which also act to create a bond between policy-makers and journalists, as the cold war anti-communist consensus did. For example, over the course of the 1990s the idea of humanitarian intervention became important in a foreign policy community more sensitive to the notion of humanitarian war. By the end of the 1990s, this idea had become a significant feature in Western foreign policy.[15] In short, if the early 1990s witnessed a more influential news media that helped to persuade policy-makers to engage in humanitarian intervention (Bahador, 2007; Robinson, 2002), by the late 1990s the concept had developed into a tool that Western leaders employed in order to justify armed intervention in the internal affairs of another state (Chandler, 2005; Chomsky, 1999; Hammond, 2007a). This could be observed during the 1999 NATO air war against Serbia: although this was primarily an act of coercive diplomacy that had the unintended effect of exacerbating a humanitarian crisis, it was promoted and justified to Western publics, quite successfully, as a humanitarian war.[16]

Subsequently, with the events of 11 September 2001 (9/11), followed by the Bush administration's declaration of a 'war on terror', the geo-political landscape was further, and dramatically, transformed. According to some, the 'war on terror' frame provided journalists with a new template with which to understand global events and a powerful rhetorical tool with which to justify particular foreign policy agendas (Domke, 2004; Jackson, 2005). One example could be seen during the build-up to war against Iraq. The US government worked hard to associate Saddam Hussein with Al Qaeda in the eyes of the US public, even in the absence of any firm evidence, while mainstream US news media often reported this claim uncritically and left some Americans actually unsure of the difference between Hussein and Bin Laden.[17]

In summary, the decline of old and the possible rise of new ideological imperatives injects a degree of uncertainty into our understanding of wartime media–state relations, raising questions about the extent to which they are influenced nowadays by dominant policy frameworks such as the 'war on terror' and 'humanitarian warfare'.

New technology and the media-empowerment thesis

The period since the mid-1990s has seen the rise of the 24-hour news channel, the associated proliferation of advanced news gathering equipment which enables real-time TV coverage, the growth of transnational news media organisations (global news media) and the arrival of the Internet. According to many advocates of what we label the *media empowerment thesis* (e.g. Annis, 1991; Deibert, 2000; Herrera, 2002; Nye, 1999; Rothkopf, 1999; Shapiro, 1999; Volkmer, 1999), these technological developments have led to a reduction in government control over the information environment, with news media now more likely to be adversarial and 'off-message'. A colourful lexicon sustains the discourse surrounding new communication technology and contemporary conflict – '"virtuous war", "new war" (including "network" and "spectacle" warfare) and "information war"' (Matheson and Allan, 2009: 18).

However, the key assumption underpinning this debate is the claim that the ability to report in real time, 24 hours a day, enables media to be less dependent on government information sources in covering events and in defining the news agenda and, consequently, more likely to include alternative viewpoints.[18] As Livingston and Bennett (2003: 364) put it: 'technologies such as the videophone and portable recording and transmission systems potentially free reporters to roam widely, and to cover events at their own discretion without filtering them through officials or along beats or well-cultivated source networks'. Brown (2003: 88) argues that the development of transnational media organisations 'challenges the ability of states to control information flows', and, according to Shaw (2000: 33), this 'diffusion of information through the increasingly global media cannot be contained within the bounds that even the most powerful state leaders would prefer'.

Volkmer (1999: 4–5) takes this analysis one step further by arguing that

CNN International is actually facilitating the emergence of a global public sphere. Finally, many have argued that the Internet has made alternative information sources much more readily available to journalists and the public, and that it has served as a tool to empower non-elite voices. For example, analysing the David and Goliath struggle between the indigenous Chiapas guerrilla army and the Mexican state, Douglas Kellner (1998: 182) claims that: 'From the beginning, the peasants and guerrilla armies struggling in Chiapas, Mexico, used computer databases, guerrilla radio, and other forms of media to circulate news of their struggles and ideas.'

Of course, claims that present the impact of new technology as transformative and empowering need to be treated with some caution.[19] The extent to which new technology actually does create the space for more critical and oppositional news media reporting in the realm of foreign policy and international affairs has been called into question by recent research (Bennett et al., 2006; Livingston and Bennett, 2003). Nevertheless, the suggestion that technological developments have reduced the ability of governments to influence news media is persistently invoked. For example, Tumber and Webster argue that:

> Globalisation has made nations markedly less self-contained and exclusive than ever and less able to contain the information that people receive and transmit . . . With cable and satellite televisions, computer communications facilities and the Internet readily available, it is increasingly difficult for nations to restrict the amount and type of programmes and information that their populations watch and send. (Tumber and Webster, 2006: 24)

While measured debate has continued over the effect of these technological developments upon media–state relations, the last few years have witnessed the emergence of a more radical proposal that there has been a paradigm shift in the relationship between news media and political power. As a result, advocates of this claim contend that it is not enough to consider new communication technologies as but one variable in the media–state relationship. Instead, our understanding of media and its connection with political power and individuals will have to change fundamentally. Most accounts of this sort arise from a belief that the proliferation of Internet-based digital communications has enabled a radical pluralisation of power and, consequently, the emergence of a 'new media ecology' (Castells, 2009; Cottle, 2006) in which interconnected and all-pervasive communication technologies (Internet, mobile phones, digital cameras, and so on) constantly shape the behaviour of everybody from ordinary citizen to Prime Minister.

For example, in their book, subtitled *The Emergence of Diffused War*, Hoskins and O'Loughlin (2010) herald the passing of the era of 'big' media (traditional broadcast media) and the arrival of the post-broadcasting era. It is the proliferation and diffusion of information facilitated by the Internet, digital recording devices and the emergence of online versions of traditional news media that, for them, represents a paradigm shift. The emergence of non-linear and non-hierarchical communication flows means that power is more pluralised in the resulting 'new media ecology'. 'Today', they explain,

> communication is less uniformly linear. Flows can go from broadcaster to audience, but also back again; or communication can begin with the soldier in the field producing a blog that leaks important information that military leaders would prefer remained un-broadcast. (Hoskins and O'Loughlin, 2010)

The implication of these more radical claims is that people come to experience war in a manner that is fundamentally different from earlier eras, in that traditional patterns of elite dominance of media are redundant. However, such claims are not measured assessments of the degree to which new communication technology impacts upon political processes, but rather bold, dramatic and largely untested declarations.

Overall, the impact of new technology raises new questions as to whether wartime media–state relations are less restricted today than they were during the 1960s and 1970s when the US news media covered the Vietnam War, as surveyed by Daniel Hallin (1986). For some proponents of the media-empowerment thesis such changes are likely to be incremental, while for others these changes suggest a radical transformation in the way people experience war. Attention will be paid to these claims as we discuss findings and reach conclusions throughout this book.

Media management, 'spin' and embedding

Even if, over time, new communication technologies have increased the potential power of news media outlets, increasingly professional government media-management techniques may have been effective in countering these developments. During the Falklands conflict in 1982, the British government demonstrated the utility of placing journalists alongside combatants as a means to foster sympathetic reporting. Learning in part from the British experience, the US military adopted the pool system in the 1991 Gulf War, allowing selected journalists to accompany frontline units while others were channelled towards the memorable set-piece press briefings. It was largely the use of dramatic images of 'smart' bombs and sanitised language (such as the use of the terms 'collateral damage' and 'surgical strikes') during these briefings that ensured that media coverage did not relay too much of the grim reality of war.

Since the 1999 Kosovo conflict, attempts to manage the information environment during wars and crises have been strengthened. Coalition military operations in Kosovo, Afghanistan and the 2003 Iraq War have been accompanied by sustained and highly organised attempts to influence media agendas by promoting coverage of some issues rather than others and by encouraging the framing of stories in ways that support the government's cause. At least some of the impetus for these attempts during the 2002 war in Afghanistan came from the UK government's Director of Communications and Strategy, Alistair Campbell, whose:

> solution was to create Coalition Information Centres (CICs) in Washington, London and Islamabad that would coordinate the release of information, attempt to control the news agenda and rebut opposition claims in exactly the way that the Clinton-Blair 'war room' model operated in domestic politics. (Brown, 2003: 93)

Other activities inherent in the 'war room' model include the coordinated use of press releases, news media appearances, press conferences and speeches. In strategic terms, these activities seek to encourage the development of common news media frames over time. In tactical terms, they serve to minimise coverage of damaging or hostile stories and to discredit oppositional counter-narratives.

Since 9/11, media management has remained a high priority for both the US and British governments. With respect to the 2003 Iraq War, the CIC in Washington morphed into the Office of Global Diplomacy and then into the Office of Global Communications (OGC), designed to explain the US strategic goals in the 'war on terror'. The OGC included not just senior diplomats and military personnel but also public relations experts, notably Victoria Clarke, and also coordinated with Alistair Campbell's group in Downing Street.[20] These Washington and London command-and-control propaganda groups were linked to Central Command (CENTCOM) in Qatar, to the Forward Press Information Centre in Kuwait and then, finally, to the minders on the ground – the US public affairs officers and British media operations personnel. While CENTCOM provided the focal point for the dissemination of coalition information to journalists via news conferences, a consistent range of messages was communicated across a variety of briefing forums – including statements to the British Parliament, and press conferences held in Downing Street, at the UK Ministry of Defence (MoD) and the US Departments of Defense and State, as well as by the White House Office of Global Communications. From the British perspective, according to Angus Taverner (at the time a Lieutenant Colonel and responsible for planning the MoD media operations policy), media strategy sought to communicate information to three key audiences: the British public, the families and friends of British service personnel and the Iraqi civilian population. In London, this was done via press briefings timed to 'make sure we would hit all the [media] deadlines around the world', and in Qatar at the CENTCOM headquarters headed up by General Tommy Franks (Commander CENTCOM), Air Marshall Brian Burridge, Brigader General Vince Brooks and Group Captain Al Lockwood. In general terms, the strategic picture was delivered in London while the operational picture was delivered in Qatar.[21]

Complementing strategic attempts to communicate the government's agenda, of course, was the high-profile tactic of embedding journalists with military units. While the policy of embedding was not unprecedented, it was unusual in terms of the numbers of journalists deployed to frontline units and the extent of systematic pre-planning devoted to it by the military. Generally seen as a successful strategy from the coalition's point of view, embedding journalists with frontline units enabled them to file reports based on their first-hand experience alongside coalition troops without having to rely on information provided in coalition press briefings.[22] With its promise of dramatic and immediate coverage of coalition soldiers in action, embedding was also attractive to news organisations. As Cortell et al. (2009: 673) demonstrate, a central factor driving the embedding policy was the desire to regain the initiative in the information war amid concerns that it would prove more difficult to control the battlefield information environment because of the numbers of journalists involved and their technological ability to report live from the front. According to Bryan Whitman, Deputy Assistant Secretary at the US Department of Defense:

> We need to tell the factual story – good or bad – before others seed the media with disinformation and distortions, as they most certainly will continue to do. Our people in the field need to tell the story . . . [Embedding counters] giving any credibility to what the Iraqi Defense Ministry might be putting out. (from interviews quoted in Cortell et al., 2009: 668)

As both Lewis et al. (2006: 188–94) and Aday, Livingston and Hebert (2005: 15–16) argue, the overall value of embedding for coalition media-management operations was that coverage remained more focused on the war and its day-to-day progress than would otherwise have been the case. As a consequence, more problematic stories for the coalition, such as civilian casualties or the rationale for war, were less likely to find their way into the news.

Summing up, the conclusion that the intensification of media-management operations has counterbalanced any empowering effects that might have occurred as a result of the end of the cold war and developments in communication technology remains a plausible one.

Concluding comments

Emerging debates surrounding new and old ideological imperatives, new communication technology and strengthened government approaches to media-management have injected a great deal of argument and uncertainty into discussion of wartime media–state relations. These developments might undermine, or might reinforce, the patterns of wartime media deference that have been argued to exist by many scholars, and their existence makes it harder to be certain of what we think we know about news media and war. Moreover, although there is a large literature that examines a wide variety of issues pertaining to the topic of news media and war, relatively few studies offer systematic and detailed content and framing analysis of news media coverage of war. Much of this literature, with the exception of Hallin's detailed account of US coverage during the Vietnam War, is mainly concerned with empirical analysis, neither theory-driven nor attentive to normative issues (Palmer, 2005: 380), and provides only uneven or incomplete accounts of wartime news media performance. Recent studies of the 2003 Iraq War (Aday, Livingston and Hebert, 2005; Lewis et al., 2006, Tumber and Palmer, 2004) offer greater levels of sophistication compared to earlier work but, due to varying definitions and operationalisations, as well as methodological shortcomings, these studies suggest strikingly different conclusions about news media performance during this conflict.

So, there is considerable value in devising and applying a theoretically-informed analytical framework which can, by providing for a systematic and rigorous analysis of wartime news media performance, offer answers to the debates and uncertainties described in this chapter. Such a framework should integrate the descriptive and explanatory insights into wartime coverage that are indicated across the literature, as well as addressing the normative question of what role news media *should* perform during war. It is to the design of such a framework that we now turn.

Notes

1 The concept of framing refers to the idea that the language, subject matter and visuals of a media narrative encourage audiences to develop particular understandings of an issue. See Chapter 3 for more details.
2 For a journal committed to this broad field of scholarship, see *Media, War and Conflict* (Sage), edited by Andrew Hoskins, Barry Richards and Philip Seib.
3 Generally, this type of research involves the use of codebooks, which show precisely how the analysis is undertaken, trained coders under the supervision of the researcher, and reliability testing and calculation.
4 See also Hallin, 1984.
5 See Althaus (2003: 386), and also Hallin (1986) and Mermin (1999), for further discussion of 'procedural' and 'substantive' media criticism.
6 It is worth noting that Hallin's analysis assumes an American-style, regional press in which concentration of ownership and a decline in the number of titles could easily lead to monopoly. In contrast, the UK's diverse, national press still contains a broad variety of titles.

7 See GUMG (1985: 1–4) for a more detailed account of the impact of the lobby system on reporting of the Falklands War.

8 The term 'episodic' is used to refer to coverage focusing on day-to-day events (e.g. the progress of troops), the term 'thematic' refers to news coverage dealing with underlying issues (e.g. the rationale for a war).

9 Morrison studies BBC1 and ITV evening news, BBC2's *Newsnight* current affairs programme, Channel 4 News, the non-terrestrial Sky World News and CNN's news channel.

10 Aday, Livingston and Hebert (2005) offer an explanation for the relatively rare occasions when they found instances of biased coverage. This explanation is based on the influence of culture/country of origin: for example, 'whenever Al Jazeera ran an imbalanced story, it fell on the critical side of neutrality' (2005: 14). But they make no attempt to explain the predominance of objective coverage that they find. Tumber and Palmer (2004: 162–5) draw on Hallin's (1986) conceptual/theoretical framework (discussed at the start of this chapter) in order to describe, rather than explain, their findings.

11 Telephone interview with Angus Taverner, 10 February 2009. Taverner worked within Ministry of Defence Corporate Communications and was responsible for formulating the MoD's media operations policy during operations in Iraq in 2003.

12 Their sample comprises news reports from the following newspapers: *Sun, Daily Telegraph, Daily Mirror* and *Guardian*; and the following television channels: BBC, ITN, Sky News and BBC News 24.

13 This criticism is also raised by Lewis et al., 2006: 145.

14 They analyse BBC and ITV evening news broadcasts, Channel 4 News and Sky News.

15 In particular, see British Prime Minister Tony Blair's 'Doctrine of the International Community' speech (Blair, 1999).

16 For further details on this case of intervention, see Robinson, 2002: 93–110.

17 For opinion poll data on Americans' belief in an Al Qaeda/Saddam Hussein link and President Bush's linking of the two, see Milbank and Deane, 2003.

18 For a fuller evaluation of these 'technological determinists', see Robinson, 2004.

19 For an overview of counter-arguments to the claim that technological developments are creating greater levels of news media independence, see Robinson, 2004.

20 The formal location was the Foreign Office Information Directorate, located just around the corner from the Prime Minister's residence in Downing Street.

21 Telephone interview with Angus Taverner, 10 February 2009.

22 For more detail on the embedding policy, see Tumber and Palmer, 2004 and Cortell et al., 2009.

Theorising and analysing media performance in wartime

There are two principal objectives to this chapter. In order to move beyond purely empirical analysis, the first is to describe the analytical framework that serves as the basis for our theoretically informed and systematic analysis of wartime media performance. Building initially on existing work by Hallin (1986) and Wolfsfeld (1997), the first half of this chapter synthesises a range of models, hypotheses and explanatory variables, drawn from across the literature, in order to set out a framework composed of three models of news media performance: the elite-driven model, the independent model and the oppositional model. We describe carefully the explanatory and descriptive aspects of each of these models, and discuss their normative basis. We also give an account of how the relationship between foreign policy, news media and war might be expected to operate, based on current theoretical understanding. The second objective of this chapter is to operationalise this framework, so we describe the methodology that was developed in order to implement it.[1]

Models of news media performance: elite-driven, independent and oppositional

Drawing on the work of Hallin (1986) and Wolfsfeld (1997), the analytical framework developed for this study is based on three distinct models of news media performance: the *elite-driven model*, the *independent model* and the *oppositional model*. The elite-driven model is equivalent to Hallin's (1986) 'sphere of consensus' and to Wolfsfeld's (1997) conception of news media as 'faithful servant', both of which describe situations when news media coverage is *supportive* of the government and its aims. The independent model, comparable with Hallin's (1986) 'sphere of legitimate controversy' and Wolfsfeld's (1997) 'semi-honest broker' category, describes conditions where news media remain balanced toward events and open to perspectives beyond those of the government, producing coverage that is labelled as *negotiated*.

However, our independent model is more broadly understood than Hallin's (1986) 'sphere of legitimate controversy', allowing for critical reporting occurring as a function of elite dissensus (as is the case with Hallin's 'elite-legitimated controversy'), but also embracing the possibility that journalists can succeed in negotiating and challenging claims made by political elites. In other words, the independent model, according to our conceptualisation, refers to news media reporting that succeeds in providing a balance of opinions in relation to an issue rather than merely mirroring elite debate and dissensus. Finally, the oppositional model, similar to Hallin's (1986) 'sphere of deviance' and Wolfsfeld's (1997) 'advocate of the underdog' category, represents circumstances in which news media offer a profound challenge to the legitimacy and conduct of a conflict – aligning themselves with anti-war opinion, for example. We identify coverage associated with this model as *oppositional*. Compared with Wolfsfeld's description of news media as 'advocate of the underdog', our oppositional model is conceived more broadly, referring not only to instances of news media support for non-elite groups but also to coverage that opposes government policy (whether or not it might be advocating the interests of non-elite groups).

Although we draw on the work of Hallin (1986) and Wolfsfeld (1997) in setting out three modes of news media performance, this is only the first conceptual step in devising our framework. In order that it should be fit for purpose, we also need to integrate these modes of news media performance with the wide range of explanatory, descriptive and normative insights from both the war and media literature and the broader field of political communication and international politics research. Our approach is eclectic: we draw on specific hypotheses and theories regarding news media coverage of war as well as theoretical accounts relating to both the media–foreign policy relationship and, more broadly, media and politics. Below we offer a detailed explication of each model, before summarising the current state of theoretical knowledge concerning news media coverage of war.

The elite-driven model and supportive coverage

Explanation

As our review in Chapter 2 showed, three reasons are variously invoked in order to explain the elite-driven model and the supportive coverage associated with it: journalists' reliance on official sources (Bennett and Paletz, 1994; GUMG, 1985; Hallin, 1986; Lewis et al., 2006), patriotism (Bennett and Paletz, 1994; GUMG, 1985) and ideology (Hallin, 1986). We now discuss each of these in turn.

Beyond the works reviewed in Chapter 2, the broader literature on media–state relations provides considerable backing both for journalists' reliance on official sources (e.g. Gans, 1979; Sigal, 1973) and for a causal link between sources and news media content. Herman and Chomsky's (1988) 'propaganda model', for example, identifies reliance on official sources as a key filter through which US news coverage is shaped by political elites. Most prominently within academic circles, Lance Bennett's (1990) widely cited and influential 'indexing' hypothesis describes how American journalists index news to the contours of official political debate by privileging Washington-based sources. Subsequently, Mermin's (1999) application of the indexing hypothesis to coverage of American military interventions since Vietnam found a pervasive pattern of news media deference to official policy. In his co-authored work *When the Press Fails* (Bennett et al., 2007), Bennett provides further detailed evidence in support of his indexing hypothesis and argues that, since 9/11, US journalists have indexed coverage tightly to White House sources, leading to a failure of accountability over issues such as the Abu Ghraib prison scandal. In Britain too, research points to the importance of officials, both as primary sources of information and as shapers of news agendas (e.g. Schlesinger and Tumber, 1994).

   Moreover, in addition to the increasingly elaborate media-management techniques now employed by military and government discussed in Chapter 2, there are further reasons to suggest that the circumstances of war can increase the reliance of journalists on official sources even beyond the level witnessed in times of peace. First, according to Wolfsfeld (1997: 25), news media tend to seek out information from the 'side' that holds the initiative, so governments benefit from privileged access to the media when they are able to initiate and control events. The relatively fast-moving and asymmetric nature of recent wars, where Western firepower has overwhelmed organised military opposition, fits well with Wolfsfeld's description. Second, the material reality of war zones sometimes means that journalists are forced into a dependence on official sources. During the 1982 Falklands conflict, which involved military action launched from British warships 8,000 miles from British soil, journalists had to travel with the Royal Navy and to rely on them in order to transmit their stories back home. In Wolfsfeld's (1997: 27) terms, the British military were able to 'regulate the flow of information', thereby controlling the political environment and ensuring supportive coverage.

   The influence of patriotism has been theorised in terms of the 'rally round the flag' effect (Mueller, 1973) whereby, in the US context, an American president enjoys widespread public and political support during times of national crisis. Although the validity of this hypothesis has been subjected to critical review,[2] the idea that patriotism influences news coverage of war is a cogent one. For example, in their study of Israeli coverage of the Second Intifada in 2000, Zandberg and Neiger suggest that national loyalty can overcome journalists' commitment to objectivity during times of crisis and conflict:

> The coverage of violent conflict when the journalist is a member of one of the conflicting parties invokes a professional dilemma: the journalists' traditional

paradigm – of objectivity and neutrality – is challenged and confronted by the journalist's patriotic sentiment and their ethnic and cultural belonging. (Zandberg and Neiger, 2005: 131)

According to Zandberg and Neiger (2005: 132), when events are perceived to threaten the existence of their state and society, journalists' sense of 'national community' may overpower their sense of commitment to professional journalism. Patriotism manifests itself in a number of ways. Liebes (1997) suggests that where journalists share a nationality with those going into action, they will instinctively want to be supportive of them and to celebrate when military victory occurs. In its most extreme form, patriotism can generate jingoistic reporting, such as the notorious British example during the 1982 Falklands conflict when the *Sun* reported the sinking of the Argentine cruiser *General Belgrano* with the headline 'Gotcha' (GUMG, 1985). Finally, as both Bennett and Paletz (1994: 284) and Liebes (1997) argue, commercial news media are vulnerable to the concern that patriotic publics will not welcome critical coverage during war.

Finally, as discussed in Chapter 2, ideological imperatives, such as anti-communist ideology during the cold war (Hallin, 1986; Herman and Chomsky, 1988) and, more recently, the 'war on terror' (Domke, 2004; Jackson, 2005) and 'humanitarian warfare' (Chandler, 2005; Chomsky, 1999; Hammond, 2007a), have been advanced as explanations for supportive coverage during war. Ideology functions at the broadest level, structuring frames of reference that are shared by journalists, policy-makers and the public at large. Ideological imperatives weave their effect in two ways: As well as promoting particular justifications for the substance of foreign policy, they also help to marginalise or exclude alternative positions that might destabilise the dominant official frames that justify the substance of foreign policy-making.

The ideology of anti-communism and the case of the Vietnam War serve to illustrate this effect. In that example, journalists and policy-makers shared the belief that the threat posed by communism required that its spread be combated, and ensured that the war could only be perceived as a righteous struggle to save the Vietnamese from the 'evil' of communist rule. Alternative explanations for the war – presenting it, for example, as an ongoing struggle by large sections of the Vietnamese population (North and South) against the intervention first of France and then the USA – fell so far outside the anti-communism frame that most journalists probably never entertained such an interpretation. As Hallin (1986: 207–8) notes, the idea of the war as an example of US imperialism and an act of aggression was scarcely ever voiced in mainstream US news media. The 'war on terror' offers a parallel here with respect to the 2001 invasion of Afghanistan which followed the attacks of 9/11 (Domke, 2004; Jackson, 2005). Here, a 'war on terror' frame provided the underlying rationale and justification for this offensive, with the result that military action against the Taliban regime was perceived by many US journalists and officials as an inevitable, predictable and justifiable response to the strikes on the USA. At the same time, this frame worked to exclude alternative interpretations, such as those highlighting the broader geo-strategic politics of the region. Central Asia is a key oil-producing region and stands at the crossroads between the USA, Russia and China, so the projection of US influence in the region represents a plausible alternative to the 'war on terror' as an explanation, and indeed justification, for the war in Afghanistan.[3]

Of course, the same 'alternative' geo-political analysis can be applied to the 2003 Iraq War. It, too, was presented publicly by the USA as part of the global 'war on terror' despite the suggestions of those opposing it that influence over oil was a more important explanation. It seems likely that the great mass of mainstream US news media and public opinion understood Iraq through the 'war on terror' lens and did not entertain such alternatives (see Rojecki, 2008). Tellingly, in 2007, when Alan Greenspan (formerly Chairman of the US Federal Reserve) ventured an alternative explanation for the war in Iraq, he created a significant amount of controversy. In his memoirs, Greenspan wrote:

> Whatever their publicised angst over Saddam Hussein's 'weapons of mass destruction', American and British authorities were also concerned about violence in the area that harbours a resource indispensable for the functioning of the world economy. I am saddened that it is politically inconvenient to acknowledge what everyone knows: the Iraq war is largely about oil. (Greenspan, 2007: 463)

In short, by providing straightforward and widely acceptable explanations for military action, ideological discourses such as the 'war on terror' and the 'struggle against communism' limit the spread of more complex and controversial explanations for war. Once journalists have accepted or internalised such a discourse, the focus of news coverage departs from substantive discussion about whether a particular foreign policy can be justified and concentrates instead on the procedural question of whether a policy can achieve the desired outcome. Accordingly, ideological imperatives might manifest themselves not only through journalists explicitly and implicitly reinforcing particular 'official' justifications for a war, but also in the relative absence of reports focusing on substantive issues during war.

Description

Drawing on the studies reviewed in Chapter 2, four key characteristics of supportive coverage can be determined. First, access to news media is largely dominated by government officials and the military of the country to which the journalist belongs (GUMG, 1985; Hallin, 1986; Lewis et al., 2006; Tumber and Palmer, 2004). For example, Wolfsfeld (1997: 69) identifies news media coverage of war as conforming closely to his 'faithful servant' type, with journalists relying 'almost exclusively on official sources', whereas access provided to other actors – for example, domestic dissenters (Hallin, 1986: 198) – is negligible. Second, the subject matter of news reporting reflects a narrow agenda, focusing largely on the military progress of 'our side': We have seen how Hallin's descriptive analysis of news media showing support for US war objectives in Vietnam identifies the central story for journalists as that of 'American boys in action' (1986: 129), with coverage tending to present the USA as 'holding the military initiative' (1986: 146). Similarly, Morrison's UK-based study of the 1991 Gulf War describes coverage as dominated by a concentration on the progress of the war, speculation over coalition strategy and concern regarding air and missile attacks on coalition forces (Morrison, 1992: 68). A third characteristic of supportive coverage is reporting that reinforces official justifications for war and avoids substantive criticism: as described in Chapter 2, Hallin (1986) argued that the Vietnam War raised fundamental questions for some about the legitimacy of US foreign policy, but such doubts are rarely aired within mainstream media. Finally, supportive coverage tends to play down or ignore the bloody reality of war, with few images of civilian and military casualties reaching the news (Morrison, 1992: 68).

In sum, the essence of supportive reporting of war is patriotic, giving support to the military campaign and viewing it from the perspective of 'our' soldiers. Criticism of government and military is minimal, with little attention given to wider political and historical contexts and few images of death reaching press or television bulletins.

Normative foundations

While many liberal academics might condemn news media for taking a supportive line in wartime, those in government, and particularly the military, often perceive the elite-driven model to represent an appropriate attitude for wartime news media to adopt. This attitude can clearly be seen where Lieutenant General Thomas W. Kelly discussed US news media and the 1991 Gulf War in the introduction to *Taken by Storm* (Bennett and Paletz, 1994). His view of news media coverage was that 'the truth was quite healthy during the war, the government told its story, and the American public believed it. The war was quick, it was successful, and there were blessedly few casualties' (Kelly, 1994: 8). Kelly then praised the US press for doing a 'good job' in covering the war, reminding the reader that 'military people are Americans too. We work pretty hard to keep our country free' (Kelly, 1994: 8).

However, it is also important to note that this normative position has a significant intellectual grounding in the school of Realism, which holds that foreign policy should be immune from public (and news media) influence.[4] The Realist position asserts that foreign policy elites are best placed to decide what should be done to further the national interest; and that publics are ill-informed about international affairs and, therefore, ill-equipped to understand foreign policy. At least in the US context, Holsti (1992) locates this belief in a long-standing hostility among US political elites towards public involvement in foreign policy formulation. He quotes Walter Lippmann:

> The unhappy truth is that the prevailing public opinion has been destructively wrong at the critical junctures. The people have impressed a critical veto upon the judgements of informed and responsible officials. They have compelled the government, which usually knew what would have been wiser, or was necessary, or what was more expedient, to be too late with too little, or too long with too much, too pacifist in peace and too bellicose in war, too neutralist or appeasing in negotiations or too intransigent. Mass opinion has acquired mounting power in this country. It has shown itself to be a dangerous master of decision when the stakes are life and death. (Lippmann, 1955: 20, quoted in Holsti, 1992: 442)

A second normative component contends that it is morally correct for public and news media to be mobilised in support of the national interest. Here, Realists promote the position that moral communities are defined by state boundaries and that both news media and public opinion should reflect this. Indeed, as we noted earlier, when discussing the impact of patriotism on wartime reporting, Zandberg and Neiger (2005: 131) highlight a conflict between journalists' professional commitment to objectivity and their 'patriotic sentiment and their ethnic and cultural belonging'. For Realists, there should be no such conflict and journalists should naturally support 'their side' in war.

So from the Realist perspective, for reasons both of sound foreign policy formulation and of moral affinity to one's nation, when a state goes to war it is right that news media help to mobilise the public in support of their troops and government.

The independent model and negotiated coverage

Explanation

At least as an ideal, journalists are often supposed to strive for detachment and 'objectivity', based on their professional standards and training. Despite this, the notion of an independent and objective news media, especially in the realm of foreign affairs coverage, has traditionally received little in the way of empirical and theoretical support from the field of political communication. Particularly in the case of war, the elite-driven model, and its prediction of supportive coverage, is expected to hold true. At most, more independent and critical journalism is usually assumed to occur only when political elites are in disagreement with each other (Bennett, 1990; Entman, 2004; Hallin, 1986; Mermin, 1999; Robinson 2002; Wolfsfeld, 1997).[5] As such, elite political dissensus is seen as a key variable in determining whether greater levels of criticism and debate may occur within news media. However, according to the work of Hallin (1986), Bennett (1990) and Mermin (1999), while journalism during periods of elite dissensus may be more critical, it remains beholden to elite political debate. In Hallin's analysis of news media and the Vietnam War, critical reporting came to reflect the debate between hawks and doves in Washington but largely failed to represent the viewpoints of the anti-war movement. The 'political contest', 'policy-media interaction' and 'cascading activation' models, advanced by Wolfsfeld (1997), Robinson (2002) and Entman (2004) respectively, are less restrictive vis-à-vis the potential independence of journalists. For example, Wolfsfeld (1997) argues that news media do, at times, advocate the interests of non-elite groups against the interests of the state; as an example, he provides evidence that news media produced coverage to challenge the Israeli government and advocate the interests of Palestinians during the 1989 Intifada. At points of policy uncertainty, when elites are unsure over policy, Robinson (2002) argues that news media can become more critical and influence policy outcomes. Most recently, Entman's (2003, 2004) cascading activation model 'explains how interpretive frames activate and spread from the top level of a stratified system (the White House) to the network of non-administration elites, and on to news organizations, their texts, and the public – *and how interpretations feed back from lower to higher levels*' (Entman, 2003: 415; emphasis added). Accordingly, Entman argues that his model demonstrates how 'media are *not entirely passive receptacles for government propaganda*'.

However, each of these accounts makes clear that independent journalism can occur only as a function of elite political disagreement and/or uncertainty. Wolfsfeld argues that the 'ability to mobilize elite support' (1997: 25) is a key variable in determining the ability of non-elite groups to control the news media and political environment:

> Whereas elites are the most common sources for journalists, those who mobilize them capture an important part of the public space on the issue. When the various factions within a government are promoting different frames about a conflict, it is more difficult to control the informational environment because journalists can choose among a variety of sources. When, on the other hand, the official frame is the only frame available among elites, journalists will have little choice but to adopt that frame. (Wolfsfeld, 1997: 29)

Entman argues that oppositional news media coverage can occur when each of the following conditions are met: dissensus exists among officials at the top level of government, mid-level officials promote challenges to existing government policy, and events occur that are culturally ambiguous and open to contestation (Entman, 2003: 422–3). As such, his model remains consistent with indexing theory in that 'elite discord is a necessary condition for politically influential frame challenges' (Entman, 2003: 415).

So, according to most key accounts of the media–foreign policy relationship, independent journalism is theorised and explained only as a function of elite political disagreement, truly independent journalism is more imagined than real, and the possibility that journalists can routinely negotiate and challenge policies put forward by political elites is played down.

However, the elite-driven model is not unassailable. In recent years, new institutionalism has articulated the importance of understanding news media as an actor that, at the very least, is semi-autonomous. At the core of this approach is an attempt to take seriously the analytical and explanatory significance of media systems, considering them to be more than just passive transmitters of political and economic elite interests. For example, Timothy Cook's (1998) *Governing with the News* argues that news media collectively, 'because of their historical development . . . shared processes . . . and predictable products across news organizations' (Cook, 1998: 2–3), can be understood as a *political institution,* neither entirely separate from government nor wholly lacking in independence from political power. Consequently, while news media have become sufficiently 'intertwined with the work of official Washington that the news itself performs governmental tasks', such as the publicising of government policy initiatives, policy itself is often 'the result of collaboration and conflict among newspersons, officials, and other political actors' (Cook, 1998: 3). Describing this interdependence, Cook writes:

> Official sources may instigate the news and direct the attention of reporters toward particular events and issues, without controlling the ultimate story. Each side relies on the other in the negotiation of newsworthiness, and neither fully dominates, because officials and reporters alike hail from at least partially independent institutions that command important and unique resources. (Cook, 1998: 105)

A particularly useful augmentation of the institutionalist approach can be found in the work of scholars such as Rodney Benson (e.g. Benson and Neveu, 2004; Benson, 2006) and David Michael Ryfe (e.g. 2006). In particular, Benson (see 2006, 2004) has drawn upon new institutionalism and Bourdieu's (1998) work on fields. Recognising the similarity between Bourdieu's concept of the field and the idea of media as an institution,[6] Benson (2006) describes how the field of journalism is constrained by broader political and economic forces or fields (along the lines predicted by the elite-driven model). At the same time, with its own internal rules and goals, the journalistic field is partially autonomous from these forces. One aspect of this autonomy concerns the significance of unique 'system characteristics' (Benson 2004: 284) which shape the behaviour and output of media. For example, acknowledging Hallin and Mancini's (2004) influential *Comparing Media Systems*, Benson (2004: 284–5) emphasises how differences in the structure, history and organisation of national media systems generate different patterns of media performance and different levels of independence and autonomy. For example, national media systems with a significant public service ethos and structure are likely to generate news that is less commercial and sensationalist than a media system dominated by commercial media.

Another important aspect of this autonomy, for Benson (2006), Bourdieu (1998) and Hallin and Mancini (2004: 33–45), lies in the culture of journalistic professionalism (referred to in this book as the professional autonomy thesis): 'Though journalists no doubt draw their intellectual, moral, and professional resources from external sources . . . they also draw strength and indeed a certain autonomy, no matter how feeble, from their colleagues' (Benson, 2006: 196). Elsewhere, Benson (2004: 284) suggests that: 'professional reform movements that institutionalize such things as journalism schools, awards for journalistic excellence, ombudsperson positions, and critical journalism reviews may have a significant semi-autonomous power to shape the news'.

Earlier work by Hallin (1994, 2000) has also encouraged greater attention to the independent role of journalists. For example, in his 1994 book, *We Keep America on Top of the World,* Hallin argues that the best journalism combines 'professional commitment to accuracy, balance . . . with a sense of justice and compassion' (1994: 6–7). He goes on to argue that the 'professional ideology of journalism' (1994: 13) can act as a countervailing force to the constraints (such as reliance on elite sources, patriotism and ideology) that have been hypothesised to cause the kind of news media deference predicted by the elite-driven model.[7] In saying this, Hallin is drawing attention to the deterministic character of the elite-driven model and suggesting that it places too much emphasis on structures that constrain journalists and not enough on those that might enable journalists to achieve greater autonomy.

Investigative reporting, including leaks, is identified by Bennett et al. (2007: 65–7) as a key factor in disrupting patterns of indexing and the elite-driven model and thus as an important element of professional and independent journalism. Bennett et al. (2007: 63–5) emphasise the rarity of investigative reporting in the US context, but it is plausible to contend that it might be more significant in the UK. Although not strictly investigative, a particularly high profile and relevant example based on leaked information concerns Andrew Gilligan's notorious BBC report of the views of the British weapons inspector, Dr David Kelly (detailed in Chapter 4).

Some empirical support for the professional autonomy thesis can be found in Scott Althaus's (2003) article 'When News Norms Collide'. Here, Althaus disaggregates between 'ends discourse' (referring to discussion about how to achieve policy success) and 'oppositional context discourse' (referring to substantive level debate). Contrary to the predictions of Bennett's (1990) indexing hypothesis, Althaus observes that journalists during the 1991 Gulf War were often an independent source of subtle forms of critical reporting with respect to 'oppositional context discourse'. For example, he finds that they often invoked the Vietnam War as an 'appropriate parallel or analogy' (Althaus, 2003: 414) to the situation in the Gulf in 1991. Colourfully, Althaus (2003: 402) concludes that 'if the ship of state has government officials at the helm, then television journalists behaved more like dolphins riding the bow wave than mussels stuck to the rudder'. Furthermore, as mentioned in Chapter 2, scholars such as Entman (2003: 423) have suggested that the ending of the cold war increased the scope for independent journalism, while others – including Tumber and Webster (2006: 163) – argue that the decline of patriotism has ushered in greater levels of journalistic independence.

In short, insights from new institutionalism and field theory provide theoretical grounding for understanding media systems as possessing an important degree of autonomy as a result of distinctive system characteristics and significant levels of journalistic independence. Other scholars have also identified journalists' professionalism as a key factor in enabling news media, at times, to act in a manner that is independent of governments and have offered some empirical support for this.

Description
While supportive coverage can be defined and operationalised with relative ease through reference to existing descriptive studies of wartime news media coverage, few studies provide a clear idea of what negotiated coverage might look like. However, Wolfsfeld's (1997) political contest model offers a useful starting point for describing such coverage. According to Wolfsfeld, while news media are often deferential to political elites, they may adopt a more balanced stance in relation to controversial issues. In these circumstances, he ascribes to them the role of 'semi-honest broker', whereby a range of relevant political actors 'are given a significant amount of time and space to air their views' (Wolfsfeld, 1997: 69). Coverage of this type would conform most closely to the ideal of objective or impartial journalism and involve a balance between official sources and viewpoints emanating from both sides of the conflict so that the perspective of all parties is represented. As such, what we have called negotiated coverage would give access to opinions from other involved parties, including civilians, humanitarian organisations, anti-war movements and international actors such as the UN. Following Boyd-Barrett (2004), Maltby (2007: 5) asserts that the relative absence of such alternative

perspectives is important in rendering news media 'vulnerable to manipulation' by officials. Of course, media do generally cover these actors during war, but the amount of attention that they are accorded in news coverage is an indicator of how far news media are prepared to act as a 'semi-honest broker' between government perspectives and alternative viewpoints.

In offering negotiated coverage, journalists could be expected to remain neutral towards the outcome of war, avoiding a simplistic focus on 'our' military victories and covering also military problems and failures. Examples of such an approach include the editorial decision by the BBC during the Falklands War to avoid using the words 'we' and 'us' when referring to the British (GUMG, 1985: 14), the positioning of correspondents in Baghdad in 1991 and 2003 so as to provide reports on civilian casualties and the humanitarian situation, and the use by Channel 4 News in the 2003 Iraq War of reportage from journalists accompanying groups fighting US forces in Baghdad (on 8 April 2003). Finally, unlike supportive coverage, negotiated coverage would remain relatively dispassionate and even-handed towards the substantive issue of whether a conflict is justified.

Normative foundations

Behind the independent model and negotiated coverage is a normative position that objectivity and detachment represent appropriate aspirations for journalists even in war. Returning again to the introduction to *Taken by Storm* (Bennett and Paletz, 1994), US journalist Marvin Kalb – providing a starkly different analysis to that of Lieutenant General Kelly – reflects this 'independent' position when he condemns the same coverage that had been so ardently praised by Kelly. Kalb asserts: 'Unfortunately, during the Gulf War, the American people were short-changed, in part because the press engaged in that most dangerous of professional practices, namely patriotic journalism' (1994: 4). He suggests that US reporters failed in their 'most important function during the spilling of blood in pursuit of national objectives: the ability to think critically, act in a detached manner, ask questions, remain unemotional, and resist . . . the strong temptation to cheer for the American side and denounce the enemy' (Kalb, 1994: 4).

A normative foundation for the independent model and negotiated coverage can be found in liberal international relations theory and, more generally, in liberal political theory. With respect to international relations theory, the idea that public opinion *should* influence foreign policy formulation can be traced back to the early twentieth century when US President Woodrow Wilson articulated the importance of public scrutiny of foreign affairs in his famous 'Fourteen Points'. Here, he called for: 'Open covenants of peace, openly arrived at, after which there shall be no private international understandings of any kind but diplomacy shall proceed always frankly and in the public view' (Wilson, 1918). Central to Wilson's position was the belief that public scrutiny of the foreign policy establishment was a way of alleviating irrational decision making and preventing mistakes. Holsti quotes this 1922 explanation by US Secretary of State Elihu Root:

> When foreign offices were ruled by autocracies or oligarchies the danger of war was in sinister purpose. When foreign affairs are ruled by democracies the danger of war will be in mistaken beliefs. The world will be gainer by the change, for, while there is no human way to prevent a kin from having a bad heart, there is a human way to prevent a people from having an erroneous opinion. (quoted in Holsti, 1992: 440)

So, according to liberal international relations theory, public opinion is a 'force for enlightenment – indeed a necessary if not sufficient condition for sound foreign policy' (Holsti, 1992: 439). More broadly, of course, liberal political theory advocates the importance of the marketplace of ideas whereby diverse opinions and viewpoints are able to circulate and these, in turn, facilitate rational and full deliberation: good policies can only come from full and open public debate. From the point of view of journalists, the overwhelming objective should be to ensure that reporting seeks to be unbiased and fair, and that the full range of opinions on a given subject are represented in a balanced way. As Habermas argued in his seminal study *The Structural Transformation of the Public Sphere* (1989), media provide a vital platform for this full and open debate to occur. Objective and independent journalism, which enables a full range of perspectives and opinions to be aired, is the vital component of this so-called public sphere.[8]

In sum, the liberal perspective argues that governments are not to be trusted unquestioningly with foreign policy and that the scrutiny of media and public is essential. In wartime, even after the 'first shot is fired', the public must remain fully informed as to the progress, consequences and continued rationale for war, so that governments can be prevented from pursuing 'immoral or unnecessary wars' (Aday, Livingston and Hebert, 2005: 4). In order to achieve this, balanced and independent reporting is vital.

The oppositional model and oppositional coverage

If the idea of an independent and objective news media receives little empirical support from the field of political communication, media acting as a source of fundamental opposition to foreign policy is understood as an even rarer phenomenon. Of course, it is reasonable to assume that professional autonomy and particular media system characteristics might enable news media to adopt an oppositional stance. In recent years, however, significant scholarly attention has also been paid to discussing the circumstances in which unexpected events cause news media to abandon their deference to political elites, and instead to adopt either an independent or oppositional stance. Most prominently, in *The Politics of Force*, Lawrence (2000) suggests that unexpected, dramatic and disturbing occurrences can 'provide legitimizing pegs to support relatively independent and critical news narratives' (Bennett et al., 2006: 468; and see Wolfsfeld, 1997: 25). To illustrate this, Lawrence notes how the now infamous assault by Los Angeles police officers on a black motorist, Rodney King, was captured on a handheld video camera and, in turn, generated substantial space for marginalised groups to influence media and political debate. In an example drawn from wartime coverage, Wolfsfeld describes how the allied bombing of the Amiriya air raid shelter during the 1991 Gulf War, with the loss of many civilian lives, generated an event beyond the control of US officials:

> This is a story that could only partially be controlled by the US military; it was one that got away. The President's 'spin patrol' . . . was dealing with damage control, and while they seem to have done an admirable job, important limits were being set by the images and information of civilian victims . . . However few and brief, these windows of opportunities did provide Iraq with some moments of international sympathy for their claims against their powerful enemies. (Wolfsfeld, 1997: 180–91)

As noted earlier, Entman's (2003, 2004) cascading activation model describes the conditions under which oppositional news media coverage can arise, namely when each of the following occurs: there is dissensus among officials at the top level of government, mid-level officials promote challenges to existing government policy and *events occur* that are culturally ambiguous and open to contestation (Entman, 2003: 422–3; emphasis added). Finally, Bennett et al. (2007: 64) note that patterns of indexing can be disrupted when 'highly dramatic events may contain other properties that embolden news organisations to step, if only briefly, outside government definitions of reality, and report alternative views'. To demonstrate their case, they describe how US news media reporting of Hurricane Katrina operated in a 'no spin-zone . . . [where] they had nearly a week to report what they actually saw' (Bennett et al., 2007: 64).

The important thread running through these accounts is the notion that events that are outside the control of elites can create conditions in which oppositional (and also independent) news media coverage may occur. Bennett et al. (2006: 467) have labelled the insights provided by Lawrence (2000) as the 'event-driven' news model, while Livingston and Bennett (2003: 364–5) have defined event-driven news as 'coverage of activities that are . . . spontaneous and not managed by officials'. By their nature, many events in wartime – including civilian casualties and 'friendly fire' incidents – are beyond the control of governments and can, potentially, weaken their influence over news media (Livingston and Bennett, 2003: 366; Wolfsfeld, 1997: 25). Moreover, in keeping with the media empowerment thesis (see Chapter 2), the proliferation of advanced news-gathering equipment, 24-hour news channels including non-Western based outlets such as Al Jazeera, and the Internet may have increased the occurrence of event-driven news by making journalists less dependent upon official sources.

Description

Oppositional coverage would emphasise military problems and failures, grant significant space to alternative 'non-official sources' and perhaps even allow the war to be presented from the position of the opponents or the 'enemy'. Indeed, it is common for reporting that emphasises problematic events, such as military problems and loss of life, to be viewed as undermining the war effort and aiding the enemy. For example, in the Wolfsfeld quotation above, media reporting of the US bombing of the Amiriya air raid shelter during the 1991 Gulf War is said to have provided Iraq with ammunition in the propaganda war. Similarly, with respect to Vietnam, Richard Nixon (1978: 35) argued that: 'television showed the terrible human suffering and sacrifice of war . . . the result was a serious demoralisation of the home front, raising the question of whether America would ever again be able to fight an enemy abroad'. Indeed, it is this supposedly literal and bloody reporting of war that underpins the Vietnam Syndrome.

We would expect to find oppositional reporting giving predominant coverage to the human consequences of the conflict for combatants and civilians alike, and emphasising its negative humanitarian impact. We would also expect coverage to offer a robust challenge to the official justifications put forward for military action. As such, this form of coverage would contain a preponderance of 'substantive' criticism.

Normative foundations

Two perspectives offering normative justifications for the oppositional model can be identified – one deriving from critical theory, the other from a more radical interpretation of the role of news media in a democracy. Critical approaches through which oppositional coverage can be justified raise fundamental questions about the legitimacy of particular conflicts and of existing political and economic orders, including those defined by the state system (Cox, 1981). For example, Marxism and critical theory question existing political and economic orders through a process of explaining and understanding their origins. From these perspectives, the state is a function of political and economic structures that enable domination by a socio-economic elite. The mass media play a central role in maintaining this inequality – reflecting and propagating the interests of elites, and transmitting an elite world-view that serves to manipulate or 'manufacture' the opinions of ordinary people.

Herman and Chomsky's *Manufacturing Consent* (1988) is a provocative account that represents this position well. Its authors emphasise the significant overlapping interests between the US state and major US business conglomerates, including media corporations themselves. This set of common interests creates commercial imperatives which lead news organisations to avoid news stories that run contrary to these interests. As a result, argue Herman and Chomsky, mainstream US news media perpetuate an image of an inherently benign, peaceful USA, committed to high moral standards, while its foreign policy is actually riddled with self-interested economic and political objectives that lead it to conduct violent and illiberal policies. In keeping with their profound criticism of the status quo, critical scholars and commentators argue that news media should adopt a far more oppositional and questioning stance than they usually do. Not doing so leaves governments free to pursue violent and illiberal foreign policies (Herman and Chomsky, 1988), while supportive news media, as the critical British journalist Robert Fisk argues, become 'a lethal weapon supporting governments that want to go to war'.[9]

However, justification for the oppositional model does not necessarily rest upon the cogency of a radical critique of the existing economic and political order. The idea that news media should adopt an oppositional stance towards powerful elites can also be seen as part of their democratic 'watchdog' function, whereby journalists actively scrutinise and challenge those in power. This involves more than simply providing a degree of balance between elite and non-elite perspectives, as the independent model would require. Instead, the argument underpinning oppositional journalism is that news media in a democracy are there to hold those in power to account by persistently asking difficult and challenging questions.

News media, theory and war

To summarise our discussion so far, there is widespread support for the predictions of the elite-driven model. Many studies, discussed here and in Chapter 2, reason that news media in wartime will produce coverage that supports the state. Hallin's (1986) study of Vietnam predicts criticism occurring only as a function of elite disagreement. Genuinely independent or oppositional coverage is not expected to occur at all. Wolfsfeld's political contest model also predicts that in wartime media adopt the role of 'faithful servant' to the state. Also, it is plausible that strengthened media-management operations, discussed in Chapter 2, reinforce media deference to the state. Nevertheless, and as shown in the previous chapter, our empirical knowledge is uncertain, while recent studies (i.e. Aday, Livingston and Hebert, 2005; Tumber and Palmer, 2004) and debates raise possibilities for the existence of a more independent and/or oppositional news media. In their most extreme form, arguments about the transformation or paradigm shift generated by the arrival of digital communication technologies predict a radically pluralised relationship between news media and the state. Here, the event-driven news thesis in particular captures the idea of how information circulation might generate both negotiated and oppositional coverage. Some have also argued that the passing of the cold war has freed up journalists to adopt a more independent stance. In theoretical terms, new institutionalist thinking about professional autonomy and media system characteristics provides ways of understanding journalists as being more than mouthpieces for government officials. The extent to which these alternative hypotheses and models are applicable in times of war, however, is unknown. The framework set out here, once applied, will provide at least some answers to all of these questions. It is to the operationalisation of this framework that we now turn.

Measuring wartime news coverage: operationalising supportive, negotiated and oppositional coverage

Overview of methodology

In order to operationalise supportive, negotiated and oppositional coverage, we drew on and developed a range of approaches, including those used in Hallin's (1986) study of the Vietnam War and those developed for analysing the news agenda and media autonomy during election campaigns (see Goddard et al., 1998; Semetko et al., 1991). The strengths of Hallin's analysis (see Chapter 2) lie in its systematic and codified approach, identifying the subjects and sources employed in US news media coverage of the Vietnam War, and assessing the tone of each news story. The election campaign framework shares some of these features and has been widely adapted for use internationally. In devising our methodology, it was important to develop a set of measures that would enable a reliable, valid and qualitatively-rich analysis of news media coverage. So we included a variety of measures ranging from those commonly used in traditional quantitative content analysis (such as airtime/word counts accorded to news sources), through to qualitative assessments of reporter tone, and on to in-depth qualitative analysis with regard to the use of visuals and the framing of news media reports. In combination, these approaches provide a detailed and rich insight into how the war was reported. In developing the methodology, we also took care to avoid the shortcomings identified in Chapter 2: specifically, we ensured that our measures were sensitive to procedural and substantive forms of criticism and subtle forms of bias that occur through framing. Following Althaus (2003), we also drew on measures that could determine the extent to which journalists themselves made critical contributions to news reports. In the following pages we provide detailed descriptions of our measures and methodology. Further details and technical aspects can be found at Appendix A.

Detailed methodology

In order to measure news media coverage, we analysed the range of *story actors* and *sources* and assessed the extent to which journalists themselves made 'critical contributions' (Althaus, 2003: 385–8) through an analysis of *reporter approach*. We also identified the subject matter of news reports (*story subjects*) and analysed the *visual* representation of the war. Finally, we assessed the overall *framing* of news reports in order to determine the extent to which reports reflected or challenged official narratives regarding the war.

Story actors and sources

These measures provide a precise assessment of which actors were focused on and prioritised by different news media outlets during the war. Stories were coded for the presence of relevant actors, from George Bush and Tony Blair as leaders of the coalition through to representatives of the Iraqi regime (e.g. Tariq Aziz and Saddam Hussein) and domestic anti-war protesters.[10] Quoted or cited sources were also identified and the length of quotes recorded. Actors were grouped into one of fourteen main categories, such as 'coalition', 'expert' or 'anti-war'. Using these measures, we were able to assess which actors were most successful at accessing the news media, illustrating the extent to which journalists achieved balance between competing sources. As such, these variables allow us to gauge the extent to which each model (elite-driven, independent and oppositional) prevailed. A predominant focus on UK and US officials as sources would offer evidence for the elite-driven model, but a substantial focus on, say, the anti-war movement, humanitarian organisations or Iraqi authorities would point towards the independent or oppositional models being in play.

Reporter approach

In addition to subject framing, we recorded reporter approach towards story actors. This measure provides an indicator of the way in which journalists refer to actors, identifying the extent to which they engage in 'straight' (i.e., non-evaluative) reporting, or use 'deflating' or 'reinforcing' language toward actors. Each story actor was given a code ('deflating' through 'mixed/straight' to 'reinforcing') to reflect how their actions and words are treated. Where actors were referred to without evaluation, a code of 'straight' was used. In this way, we are able to capture how often reporters make judgements and to whom they are directed. These measures are derived from the coding schema for election surveys (Semetko et al., 1991) and are equivalent to the measure of objective reporting employed in the study by Aday, Livingston and Hebert (2005). The aim here was to assess whether journalists adopted either adversarial language or, alternatively, deferential or reinforcing language towards story actors. As recommended by Althaus (2003: 385–8), this measure provides an insight into the extent to which journalists themselves make critical contributions to news stories.

Story subjects

This measure identifies the subject matter of news reports – for example, a news report might focus on the military campaign itself, civilian or military casualties, humanitarian operations or the background to and rationale for the war. The list of story subjects, based on Hallin's (1986) work and compatible also with the American study of the Iraq invasion by Aday, Livingston and Hebert (2005), was designed to enable the identification of the full range of potential news coverage, from subjects that the coalition sought to promote (such as coalition humanitarian relief operations) to those favourable to the anti-war movement (public protest, for example) or aid agencies (including food and water shortages in Iraq). As such, this measure enables us to assess the relative prevalence of subjects indicative of the elite-driven model (battle progress, military success, and so on) and those associated with the independent or oppositional models (casualties, anti-war protest, and so on). The list also enables us to distinguish between subjects where we might expect procedural criticism and those where substantive criticism might occur. As with the study by Aday, Livingston and Hebert (2005: 3), this measure provides a 'macro-level portrait of the war' as offered by each news outlet and identifies the constituents of the news agenda during the conflict.

Visuals

Analyses of news media content that do not code visual images – those which collate news text from databases such as Lexis-Nexis, for example – exclude a significant element of the complete news story. Even broadsheet newspapers nowadays include substantial pictorial content during wartime. For example, the Iraq-related news pages contained approximately 20 photographs or illustrations each day during the invasion. In contrast to the other two major studies on UK news media coverage of the Iraq invasion (see Chapter 2), our codebook included detailed measures for recording the occurrence of certain types of visual imagery. The main headings for the visuals measure mirror the story subject classifications outlined above (e.g. 'battle', 'humanitarian' or 'public protest') and are designed to capture the full range of subjects visually represented in television and press imagery. In addition, the measures for visuals were further refined so as to allow identification of 'live pictures' from television news and, for example, images which were particularly graphic (such as 'Civilian casualties: Body, isolation on single individual, face shown'). We also recorded where external sources for visuals, such as wire agencies, alternative media or military camera crews, were given credit. As Lewis et al. observed (2006: 120), provenance of visual imagery was not consistently credited across television outlets, and similarly we found that red-top newspapers rarely sourced photographs. However, we included a measure to record *where possible* those instances when an alternative source is accredited (whether indicated verbally or visually). When discussing visual aspects of coverage, we combine both systematic and quantitative data (as described above) along with non-systematic qualitative analysis based on a detailed and rich knowledge of how visuals were used in press and TV.

Besides coding visual subjects separately, visuals are also one of the elements that we consider in coding for the framing of news reports, as explained below. The role of visuals in providing supportive, negotiated or oppositional coverage can only be assessed when visual and verbal elements are considered together. For example, a rather innocuous press photograph depicting a British soldier alongside Iraqi children, who are neither smiling nor angry, is anchored by the caption, 'Unwelcome: A British Marine is surrounded by sullen children as he patrols the streets of Umm Qasr' (*Mail on Sunday*, 6 April 2003: 10). As a result, a message of Iraqi wariness or hostility toward the soldiers emerges from this picture rather than a possible supportive interpretation. Similarly, the meaning of television visuals can be pre-empted and closed to some degree by the verbal narrative offered by the reporter or other sources. Audiences are, of course, active players in the interpretations of media messages; nevertheless, in coding for the framing of news stories, we take into account the way in which language *and images* have been combined to offer readers and viewers a certain take on the events depicted. The observable patterns of 'selection, emphasis, and exclusion' (Gitlin, 1980: 7) – of both verbal and visual elements in the news – offer the researcher insights into the subjects and frames deemed newsworthy, suitable and consonant by each news media outlet.

Framing

The measures already described allow us to assess the news agenda during the conflict and to assess who gains access to the news media and how independently journalists report. But it is also necessary to evaluate more subtle types of partiality. As Wolfsfeld (1997) argues, access is only one part of the contest over news media and it is equally important to assess the extent to which actors were successful at framing the news media agenda, the 'cultural contest over meaning'. The concept of framing refers to the 'specific properties of . . . [a] narrative that encourage those . . . thinking about events to develop particular understandings of them' (Entman, 1991: 7). By employing particular types of language, visuals and information, news reports can be framed so as to privilege one understanding of events over another. For example, in what was widely perceived as a public relations victory for the US military during the 1991 Gulf War, the deployment of coalition language such as 'collateral damage' instead of civilian casualties, images of laser-guided bombs hitting their targets and a focus on battle tactics and military progress helped to frame the war as a clean, fast and efficient one (Baudrillard, 1991; Bennett and Paletz, 1994). Analysing news media frames is particularly important because, even if journalists allow equal access to all relevant actors and avoid reinforcing or deflating language, news reports may still favour one actor over another, whether explicitly or implicitly. As shown in Chapter 2, for example, a news story might be assessed to be straight or 'objective' (Aday, Livingston and Hebert, 2005) but, in emphasising coalition attempts to encourage a focus on its humanitarian activities, it will nevertheless reflect a coalition perspective.

In order to increase the ability of coders to assess story framing accurately, we developed a detailed set of criteria for determining the extent to which reports favour the coalition perspective, either implicitly or explicitly, or reflect alternative viewpoints. Our criteria were developed only for key themes in coverage by which the range of news media debate during the war could be assessed, namely *battle, civilian casualties, military casualties, humanitarian issues* and the three principal justifications for war – *WMD, humanitarian* and *'war on terror'*. In addition, the themes chosen enabled us to distinguish between areas where procedural criticism might occur (battle, civilian casualties, etc.) and where substantive criticism might occur (justifications for war). In assessing the framing of themes, we drew on our measures for story actors, story subjects and reporter approach, as well as visuals and any prognoses about the progress of the war, in conjunction with our predetermined criteria. A summary of our framing criteria is given in Table 3.1 and we describe our approach to coding in relation to each of these frames below. Detailed criteria that were developed for two of these frames (battle and the humanitarian rationale for war) are shown in Appendix B. As not all stories could be coded according to this list of themes, coders also identified the way in which the subjects within each news story are framed (*subject framing*) and the framing of each story as a whole (*overall story framing*). Although still reliable and valid, no explicit coding criteria were produced for these two measures, which we draw upon quite rarely in the analysis that follows and identify clearly when we do.

For each *theme, subject* and *story* identified, we awarded a framing code to indicate how coverage played for the main political actors involved. Framing codes could be applied to each main actor – coalition, Iraq, UN, anti-war,

Table 3.1 Coding criteria for thematic frames (from the perspective of the coalition)

Supportive (elite-driven model)	Negotiated (independent model)	Oppositional (oppositional model)
Possible reinforcing tone/ acceptance of coalition language (e.g. 'liberation')	Mixed or straight tone	Possible deflating tone/ challenge to coalition language (e.g. 'invasion')
Subjects: **Battle**: military success, battle progress as the central organising narrative.	*Subjects:* **Battle:** mix of positive and negative codes, or unclear position on outcome.	*Subjects:* **Battle:** military failure, unexpected and successful resistance, strategic errors.
Civilian casualties: responsibility attributed to Iraqi tactics/emphasis on precision bombing/ coalition denial accepted. Visuals of casualties at a minimum.	**Civilian casualties:** balance of positive and negative perspectives, Iraqi claims of coalition-attributed casualties countered by coalition sources.	**Civilian casualties:** civilian suffering prioritised, with responsibility attributed to coalition/questioning of accuracy of targeting/ graphic visuals.
Military casualties: bravery and heroism of deceased soldiers/family supportive of war.	**Military casualties:** straight reporting of deaths as statistical facts, or bravery balanced with criticism.	**Military casualties:** emphasis on procedural errors or 'friendly fire', families questioning the reasons for war.
Humanitarian issues: coalition success in delivering aid and winning 'hearts and minds'.	**Humanitarian issues:** possible problems or delays but not significant criticism of efforts.	**Humanitarian issues:** failure to deliver aid/lack of crucial supplies for Iraqi civilians/pessimism about humanitarian situation.
Justifications – WMD: relaying coalition claims regarding Iraq's WMD capability unproblematically, assuming they would be found/ reporting finds.	**Justifications – WMD, humanitarian, 'war on terror':** mix of arguments presented, coded for each separate justification frame.	**Justifications – WMD:** questioning of coalition evidence and likelihood of finding WMDs.
Humanitarian: bringing freedom and democracy/referencing the moral case for war and the brutality of the Iraqi authorities.		**Humanitarian:** challenge to humanitarian narrative for the war, setting out alternative explanations (US imperialism, oil reserves).

Table 3.1 (continued)

Supportive (elite-driven model)	Negotiated (independent model)	Oppositional (oppositional model)
'war on terror': unproblematic reference to official claims connecting Saddam to 9/11 and Al Qaeda, or more generally to funding terrorism.		'war on terror': link between war in Iraq and 'war on terror' rejected as invalid/ war will increase world terrorism.

other – on a three-point scale: supportive, negotiated and oppositional. In presenting our findings in Chapters 5, 6 and 7, however, we have generally reported our framing measures from the perspective of the coalition.[11]

Framing of battle

Predictably, promoting a positive image of coalition military progress was a central goal of the coalition. In addition to the strategy of embedding journalists, the coalition focused heavily on the subject of battle during press briefings, with 40 per cent of all coalition briefing subjects related to it (Robinson, Goddard and Parry, 2009: 682).[12] While briefings conducted in London were particularly focused on 'giving out a very positive line' which was 'always very much about forward progress', the entire media operation was coordinated so as to ensure that coalition officials spoke with a common voice in encouraging a narrative based around success, forward progress and momentum.[13] The following quote from the CENTCOM briefer Brigadier General Vincent Brooks demonstrates this strategy:

> I want to take a few minutes to brief you now on some of the operations that have occurred by the coalition over the last several days. The operation of course began on the 19th of March, and since that time, coalition forces have already achieved a number of key objectives. Our first effort is aggressive with direct attacks to disrupt the regime's key command, control, communications, integrated air defense and ballistic missiles using various targeting and methods that will achieve the desired effects. This video shows an attack against an Ababil-100 in southern Iraq, and resulted in its destruction. . . . I should add that the power of information has been key throughout this operation, and it is truly having the effect of saving lives – of the Iraqi and military units who are choosing not to fight and die for a doomed regime. The leaders from several regular army divisions surrendered to coalition forces, and their units abandoned their equipment and returned to their homes, just as the coalition had instructed. (21/22 March 2003; quoted in Cordesman, 2003).

There were also concerted attempts to deflate over-optimistic expectations of a rapid victory (Robinson, Goddard and Parry, 2009: 682). With respect to battle, stories were coded as supportive for the coalition if they emphasised military success implicitly or explicitly. Such reports might include coalition battle successes, presented in a reinforcing manner by journalists, with an optimistic prognosis and unproblematic acceptance of coalition language. Conversely, stories were coded as oppositional for the coalition if they focused on military failures with clear disdain or critical distance in the reporter's tone. Such reports might be characterised by a rejection of coalition language and a pessimistic prognosis regarding the war. Stories that contained a mixture of positive and negative codes towards the coalition or presented an unclear position on the outcome of the war were coded as negotiated.

Framing of civilian casualties

Civilian casualties represented a key issue area in which the coalition sought to minimise the potential for negative publicity. Before the conflict began, Tony Blair told the House of Commons: 'We will do everything we can to minimise civilian casualties' (G. Jones, 'British forces will try to minimise civilian casualties, Blair tells MPs', *Daily Telegraph*, 20 March 2003: 3). Nevertheless, the coalition 'never tried to downplay civilian casualties', according to Angus Taverner: they 'always tried to say "war is a messy business; we are trying to be as careful as we can be but there are always going to be mistakes"'.[14] When such casualties occurred, emphasis would be placed on the precision targeting of weapons and dubious Iraqi tactics. Following a marketplace blast in early April, for example, coalition briefers told journalists:

> Coalition aircraft used precision weapons to target nine Iraqi surface-to-air missiles and launchers . . . The missiles and launchers were placed within a residential area. Most of the missiles were positioned less than 300 feet from homes. While the coalition goes to great lengths to avoid injury to civilians and damage to civilian facilities, in some cases such damage is unavoidable when the regime places military weapons near civilian areas. ('14 killed in Baghdad raid, says Iraq', *Daily Telegraph*, 12 April 2008)[15]

So, although civilian casualties might be considered to be an inherently negative subject for the coalition, their occurrence could still be presented in strikingly different ways. Reports were coded as supportive for the coalition if they attributed responsibility for civilian deaths to Iraqi actions (military hardware in civilian areas, for example) and emphasised attempts to keep casualties to a minimum through precision bombing. Such reports were also likely to contain few visual images of death or injury. Conversely, reports that prioritised the suffering of civilians through dramatic visuals and emotive language, and, for example, questioned the accuracy of coalition targeting, were coded as oppositional for the coalition. Reports that remained more detached, perhaps by balancing Iraqi claims against coalition claims, were coded as negotiated.

Framing of military casualties

The subject of military casualties was also open to differing interpretations in news reports despite being an inherently negative matter. The coalition was careful to give due respect and deference to soldiers killed in combat. For example, following his death, the regiment of one British soldier described him as: 'an all-round professional soldier. A first-class tank commander, a strong and effective man manager with a great depth of character, who excelled under pressure' ('Steve died doing the right thing, says widow of sergeant', *Daily Telegraph*, 26 March 2003: 5). At other times, there were instances where the coalition requested that news media did not show footage that had become available of soldiers being killed or wounded.[16] Reports that concentrated on the bravery of deceased soldiers, reinforced through the language employed by the reporter and avoiding distressing images, were coded as supportive for the coalition. But at other times, news stories adopted a far more critical stance, focusing on the angry reaction of relatives, for example. Such reports, relying on family or anti-war sources that questioned the coalition's rationale for the war or procedural mistakes that could have caused the deaths, were coded as oppositional. Reports that merely relayed facts without evaluation, or where the highlighting of bravery was balanced against criticism, were coded as negotiated.

Framing of humanitarian issues

A principal aim of the coalition media-management agenda was to promote the humanitarian operations carried out by allied forces. After the issues of battle and the post-war rebuilding of Iraq, humanitarian operations represented the next largest category of briefing with 9.1 per cent of briefing subjects dealing with this area (Robinson, Goddard and Parry, 2009: 682). As Angus Taverner explains, humanitarian operations were very much in 'our heads and in our plans', partly because the coalition 'anticipated the likelihood of a major humanitarian disaster' following the collapse of the regime.[17] The following quote from US Major General Vincent Renuart (CENTCOM) provides an example of the coalition's approach:

> At the same time, combat operations were ongoing. Humanitarian aid – I mention this repeatedly because that is really one of the two great pillars of this combat operation – at the same time you're exerting combat power against a very focused enemy, you want to be able to infuse into that fight humanitarian assistance that will begin to normalize the lives of the people in the towns that you're liberating. And things like bringing in wheat to Umm Qasr,

bringing in humanitarian aid overland from Kuwait – great support from the Kuwaitis to infuse that aid into the fight was noted as early as the second or third day after combat operations began. The water pipeline was constructed and is completed now from Kuwait into Umm Qasr, up to Zubair, and we now have a situation just a few days ago, a couple of days ago, where water into Basra is almost completely restored. (5 April 2003; quoted in Cordesman, 2003)

In our analysis of news media coverage, reports dealing with coalition efforts to distribute aid that were delivered in a reinforcing manner by journalists, with an optimistic prognosis and unproblematic acceptance of coalition language (e.g. 'battle for hearts and minds'), were coded as supportive for the coalition. Conversely, reports dealing with the failure to deliver aid, emphasising problems facing coalition aid efforts and offering pessimistic assessments of the humanitarian situation were coded as oppositional. Reports that identified problems and delays concerning humanitarian relief but did not criticise coalition efforts were coded as negotiated.

Framing of justifications for war – WMD, humanitarian, 'war on terror'
We were also particularly interested in assessing the extent to which news reports promoted or challenged the official justifications for the war in Iraq. Although coalition briefings contained details of specific aspects of military and humanitarian operations, the broader rationale for the war was also an important part of the coalition media campaign[18] and was included in official statements and lines. At the start of the military campaign, US Secretary of Defence Donald Rumsfeld outlined the coalition's objectives:

- First, [to] end the regime of Saddam Hussein.
- Second, to identify, isolate and eliminate Iraq's weapons of mass destruction.
- Third, to search for, to capture and to drive out terrorists from that country.
- Fourth, to collect such intelligence as we can relate to terrorist networks.
- Fifth, to collect such intelligence as we can relate to the global network of illicit weapons of mass destruction.
- Sixth, to end sanctions and to immediately deliver humanitarian support to the displaced and the many needy Iraqi citizens.
- Seventh, to secure Iraq's oil fields and resources, which belong to the Iraqi people.
- And last, to help the Iraqi people create conditions for a transition to a representative self-government.
(21/ 22 March 2003; quoted in Cordesman, 2003)

Running throughout Rumsfeld's objectives are the main 'official' justifications for the invasion of Iraq: the elimination of the threat posed by Iraq's possession of WMD, the idea of saving the Iraqi people from a brutal dictator (the humanitarian rationale for war), and the claim that the campaign was part of a broader 'war on terror'.

Regarding the WMD justification for war, reports were coded as supportive for the coalition if they implicitly or explicitly reinforced coalition claims concerning WMD – for example, by relaying British or American claims about Iraq's WMD capability in unproblematic terms and incorporating clear assumptions that WMD would be found. Alternatively, if a report played down coalition claims, questioning the likelihood of finding WMD, it was coded as oppositional. In relation to the humanitarian justification for the war, reports that implicitly or explicitly reinforced official claims about the moral case for war, spoke of bringing democracy and freedom to the Iraqi people and contained unproblematic acceptance of coalition language ('freedom', 'democracy', 'liberation') were coded as supportive. Similarly, reports highlighting past atrocities committed by the Iraqi regime in the context of reinforcing the humanitarian narrative, either implicitly or explicitly, were also coded as supportive. Conversely, reports challenging this official narrative through deflating commentary or by setting out alternative explanations for the war – US imperialism, economic benefit (including oil), regional influence, US domestic political considerations – were coded as oppositional. Finally, with respect to the 'war on terror', reports that referred unproblematically to official claims linking Saddam with al-Qaeda, 9/11 or the 'war on terror', and accepted coalition language, were coded as supportive for the coalition. However, reports that challenged such connections – for example, in giving a voice to anti-war commentators who questioned the validity of the claimed link between Iraq and the 'war on terror' – were coded as oppositional for the coalition. Finally, in relation to all three justifications for war, reports that avoided either condoning or challenging the arguments for war, or contained a mix of pro- and anti-war arguments, were coded as negotiated.

Case selection and additional research strategies

Case selection

Our tripartite analytical framework provides a theoretically informed grounding for the analysis of news media coverage during the 2003 invasion of Iraq. By applying the framework to British coverage of the invasion, we are assessing the UK news media's performance in covering this war but also testing the validity of the three models. So, besides its focus on British news media coverage, our study also has considerable theoretical implications. Consequently, we need to identify the type of case represented by the 2003 invasion of Iraq: whether it amounts to an easy or a hard case in relation to particular theories and models. Of course, any judgement about the type of case that we are examining depends on how we categorise it – as part of the domain of cases of news media-and-war, or the domain of cases of media-and-foreign-policy.

If considered as part of the domain of cases that fit the category of media-and-war, the 2003 invasion of Iraq is at face value a hard case (or critical case)[19] for the elite-driven model. The war was unusually controversial and was associated with high levels of dissent throughout British society when compared with other wars such as the 1982 Falklands conflict and the 1991 Gulf War. To the extent that our findings support the elite-driven model, we can be confident that this model will work well in other, easier (or less critical) cases of media and war. At the same time, just as the case is a hard one for the elite-driven model, it is an easy one in which to find evidence for the independent and oppositional models: Given the controversy and extent of anti-war sentiment, we may find evidence of journalists challenging the government even when British troops were in action. It follows that evidence that we find for the independent and oppositional models is less likely to be repeated in other, harder, cases of media and war where lower levels of controversy exist.

However, with respect to the domain of cases that fit the broader category of media-and-foreign-policy, since news media deference to government is often argued to be the norm during wartime (see Chapter 2), British coverage of the 2003 invasion of Iraq is at face value an easy one for the elite-driven model. So, whatever our findings here, we would be less likely to find evidence for the elite-driven model as we move to low intensity conflicts and non-wartime cases of media-and-foreign-policy. Conversely, because it concerns a war, British news media coverage of the 2003 invasion of Iraq is a hard one (or critical case) for finding evidence of independent and oppositional coverage in comparison with other cases of media and foreign policy. So finding evidence for the independent and oppositional models in this case would be extremely important and indicate that we would be likely to find even more evidence for these models as we moved to easier cases drawn from the broader category of media-and-foreign-policy. We return to these issues and associated questions regarding the generalisability of our study in Chapter 8.

Additional research strategies and interviews

While the centrepiece of our study was a detailed content and framing analysis, we employed other research strategies in order to make sense of our findings and place them in context. Semi-structured interviews were conducted with journalists from almost all of the news media outlets that we surveyed[20] in order to give us further insights into news coverage of the war and, more importantly, to explore how journalists perceived their role and function. In addition, we have drawn on a range of primary sources, official documents (including US Congressional hearings concerning the Jessica Lynch case) and published memoirs of policy-makers, journalists, editors and military personnel. Secondary accounts – in particular academic analysis of the military campaign – were used to provide non-media insights into the military dimensions of the invasion.

Concluding comments

In this chapter we have defined, detailed and operationalised the analytical framework that serves to structure our analysis of UK news coverage of the 2003 invasion of Iraq. Three models of news media performance – the elite-driven model, the independent model and the oppositional model – form the basis of this analytical framework. The framework and its constituent models are designed to overcome weaknesses in the existing literature on news media and war, particularly deficiencies in both methodological and theoretical support, as well as to consolidate the range of explanatory variables and hypotheses available to explain news media performance both in wartime and more generally. In addition, the framework is able to engage explicitly with normative questions about how news media *should* report on war. The framework also specifies the observable implications of the three models and consolidates a range of existing methodologies in order to provide for a sophisticated and sensitive analysis of news media coverage.

Notes

1 Appendix A contains more detailed information about some aspects of the methodology applied here.
2 For a recent challenge, see Groeling and Baum (2008).
3 See Rogers (2002) for a useful and prominent account of the geo-politics of the twenty-first century.
4 See Holsti (1992) on Realist and Liberal positions on public opinion and foreign policy.
5 For a review of this literature, see Robinson (2001).
6 Fields and institutions are similar in that both identify distinct rules which govern the conduct of actors – rules which in turn define the existence of a field/institution as a unified entity.
7 Hallin's comments here are actually directed at the propaganda model, devised by Herman and Chomsky (1998). Regarding the similarity between the propaganda model and other elite-driven theories of media–state relations, see Herring and Robinson (2003).
8 For useful discussions on questions of balance and impartiality, see Althaus (2003: 402–5), Gavin (2007: 47-73) and Starkey (2007).

9 Speaking in *Iraq: The Hidden Story* (Zenith Entertainment), broadcast 8 May 2006 by Channel 4.

10 In reporting our findings, we include all actors who had a central or subsidiary role in a story, but not those whose roles were judged to be peripheral.

11 In reporting our framing measures from the perspective of the coalition, we have combined the results for 'supportive' framing towards the coalition with those for 'oppositional' framing towards the Iraq government to calculate our overall 'supportive' coalition figures. Likewise, 'oppositional' coalition results also include any 'supportive' framing codes for Iraq. 'Other' codes indicate subjects whose main orientation made coding for framing towards the coalition or the Iraq government inappropriate (for example, where only the UN, Iraqi citizens or other world leaders were concerned).

12 The research on coalition media-management strategy and press briefings was conducted by Robin Brown and Philip M. Taylor at the Institute of Communications Studies, University of Leeds. The results of this work are documented in the form of a research report at the ESRC website (www.esrc.ac.uk) and also published in Robinson et al., 2009.

13 Telephone interview with Angus Taverner, 10 February 2009.

14 Telephone interview with Angus Taverner, 10 February 2009.

15 This article was only published in the online version of the *Telegraph*: www.telegraph.co.uk/news/1425685/14-killed-in-Baghdad-raid-says-Iraq.html (accessed 4 September 2009).

16 Anonymous coalition source.

17 Telephone interview with Angus Taverner, 10 February 2009.

18 Telephone interview with Angus Taverner, 10 February 2009.

19 For an excellent discussion of single case studies and generalisation, see Flyvbjerg (2006).

20 Despite attempts, we were unable to obtain an interview with a journalist who covered the war for one of the *Mail* newspapers.

4

Placing coverage of the invasion in context

Overview

In order to place British coverage of the invasion in context, this chapter offers brief summaries of the structure and character of Britain's television news services and its press. It is also important to offer a context for understanding the events surrounding the invasion itself. In the latter part of this chapter, we summarise key events in the run-up to the invasion, its main combat phase and its aftermath.

'Serving the public': the character of British television news

British television is founded on the notion of public service broadcasting, in which news is seen as a crucial democratic resource for citizenship, with its reliability underpinned by a robust system of regulation. As a consequence, British broadcasters are required to report with 'due accuracy and impartiality' concerning 'matters of political or industrial controversy; and matters relating to current public policy' (Broadcasting Act, 1990: 6(b) and (c)).[1] As a result, broadcast news differs from press news in two important ways: first, it is subject to a specific tier of legislation beyond the law of the land which recognises 'the continued special status of broadcasting' (Kuhn, 2007: 116); second, and partly as a consequence, it is regarded by audiences as more authoritative and trustworthy.[2]

Of course, the concept of 'due impartiality' is an ideal. In practice, British television news is generally expected to be 'balanced' between different perspectives on events.[3] This notion of 'balance', as a means of achieving fairness, is associated with what we have labelled 'negotiated' reporting and the independent model (see Chapter 3). In the absence of balance, we would expect to find coverage that has the effect of supporting one side or one perspective over others – in other words, coverage that our analysis would categorise as 'supportive' or 'oppositional'.

A further consequence of regulation is that news programming from different broadcasting outlets remains quite similar in orientation and style. Unlike the wide variations found in the more partisan British press, broadcast news seeks to satisfy the information needs of a mass of viewers drawn from across the class spectrum. As Curran and Seaton note (2003: 339), 'the audience of BBC or ITV news includes most readers of tabloids, but these programmes' political values are closer to those of *The Times* and the *Observer*'. So news broadcasters face the challenge of producing news that is accessible and popular, but which contains an analytical edge and is contextualised sufficiently well that a broadsheet audience will not be dissatisfied.

In surveying British television news coverage of the Iraq invasion, we examined the flagship news programmes of four principal nationally broadcast networks – three of them (BBC, ITV and Channel 4) from long-established, terrestrially broadcast television channels, the fourth (Sky) available by subscription via satellite, cable or digital terrestrial platforms. The character, ownership and regulatory framework of each are discussed in turn below:

BBC

Known throughout the world and highly regarded for the extent and accuracy of its news operation, the BBC is a public corporation funded by a compulsory licence fee whose programme content obligations are enshrined in its Royal Charter and Agreement. Under the terms of the Agreement in force at the time of the Iraq invasion, the Corporation was required to offer 'comprehensive, authoritative and impartial coverage of news and current affairs in the United Kingdom and throughout the world to support fair and informed debate at local, regional and national levels' (Department of National Heritage, 1996: 6). Consequently, the BBC considered itself to have a 'special responsibility to its audiences . . . who turn to us in large numbers for accurate news and information', as its editorial policy guidelines for Iraq War coverage explain: 'They . . . look to the BBC to help them make sense of those events by providing impartial analysis and by offering on our programmes a range of views and opinion, including the voices of those who oppose the war in Britain and elsewhere' (Whittle, 2002). As these guidelines suggest, the BBC owes its allegiance to 'the public interest' and guards its independence from government interference fiercely despite its statutory basis. Greg Dyke, BBC Director General in 2003, confirms the importance of balanced coverage of the invasion:

> Our job was to report the events leading up to the war, and the war itself, as fairly as we could. It was certainly not the job of the BBC to be the Government's propaganda machine, but nor was it our job disproportionately to represent the views of those protesting against the war. (Dyke, 2005: 251–2)

We analysed BBC1's main evening news programme at 10 p.m. For much of the period of this study, its running time was doubled to 60 minutes.

ITV

The BBC's rival since 1955, ITV is commercially owned and derives its revenue from advertising. Its news service is provided by Independent Television News (ITN), originally a wholly owned subsidiary. Until the early 1990s, British broadcasters were not in direct competition for income, which helped to safeguard their 'public service' orientation and enabled ITV News to develop a reputation for quality that rivalled the BBC's. But as multi-channel and digital television developed in Britain, bringing competition from hundreds of additional commercially funded channels, ITV's news agenda seemed to focus more on audience maximisation, becoming more populist with less foreign coverage (see Tumber, 2001: 99). Nevertheless, ITV News gave comprehensive coverage to the Iraq story, moving its late evening news programme (which we analysed) to 9 p.m. and extending it to one hour for much of the invasion period.

Channel 4

Launched in 1982, and funded wholly by its own advertisement sales since 1998, Channel 4 is a public trust. It has a unique remit, established by statute, which requires its programming to offer distinctiveness, innovation and diversity when compared to other channels. Accordingly, Channel 4 News aims to 'provide a broadsheet news service which reflects Channel 4's own spirit of innovation and scepticism', with a commitment to 'set our own agenda', 'come up with a distinctive take on events' and 'challenge existing assumptions'.[4] Like ITV, its news service is provided by ITN, although the two services have separate editors and dedicated correspondents. Although it is not unusual for news material to be pooled among broadcasters internationally in a war situation, the sharing of material between ITV News and Channel 4 was quite common. Even when this occurred, however, each news service framed, edited and incorporated it into bulletins differently. They also worked to different formats: our analysis was based on Channel 4's main news programme, which retained its standard 7 p.m. slot and 55-minute running time throughout the invasion period. In keeping with its remit and length, Channel 4 News was more likely to include studio interviews and discussions than the other news programmes surveyed and its field reports were often longer – 4 or 5 minutes compared with 2 or 3 minutes on other channels. It was also the only news programme surveyed that was broadcast before the 9 p.m. 'watershed', considered in Britain to mark the point in the evening's schedules when content can be broadcast that may be unsuitable for younger viewers.

Sky News

Sky News, a 24-hour rolling news service, is operated by BSkyB, the UK's largest pay-TV provider and a key player in the rise of multi-channel television through its satellite TV service. Sky News is also available on other digital platforms and is notionally free-to-air, although until October 2002 all digital platforms required subscription access in the UK.[5] Rupert Murdoch's News Corporation is the largest shareholder in BSkyB, which means that Sky News can call upon News Corporation's resources and global presence when required. At least at the time of the invasion of Iraq, Sky News had a stronger reputation for breaking news even than the BBC (see Beers and Egglestone, 2007: 141–2). We chose to analyse the 10 p.m.–10.30 p.m. segment of Sky's rolling news service, which comprises its main late evening news round-up, although we were unable to obtain weekend coverage for this channel.

Television news audiences generally rose substantially for the period of the invasion, with the BBC and ITV news programmes in our survey averaging between 6 and 7 million viewers and with peaks as high as 9.3 million. Channel 4 News, averaging approximately one million viewers in normal circumstances, peaked at 1.6 million, while Sky News' 10 p.m. audience would have been considerably smaller despite a peak for the channel of 1.2 million as the invasion was launched and a reach of 6.1 million (see Timms, 2003; Cozens, 2003c; Wells, 2003).

'Opinionated, partial and imbalanced': the character of the British press

The claim that Britain has 'the largest national newspaper press in Europe' (Deacon, 2004: 10) is broadly correct, although the Nordic countries and Switzerland have greater daily sales per head (Hardy, 2008: 37). So, not only does Britain have an unusually high proportion of newspaper readers but, unlike the USA and many European countries, its press is predominantly national, sustaining 10 daily and 10 Sunday titles. By comparison, sales of regional and local newspapers are small and their impact relatively minor. Consequently, Britain's newspaper market contains powerful competitive pressures, depends heavily on brand image to attract and maintain reader attention and gives strong commercial incentives for newspapers to pursue editorial strategies that differentiate them from their competitors. The absence of any statutory requirement for 'impartiality', in contrast to television, increases the scope for differentiation and partiality. Besides journalists' professional ethics, the market is the main driver that might encourage 'fair' or balanced reporting. As Starkey (2007: 49) puts it: 'because newspaper purchase is voluntary (rather than obligatory in the case of a broadcast receiving licence), those who disagree with a newspaper's editorial policy can simply move on to another'. A gradual decline in circulation over recent decades has further increased competition between titles.

With Britain's newspapers drawing readers from across the class spectrum (rather than just the middle classes, as in some countries) (Tunstall, 1996:

8–9), an important competitive factor in the structure of the British press is market stratification. Although it has been common to regard the market as containing two types of newspaper – tabloid and broadsheet – a division into three types more accurately reflects its reporting styles and the social class divisions of its readership:[6]

Red-tops

'Red-tops', most notably the *Sun* and the *Daily Mirror,* are mass circulation tabloids with a populist news agenda. Their stories tend to be short and sometimes picture based, specialising in celebrity, crime and personality stories. Even their reporting of hard news is characterised by a lively, 'chummy' writing style and a focus on the human interest angle. Tunstall (1996: 11) characterises the approach of these newspapers as involving 'look-at' and 'quick-read' material, featuring pictures, big headlines and stories that rarely exceed 400 words. These are newspapers designed predominantly to appeal to occupational classes C2, D and E, who make up over 60 per cent of their readers,[7] and to sell in huge numbers (the *Sun* alone outstrips the combined sales of broadsheet newspapers). We analysed the reporting of the *Sun* and *Mirror,* but omitted the *Daily Star* from our survey as containing relatively little hard news, even by red-top standards.

Broadsheets

At the other end of the market are the 'quality' broadsheet newspapers, which operate a more 'serious' approach, reflecting a readership that is more engaged by 'heavier' news topics and a more weighty reporting style. Broadsheets offer a wide variety of sports, arts, financial and features reporting, but comprehensive home, political and foreign coverage is at the heart of their news operation. Many stories may exceed 800 words and, typically, a broadsheet newspaper will contain three times as many words as a red-top (Tunstall, 1996: 12). Although broadsheets sell far fewer copies than red-tops, they tend to appeal to affluent or educated readers, 85–90 per cent of whom are from occupational classes A, B and C1. We surveyed the output of *The Times, Daily Telegraph, Guardian* and *Independent,* but omitted the *Financial Times* from our survey as its content is primarily business oriented.

Black-tops

In between are the 'black-tops' – mid-market papers whose appeal depends heavily on star columnists, interviews and human interest features. They adopt less of a 'quick-read' approach than the red-tops, generally containing somewhat more hard news as well as lengthy features and interviews. The *Daily Mail* is the runaway black-top market leader and its circulation is second only to the *Sun.* Roughly 65 per cent of the *Mail*'s readers are drawn from occupational classes C2, D and E, so its readership profile is quite similar to that of the red-tops but with a stronger appeal to female readers. We omitted the *Daily Express* from our survey for its similarity to the much larger-circulation *Daily Mail*.

Sunday newspapers tend to be more extensive than dailies and less tied to a 24-hour news cycle. The majority of Sundays, including all of those included in our survey, are stablemates of daily titles, although separately edited, and tend to have similar readership profiles and reporting styles. As a result, in presenting our findings, we have generally treated each daily and Sunday newspaper as a single entity.

British national newspapers are commercial enterprises in private or corporate ownership with the exception of the *Guardian* and the *Observer*, both owned by the Scott Trust. The Trust reinvests its profits into the business and requires that its papers eschew party affiliation and uphold the tradition of liberal journalism.[8] Despite some concentration of newspaper ownership, including the acquisition of Sunday newspapers by dailies, there has been little change in the quantity of national titles since the 1970s. Some groups own multiple titles, however – most notably Rupert Murdoch's News International which owns the *Sun*, the *News of the World* (its Sunday equivalent), *The Times* and the *Sunday Times*, accounting for roughly one-third of the overall market by circulation. A key feature differentiating Britain's national newspapers from one another is their political orientation which, at times, may reflect the commercial or political interests of their proprietors. Newspapers rarely see themselves as party political vehicles nowadays, especially with the decline of the ideological party and the rise of media-management strategies (see Kuhn (2007: 217–25) for an overview), but they still have clear political leanings, whether broadly conservative and pro-business or broadly liberal and in favour of social issues. In the case of the 2003 Iraq invasion, some papers adopted editorial positions opposed to the conflict while others keenly supported it. The newspapers surveyed in our study, together with circulation figures prior to the Iraq War, type, political orientation and attitude towards the invasion, are set out in Table 4.1.

So our analysis covers a press which is nationally based, draws readers from all social classes, is highly competitive and contains newspapers adopting a variety of political orientations. Many commentators identify more intangible factors that distinguish it from the press in other countries as well, notably its lively tone. Gavin (2007: 13) calls it 'opinionated, partial and imbalanced, often raucously so', while Lionel Barber describes it as 'like a riotous carnival' in comparison with the 'somewhat stuffy self-importance' of the American press.[9] Barber goes on to characterise the British press as 'a useful troublemaker. It's the early 20-something, doesn't wear a tie, a bit stroppy. Whereas the American press, it's rather preppy, does wear the tie, dresses correctly and is rather earnest and serious.'

Table 4.1 British newspapers included in our analysis of Iraq War reporting

Title	Circulation	Type	Orientation	Editorial attitude to the invasion
Sun/ News of the World	3,611/3,979	Red-top	Broadly right-wing/ populist	Pro-war
Daily Mirror/ Sunday Mirror	2,101/1,726	Red-top	Broadly left-wing/ populist	Anti-war
Daily Mail/Mail on Sunday	2,366/2,297	Black-top	Broadly right-wing/ populist	Pro-war
Guardian/Observer	384/438	Broadsheet	Broadly liberal	Anti-war
Independent/ Independent on Sunday	184/181	Broadsheet	Broadly liberal	Anti-war
The Times/Sunday Times	634/1,367	Broadsheet	Broadly conservative	Pro-war
Daily Telegraph/ Sunday Telegraph	930/744	Broadsheet	Broadly conservative	Pro-war

Note: Average circulation figures (in thousands) for August 2002–January 2003 inclusive.

Source: Audit Bureau of Circulations.

The 2003 invasion of Iraq: the run-up to war, invasion and subsequent events

The run-up to war

The invasion of Iraq on 21 March 2003, codenamed Operation Iraqi Freedom in the USA and Operation Telic in the UK, represented the end of a remarkable period of domestic and global debate and controversy. The run-up to war witnessed campaigns by the US and British governments aimed at promoting the perception that Iraq posed a significant threat because of its weapons of mass destruction (WMD). In the USA, the White House Iraq Group was set up in August 2002 to coordinate 'a systematic media campaign' (Bennett et al., 2007: 18) that would reveal to the American public details of the threat posed by Iraq's alleged WMD activities.[10] Although the threat of WMD was settled upon as the major official justification for war, neo-conservative aspirations to bring democracy to the Middle East, the desire to shore up US influence in a key oil-producing region and unfounded allegations of Iraqi connections with the 9/11 attacks, were also widely suggested as explanations for US policy. The British government, having already aligned itself privately with the Bush administration policy of regime change (Meyer, 2005; Sands, 2006), also spent many months attempting to persuade the British public, media and legislature of the threat posed by Iraq. A sub-text to the British case for war was the idea that the overthrow of Saddam could be justified as a humanitarian act.

In an unprecedented move, a dossier based on intelligence about Iraq was published in September 2002 (Prime Minister's Office, 2002), written by the Joint Intelligence Committee but, it later emerged, with substantial involvement from the Prime Minister's office and from Alistair Campbell, the Prime Minister's official spokesman. The news media reported its publication eagerly, giving particular attention to the now notorious claim that Iraqi WMD could be ready 'within 45 minutes of an order to use them' (Prime Minister's Office, 2002); 'Brits 45 minutes from doom' was the *Sun*'s headline.

Meanwhile, Britain and the USA sought to involve the United Nations in the campaign against Iraq. After eight weeks of negotiations, mostly aimed at overcoming French and Russian concerns that it would be used to justify an invasion, UN Security Council Resolution 1441 was passed on 8 November 2002 requiring Iraq to disarm and reinstituting a weapons inspection regime under the auspices of UNMOVIC, the UN monitoring force headed by Hans Blix. Although the text of the resolution referred to 'serious consequences' if Iraq failed to disarm, it was widely understood that a second resolution would be needed to legitimise an invasion, and Britain and the USA gave assurances to this effect (UN Security Council, 2002).

Blix and his inspection team returned to Iraq and had found no evidence of WMD by mid-February (Blix, 2003). Nevertheless, the USA and Britain continued to press for an invasion. In early February, the British government published a second dossier, which sought to highlight the deceptive nature of the Iraqi regime (Prime Minister's Office, 2003), but this was rapidly discredited as the 'dodgy dossier' when it was found that parts had been plagiarised from a PhD thesis discussing events following the 1991 Gulf War. Meanwhile, Britain and the USA pressed for a second UN resolution that would formally sanction an invasion. However, French president Jacques Chirac announced on 10 March that France would veto any such resolution, denying UN support to any military action against Iraq.

The American public favoured an invasion (Benedetto, 2003) and there were even popular moves to boycott French imports, but in Britain there was widespread public debate and protest (see the case study of the anti-war movement in Chapter 7). Between January and March, polls showed public opposition to be substantial and support to be conditional on a second UN resolution.[11] On 15 February, approximately one million anti-war protestors marched through London in the country's largest ever demonstration.[12] It was against this backdrop of continuing attempts to manage public opinion, the absence of UN support for war and popular protest that the House of Commons was asked to endorse the decision to go to war – perhaps the most controversial decision of its kind in modern British history. On 17 March 2003, on the eve of the debate, Robin Cook, Leader of the House of Commons and a prominent government figure, resigned, giving a dramatic resignation speech opposing military action and questioning claims about Iraq's possession of WMD (Hansard, 2003a). On the following evening, the debate itself precipitated a major revolt with a record number of Labour MPs voting against their own government. The government ultimately won parliamentary approval, aided by the votes of most of the opposition Conservative Party, but approximately one-third of MPs voted against military action. The invasion quickly followed, with British and American forces – leading a so-called 'coalition of the willing'[13] – entering Iraq in large numbers from Kuwait on 20/21 March. As the war began, British political leaders called for unity and support: Labour Party Chairman John Reid declared: 'Now that the democratic decision has been taken, it is time for the country and parliament to unite', and the Prime Minister's official spokesman echoed this message, saying: 'It is now time for all of us in parliament and in the country to come together and show the support our armed forces deserve' (BBC News, 2003).

Military action[14]

British military action focused on invading the southern part of Iraq with the capture of the major city of Basra as its key objective. The port settlement of Umm Qasr was an important early target for British forces, who encountered unexpectedly strong resistance, not taking full control until 25 March. As well as offering a supply corridor from the sea, Umm Qasr would allow the landing of humanitarian aid, a key component in the battle for Iraqi 'hearts and minds'. Despite widespread publicity for these aid efforts, however, it took several more days to make the port safe for ships and it proved difficult to distribute the aid that was delivered to the remainder of Iraq (D. Batty, 'Iraq aid confined to south', *Guardian*, 2 April 2003). By 6 April, after two weeks of fighting, British forces had occupied Basra, with some troops advancing northwards to occupy Amarah, which had been taken by US forces.

Meanwhile, as part of a declared strategy of 'shock and awe', US forces made early attempts to bomb locations in Baghdad, where intelligence suggested that Saddam Hussein might be present. Bombardment of Baghdad continued until ground troops arrived at the city, leading to considerable loss of civilian life. Although their origin was disputed (see Chapter 6), US bombs killed 62 in a Baghdad marketplace on 27 March, one of numerous incidents of civilian carnage reported widely by news media. Another bomb attack near Baghdad in the first hours of April injured Ali Ismaeel Abbas, the Iraqi boy whose picture came to symbolise the suffering of Iraqi civilians (see case study in Chapter 7), and killed 16 members of his family. US ground forces entered Iraq from Kuwait as the invasion began and pushed rapidly northwards, often moving around significant concentrations of resistance, including the cities of Nasiriyah and Karbala. Nasiriyah was taken by US marines on 23 March after heavy resistance. A convoy from 3rd Infantry division was ambushed near the city on the same day. Five members of the division were taken alive and shown on Iraqi TV bloodied and beaten, an incident that gave rise to international condemnation. Also captured was Jessica Lynch (the subject of a case study in Chapter 7), who was retrieved from a Nasiriyah hospital on 1 April.

Significant pauses when frontline troops were resupplied, together with bad weather during the early part of the campaign, introduced delays and some uncertainty regarding the effectiveness of military progress. This was particularly the case in the second week of the invasion, referred to by some media sources as 'the week of wobble', as US forces were moving towards Karbala. The invading force finally arrived in the Karbala area on 31 March, meeting resistance from the Iraqi Republican Guard before bypassing the city and advancing on Baghdad. The first US troops seized Baghdad airport on 5 April and began tank raids into the city. Initially, despite heavy fighting, the Iraqi Information Minister continued to insist that there were no US troops in Baghdad even when – on 7 April – they could be seen only a few hundred metres from his press briefing. By the time a statue of Saddam Hussein was famously pulled down in Firdos Square on 9 April, US forces were consolidating their presence in Baghdad. At this stage, Saddam Hussein's regime had effectively collapsed, although it was another week before his home town of Tikrit fell to coalition forces (13/14 April). It was during this period that initial high hopes regarding a rapid and peaceful transition to democracy were undermined by the wave of lawlessness and looting that gripped the country. Regardless of the widespread disorder and a nascent insurgency, on 1 May President Bush boarded a US aircraft carrier to declare that: 'Major combat operations in Iraq have ended' (Bush, 2003).

Fallout from the invasion

No WMD were found and, despite the swiftness with which Iraq had fallen, conflict in Iraq continued. This was particularly so for US forces, who bore the brunt of the insurgency. As a result, recriminations about the invasion and about the decision to go to war continued to be a focus of media and public attention in Britain, while the behaviour of the news media themselves became a source of controversy. Even before Baghdad fell, members of the British government were publicly criticising some sections of the media. For example, David Blunkett, the British Home Secretary, complained: 'we have broadcast media behind what I would describe as enemy lines, reporting blow by blow what is happening . . . on occasions as though they [the 'enemy'] were moral equivalents', while Labour Party Chairman John Reid described the BBC as acting like a 'friend of Baghdad'.[15]

But the most exceptional clash between government and media over the invasion was the Gilligan/Kelly affair. On 29 May 2003, in a report for Radio 4's *Today* programme, BBC journalist Andrew Gilligan claimed that the suggestion in the government's September 2002 dossier that Iraq could launch WMD 'within 45 minutes of an order to use them' (Prime Minister's Office, 2002: 5) had been inserted even though the government knew it to be false. The government vehemently denied Gilligan's claim and called for the BBC to withdraw it and apologise; the BBC stood by its reporter and his story. An unprecedented argument between the British government and the BBC followed, leading ultimately to the suicide of the British weapons scientist Dr David Kelly, the source for Gilligan's report. In response, the government launched a judicial inquiry chaired by Lord Hutton. Hutton's inquiry exonerated the government and condemned the behaviour of the BBC and Gilligan, who immediately resigned along with the BBC's Chairman and Director-General – an unprecedented event. So completely did the inquiry find in the government's favour that it was widely regarded as a whitewash. The inquiry itself put evidence from the government, security services and media into the public domain. This represented an exceptional opportunity for public and media to witness the manner in which the case for the 'threat' posed by Iraq's WMDs had been made, to evaluate the strength of the evidence for it and to discover the extent to which it had been influenced by considerations of media management, particularly through the involvement of Alistair Campbell. The inquiry heard, for example, that the dossier had been worded with the intention of producing the strongest possible case for war, sometimes on the advice of Campbell, and that experts within the intelligence community had reservations about the strength of evidence presented in parts of the dossier (Ministry of Justice, 2004; Morrison, 2004). As a result, the government's WMD case for war was subjected to unprecedented scrutiny. In addition, the Gilligan/Kelly affair provides a fascinating insight into the ability of the BBC to remain independent under extreme political pressure.

The decision to invade Iraq gave rise to a number of other media controversies over the years that followed as well as continued media coverage of US and UK military operations in the country. Some of these are discussed in Chapter 8, as well as future research issues related to media performance during this period. Chapters 5, 6 and 7, however, deal with our analysis of media coverage of the 2003 Iraq invasion.

Notes

1 The BBC is governed by its own Charter, although the wording on accuracy and impartiality is very similar. The 1990 Act was superseded in July 2003 by the 2003 Communications Act, although it too incorporates these requirements for accuracy and impartiality of news.

2 A poll for YouGov in February/March 2003 found that television news journalists were trusted considerably more than broadsheet journalists, while many more respondents distrusted black-top and red-top journalists than trusted them – see Gavin, 2007: 16.

3 See Starkey (2007) for a discussion of the differing implications of impartiality, balance and objectivity.

4 From the Channel 4 News website: www.channel4.com/news/about/programmes/c4news.html (accessed 21 September 2007).

5 Freeview, a free-to-air digital terrestrial television platform, was launched in October 2002 following the collapse of its subscription-only predecessor. Its package includes the Sky News channel.

6 Our division of the press into three types follows Tunstall's (1996) approach, although the 'red-top'/'black-top'/'broadsheet' terminology that we have adopted here is that employed in various works by Gavin (eg. Gavin, 2007).

7 Data on occupational class and gender of readerships from the National Readership Survey, July 06–June 07.

8 Information about the purposes, values and history of the Scott Trust is available at: www.gmgplc.co.uk/ScottTrust/tabid/127/Default.aspx (accessed 4 August 2009).

9 Lionel Barber, editor, *Financial Times*, and former managing editor of its US edition, speaking on *The Media Show*, BBC Radio 4, 12 November 2008.

10 See Pincus (2008) and McClellan (2008) for more information about the personnel and activities of the White House Iraq Group.

11 According to Ipsos-Mori, opposition had been as high as 77 per cent in January unless there was UN support, and was at 63 per cent on 14–16 March – see http://ipsos-mori.co.uk/content/polls-03/blair-losing-public-support-on-iraq.ashx; and http://ipsos-mori.co.uk/content/polls-03/war-with-iraq-the-ides-of-march-poll.ashx (both accessed 12 February 2009).

12 Estimates range from 750,000 to 2 million demonstrators.

13 Although the White House described the 'coalition of the willing' as consisting of 49 nations (White House, 2003), only five contributed troops (the others were Australia, Poland and Denmark) and some of those named were tiny and without military capability.

14 For valuable accounts of the military campaign, see Gordon and Trainor (2007) and Ricks (2006).

15 Matt Wells, 'Blunkett accuses media over reports from "behind enemy lines"', *Guardian*, 4 April 2003: 6; 'Labour Chairman says BBC is acting like "friend of Baghdad"', *Sunday Telegraph*, 30 March 2003: 6.

5

'Supporting our boys in battle': Evidence for supportive coverage and the elite-driven model

Overview

This chapter focuses on the evidence emerging from our study for the supportive coverage predicted by the elite-driven model. We draw on the range of measures detailed in Chapter 3 – sources, reporter approach, subjects and framing – together with examples from television and press coverage and interviews with journalists, in order to provide a detailed assessment of the extent to which television and the press generated supportive coverage. We then provide an analysis of the ways in which the news media's visual depictions of the war reinforced supportive coverage, and offer detailed qualitative analysis of one particular visual, which we present as indicative of the way in which the coalition's humanitarian warfare narrative was portrayed. The final section is devoted to discussing some of the evidence that emerges for the three key explanatory factors (sources, patriotism and ideology) commonly associated with supportive news media coverage and the elite-driven model. Particular attention is paid to the role of patriotism and humanitarianism in shaping coverage.

'Lapdogs to the coalition': evidence for supportive coverage during the invasion period

Heavy reliance upon coalition sources

As detailed in Chapter 3, a major feature of the elite-driven model is the propensity of news media to rely overwhelmingly on official sources, in particular under conditions of war. Our findings for sources used in both television and press conform closely to this pattern and show a clear tendency towards a supportive mode of reporting from 20 March onwards. For television coverage, the coalition was easily the most successful both at securing news media attention and at gaining airtime via direct quotation. In Table 5.1, reporting the prominence of story actors, coalition representatives are present in the vast majority of news stories. In contrast, humanitarian actors, Arab commentators and the UN each received relatively little attention, being

Table 5.1 Story actors present in TV coverage (no. of stories/as percentage)

	All channels	
All coalition	906	85.2
Iraqi regime	652	61.3
Iraqi opposition	89	8.4
Anti-war	54	5.1
International leaders anti-war	23	2.2
Arab political	50	4.7
UN	58	5.5
Experts	68	6.4
Humanitarian	55	5.2
Religious	3	0.3
Iraqi civilians	418	39.3
Terror groups	12	1.1
Opinion/citizens	92	8.7
Media	159	15.0
All other actors	82	7.7
Total no. of subjects	2,715	
No. of stories	1,063	

mentioned in only a fraction of stories. Table 5.2, which displays our findings for story sources quoted in television news, shows that a majority of direct quotes across all channels came from coalition speakers, while scarcely any other category of actor featured even in a tenth of direct quotes. There were variations between television channels. Rupert Murdoch's 24-hour satellite broadcast Sky News was by far the most reliant upon official sources, with over two-thirds of direct quotes attributable to the coalition. In part, this high figure reflects the tendency of Sky News to draw heavily on coalition press briefings, often incorporating live briefings into its news coverage unedited. But this finding also supports claims that Sky News, like almost all of Murdoch's other outlets internationally, reflected his avowed support for the war (Greenslade, 2003; Thussu, 2009: 118–22). In contrast, Channel 4 News relied least on official sources, which accounted for little more than half of its quotes. The figures for BBC and ITV News were both just under two-thirds. Despite these variations, the overall pattern here is one of coalition dominance.

In press coverage, coalition actors also dominated the picture. They received the most coverage and were the most quoted, as Tables 5.3 and 5.4 demonstrate. Coalition actors appeared in nearly nine-tenths of news stories and were responsible for just under half of all direct quotes. Repeating the

Table 5.2 Story sources quoted by TV channel (in seconds/as percentage)

	BBC		ITV		C4		Sky		All channels
	seconds	%	seconds	%	seconds	%	seconds	%	%
All coalition	2,228	56.9	2,247	59.1	8,824	52.5	2,709	70.3	56.4
Iraqi regime	168	4.3	141	3.7	738	4.4	200	5.2	4.4
Iraqi opposition	172	4.4	48	1.3	692	4.1	122	3.2	3.6
Anti-war	114	2.9	86	2.3	469	2.8	23	0.6	2.4
International leaders anti-war	26	0.7	0	0.0	27	0.2	0	0.0	0.2
Arab political	45	1.2	0	0.0	798	4.7	0	0.0	3.0
UN	0	0.0	0	0.0	196	1.2	19	0.5	0.8
Experts	178	4.5	369	9.7	2,505	14.9	46	1.2	10.9
Humanitarian	105	2.7	103	2.7	809	4.8	45	1.2	3.7
Religious	0	0.0	14	0.4	49	0.3	0	0.0	0.2
Iraqi civilians	198	5.1	276	7.3	699	4.2	369	9.6	5.4
Terror groups	0	0.0	0	0.0	0	0.0	0	0.0	0.0
Opinion/ citizens	552	14.1	272	7.1	249	1.5	155	4.0	4.3
Media	39	1.0	197	5.2	546	3.2	143	3.7	3.3
All other actors	88	2.2	52	1.4	221	1.3	23	0.6	1.4
Total (seconds)	3,913		3,805		16,822		3,854		

Note: Although the final column gives aggregate percentages, the differing lengths and formats of each news programme mean that aggregated figures could give a misleading view of overall coverage.

pattern that we found in television coverage, no other category of actor achieved even a tenth of direct quotes. The overall picture is clear, as it was for television news: Not only did coalition actors dominate coverage of the war but many other groups of actors featured little in coverage and were accessed even more rarely for quotes. Among those marginalised were anti-war actors, who were mentioned in 7.6 per cent of newspaper stories and provided just 3.4 per cent of quotes, although these figures are slightly higher than the equivalent figures for television, largely because of the greater depth of coverage available in the press. The similarity across all the newspapers in their focus on official sources is especially striking, particularly since different titles adopted markedly different editorial positions towards the war. The range of variation among newspapers in our findings for the presence of coalition

Table 5.3 Story actors by newspaper (as percentage of stories containing references)

	Sun	Mirror	Mail	Indep-endent	Guard-ian	Times	Tele-graph	All papers
All coalition	86.9	85.5	89.5	91.4	86.9	84.3	87.6	87.3
Iraqi regime	55.4	54.1	61.6	54.2	54.9	54.5	60.7	56.3
Iraqi opposition	4.0	6.8	8.7	13.9	13.6	12.6	13.3	10.7
Anti-war	5.8	6.8	6.9	9.2	9.4	8.1	6.7	7.6
International leaders anti-war	8.4	2.6	4.6	6.7	5.1	5.5	7.1	5.8
Arab political	1.8	4.3	3.3	8.2	8.2	8.4	5.2	5.9
UN	4.6	6.8	4.3	13.5	13.2	9.2	7.9	8.8
Experts	4.2	4.1	6.1	7.8	15.2	7.9	4.7	7.3
Humanitarian	2.6	7.1	4.9	11.1	10.3	8.1	5.5	7.2
Religious	0.4	0.9	0.8	1.9	4.0	3.4	2.9	2.2
Iraqi civilians	28.7	35.0	30.9	36.6	34.8	33.0	33.8	33.4
Terror groups	2.0	2.8	2.3	3.2	2.8	2.6	2.5	2.6
Opinion/citizens	16.9	20.1	12.8	9.5	9.8	14.2	13.6	13.7
Media	20.9	23.9	25.8	26.9	21.6	16.0	20.8	21.9
All other actors	14.3	12.4	10.5	22.9	18.3	19.9	19.5	17.3
Total no. of actors	1,289	1,278	1,068	1,662	1,768	1,848	1,736	10,649
Total no. of stories	502	468	391	524	574	642	595	3,696

actors in stories and for the use of direct quotes from them was very narrow (between 84.3% and 91.4%, and between 39.6% and 55.2% respectively – see Tables 5.3 and 5.4). So whether pro-war or anti-war, newspapers relied heavily upon coalition sources.

As discussed in Chapter 2, for those who advocate the transformative impact of new media technologies, the claim that there now exists a greater diversity of news sources is an essential component of their argument. Claims regarding the diversity and volume of reporters now covering war (Tumber and Webster, 2006: 17), the supposed 'information blizzard' (Keane, 1998) that accompanies contemporary war, and the idea that the 'new media ecology' (Castells, 2009; Cottle, 2006) means that: 'Nobody knows *who* will see an event, *where* and *when* they will see it, or *how* they will interpret it' (Hoskins and O'Loughlin, 2010 – original emphasis), all paint the picture of a radically pluralised information sphere in which no one source dominates. But the results we have presented here, in common with those of Lewis et al.

Table 5.4 Story sources quoted by newspaper (as percentage of lines quoted)

	Sun	Mirror	Mail	Indep-endent	Guard-ian	Times	Tele-graph	All papers
All coalition	55.2	43.3	54.4	46.0	39.6	42.3	45.4	45.1
Iraqi regime	1.7	6.8	5.4	6.1	4.0	4.3	4.6	4.7
Iraqi opposition	0.8	1.9	3.1	4.8	4.7	6.4	4.9	4.4
Anti-war	2.4	4.3	2.4	3.4	5.0	3.1	2.6	3.4
International leaders anti-war	0.4	0	0.8	1.7	1.3	1.6	1.9	1.4
Arab political	0.1	0.6	0.2	0.8	1.3	0.9	0.5	0.7
UN	0.1	0.8	0.0	1.7	1.5	1.3	1.7	1.2
Experts	3.2	2.0	4.2	3.9	8.7	3.8	2.0	4.3
Humanitarian	1.1	3.4	2.2	3.8	3.7	3.3	2.2	3.0
Religious	0.1	0.1	0.2	1.2	2.4	1.9	1.2	1.3
Iraqi civilians	5.8	14.0	6.3	9.2	10.1	9.5	9.9	9.5
Terror groups	0.0	0.4	0.0	0.2	0.3	0.1	0.0	0.2
Opinion/citizens	14.0	12.8	10.8	5.2	6.7	11.5	9.0	9.4
Media	7.6	5.8	5.9	8.0	6.5	4.8	9.2	6.8
All other actors	7.4	3.0	4.1	4.0	4.0	5.0	4.9	4.5
Total lines quoted	6,197	8,168	7,146	11,907	15,397	16,172	13,956	78,943

(2005: 120) and Tumber and Palmer (2004: 103), offer a strong challenge to these claims, at least with respect to major war fighting and high intensity conflict. In fact, we found that official sources and actors dominated television and press coverage and ensured that the story of the invasion was narrated largely through the voice of the coalition.

Reporter approach: straight reporting for everybody but the Iraqi 'bad guys'
Through our reporter approach variable, we were able to measure whether journalists remained neutral and objective towards actors (defined as straight reporting, as opposed to reporting that was overtly deflating or reinforc-ing). A very high proportion of reporting across all television channels was coded as straight (96% for BBC News, 91% for ITV News, 96% for Channel 4 News, and 94% for Sky News). These figures are consistent with the findings of Aday, Livingston and Hebert (2005: 14) who found that of all the US news networks analysed, only Fox News, at 62 per cent, reported straight less than 90 per cent of the time (see Chapter 3). Nevertheless, not all television news reporting was straight. There were instances, generally quite rare, of rein-forcing and deflating treatment on all channels towards a variety of actors in the war, but easily the most common departure from straight reporting

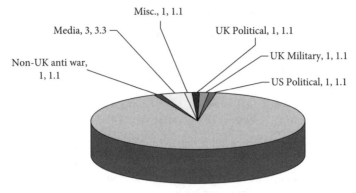

Misc., 1, 1.1

Media, 3, 3.3

UK Political, 1, 1.1

Non-UK anti war, 1, 1.1

UK Military, 1, 1.1

US Political, 1, 1.1

Iraq, 84, 91.3

Figure 5.1 Instances of deflating reporter approach towards actors (all TV channels; number/as percentage)

was deflating treatment given to members of the Iraqi regime (see Figure 5.1). Eleven of the 13 instances of deflating reporting by BBC News were directed towards Iraqi regime actors. Figures for other channels were comparable: 39 out of 41 instances in ITV News were directed at the Iraqi authorities, 19 out of 22 instances in Channel 4 News and 15 out of 16 instances in Sky News.[1] In short, straight reporting was clearly the norm, but when television journalists departed from this, it was nearly always to undermine the Iraqi authorities.

With its regulatory requirement to be 'duly impartial', we might expect British television news reporting to be overwhelmingly straight. But the proportion of straight reporting in the press, which has no such obligations, was also high across all newspapers (see Table 5.5), and particularly among the four broadsheet titles, which averaged 88.4 per cent. As with television, however, the distinction in tone between the reporting of the coalition and the Iraqi authorities was marked. As can be seen in Tables 5.3 and 5.4, Iraqi authorities were the most prominent group of actors mentioned after those representing the coalition. However, each group received very different treatment (see Table 5.6, which compares the treatment of coalition actors with those from the Iraqi regime across all of the newspapers surveyed). Coalition actors benefited from straight reporting most of the time and, where journalists took sides, they showed themselves able to side with, as well as against, them. But Iraqi regime actors were reported straight barely more than two-thirds of the time and nearly a quarter of reporting deflated them. For Richard Beeston of *The Times*, the tendency of journalists to distrust (and deflate) Iraqi official sources was partly a result of their lack of credibility:

The problem with the Iraqis is that we are not dealing with a reasonable alternative view . . . When you have the Minister of Information say: 'Oh, the

Table 5.5 Reporter approach towards all actors by newspaper (as percentages)

	Sun	Mirror	Mail	Indep-endent	Guard-ian	Times	Tele-graph	All papers
Straight	69.5	81.9	77.5	88.2	90.3	88.3	86.8	84.5
Reinforcing	10.7	2.9	4.4	0.5	0.8	1.7	1.8	2.8
Mixed	2.6	4.4	6.4	7.1	5.4	5.4	5.0	5.3
Deflating	17.2	10.7	11.7	4.2	3.4	4.6	6.4	7.5

Note: Not all columns add up to 100% due to rounding.

Table 5.6 Reporter approach towards coalition and Iraq regime actors (all newspapers; as percentages)

	Straight	Reinforcing	Mixed	Deflating
Coalition actors	86.7	4.8	5.4	3.0
Iraq regime actors	69.7	0.0	7.3	23.0

Note: Not all rows add up to 100% due to rounding.

Americans are not anywhere near here', and you can see the [American] tanks in the background just driven in to Baghdad . . . you have to be cynical.[2]

In their recent analysis of war correspondents, Tumber and Webster (2006: 20) claim that heightened media-management campaigns have served to increase the cynicism of war reporters. In turn, 'this bolsters journalists' disposition to treat *all* sources sceptically, an important factor in what and how they report from the war zone' (2006: 20, original emphasis). Our findings for reporter approach, however, suggest that any such cynicism and scepticism was far from evenly applied. Both in television and press coverage, coalition actors were much more likely than the Iraqi regime to be reported straight. In contrast, when journalists departed from straight reporting of the Iraqi authorities, it was almost always to undermine them. To put these findings more colourfully, such obvious instances of deviation from balanced or objective reporting would have been unlikely to leave viewers or readers in doubt as to the status of the Iraqi authorities as the 'bad guys' and, by implication, presented the coalition as the 'good guys'.

The subject agenda: battle stories dominate

Our findings for the story subject variable highlight the extent to which the day-to-day events of the battle itself dominated the agenda of news coverage. As Figure 5.2 shows, almost two-thirds of television news stories involved battle. In the press, it was a subject in almost half of the stories coded (see

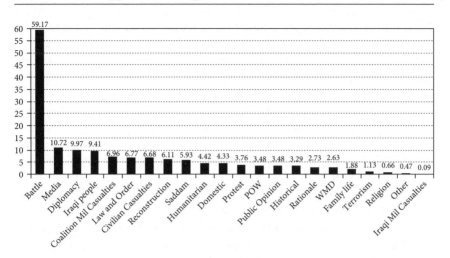

Figure 5.2 Story subjects in television news by category (all TV channels; as percentages)

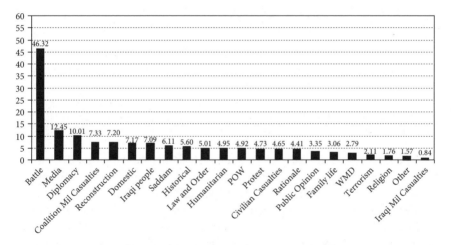

Figure 5.3 Story subjects in the press by category (all newspapers; as percentages)

Figure 5.3). Although this figure is not as high as for television, other subjects were similarly 'crowded out' of coverage. In each medium, the only other subjects present in more than a tenth of stories were media and diplomacy, meaning that relatively little coverage was given to some important aspects of the war. For example, subjects such as protest, the rationale for war and public opinion, each of which might have generated critical coverage, were significant elements in fewer than one in twenty stories in either medium. Overall, the subject agenda was remarkably similar throughout press and television coverage and the dominance of battle stories was universal. This was so even in the press, despite the much wider range of editorial positions that were adopted in relation to the war. For example, battle accounted for just over half (53.7%) of stories in the pro-war *Mail* newspapers and 42.7 per cent in the *Independent*, with the other papers occupying a range between 44.2 per cent and 48.4 per cent. There was a difference between newspapers of no more than 5 per cent for almost every subject area that we coded.

Interviews with journalists provided various explanations for the dominance of battle. In television, the highly visual nature of battle coverage created compelling reasons for its inclusion, according to Jon Snow (Channel 4 News): 'Bang-bang comes up well on TV . . . We live in a Hollywood age and when you get real life mimicking what you watch in fantasy, it is very difficult to shut it down.'[3] For Richard Sambrook (BBC), the embedding policy and new technology only enhanced this effect: 'This time round, the scale of it [embedding] and the technology [i.e. real-time] raised a number of issues that we hadn't had to face before . . . because we had some very compelling frontline coverage it did tend to dominate.'[4] But even in the press, the *Guardian*'s James Meek felt that media outlets had an obligation to prioritise battle coverage since their readers had a direct interest in its outcome:

> If you've got an army that you have paid for through your taxes, and they include people you know, or relatives of people you know, in it and they are killing people with your money and the bullets you've paid for, then I feel that's the first thing you want to know about: How is that going? How many people are they killing? . . . How deep are they in? . . . And I don't think that's unreasonable.[5]

Of course, it might be argued that empirical data showing that the subject of battle dominated coverage does not necessarily confirm that news media adopted a supportive mode of coverage. Perhaps such a focus on battle stories is a natural and unproblematic finding in war reporting, as is implied in James Meek's comment above. However, as Lewis et al. (2003) point out, the process of embedding journalists with frontline troops encouraged 'a focus on the actions of US and British troops, who would be seen fighting a short and successful war'. In other words, from the point of view of coalition media management, focus on military progress ensured that journalists were concentrated on an area liable to go well for them. Hence the story was all about winning and losing, rather than offering a consideration of the context in which the war was fought. In addition, as Aday, Livingston and Hebert (2005: 18) point out, such coverage ended up marginalising 'other important aspects of the war'.

Table 5.7 Framing of battle theme by television news programme (as percentages)

	BBC	ITV	C4	Sky	All
Supportive	49.0	59.8	43.2	76.0	53.5
Negotiated	45.5	37.0	50.9	22.7	41.8
Oppositional	5.5	3.1	6.7	1.3	4.7
No. of stories	145	127	163	75	510

Framing the war

Analysis of sources, journalist approach and subject agenda offer useful indications of news media performance. However, our framing analysis, which considered all aspects of a news report including these measures and the language and visuals used in reports, in conjunction with our predetermined criteria (see Chapter 3 and Appendix B), provides the most sensitive and valid measure of news media reporting. Here, our analysis found that battle was not merely the predominant topic of coverage; those reports focusing on it also tended to be framed in a manner that was supportive of the coalition. Table 5.7 gives our findings for the framing of battle stories in television news programmes. Here, just over half of the stories presented coalition military progress in a supportive way, while only a fraction suggested serious military problems for the coalition through oppositional framing. Indeed, coalition attacks on Iraqi forces were a frequent focus (present in 16% of all battle stories), whereas only 4 per cent of battle stories focused upon Iraqi resistance.

Examples of the sort of supportive coverage that we identified include the following account from Colin Brazier: 'This advance has been as urgent as its prelude was patient. In recent days, air power has blown a hole in Iraqi defences and the armour is now pouring through' (Sky News, 2 April). Similarly, in a report on British marines, Bill Neely explained that the 'liberating' force of the marines had established a 'tight grip' on Umm Qasr. 'Then', he continued, 'it's on to the dusty streets of a town that rebelled against Saddam twelve years ago – a revolt he brutally crushed. Street by street, town by town, in southern Iraq the marines are imposing their will and their weapons' (ITV News, 29 March 2003). Consistent with the framing criteria, these supportive battle reports tended to emphasise military success, reinforce optimistic coalition claims and sometimes to contain unproblematic acceptance of coalition language. Despite this, there were pronounced variations in the way that different programmes tended to cover battle stories. Three-quarters of all Sky News reports and almost two-thirds of ITV News reports were supportive of the coalition, whereas just under half of BBC News reports and an even smaller proportion of Channel 4 News reports were supportive (see Table 5.7).

Table 5.8 Framing of battle theme by newspaper (as percentages)

	Sun	Mirror	Mail	Indep-endent	Guard-ian	Times	Tele-graph	All
Supportive	86.4	45.4	60.9	41.2	46.2	53.4	70.5	58.1
Negotiated	9.9	36.2	28.3	47.7	41.9	36.3	23.3	31.9
Oppositional	3.7	18.5	10.9	11.1	11.8	10.4	6.2	10.0
No. of stories	162	130	138	153	186	193	193	1,155

Note: A small number of subjects coded as 'other' (5 stories in all) are excluded.

These variations are notable for the challenge that they pose to some of the more extreme claims levelled at British broadcasters by the British government, such as the notion that news media reporting treated the coalition and the Iraqi 'enemy' as 'moral equivalents' and that the BBC acted like a 'friend of Baghdad' (see Chapter 2). In fact, television news rarely adopted an oppositional stance in respect of battle, the dominant news subject, and, whereas the BBC was the focal point for government anger, it was actually Channel 4 News that adopted the more critical stance toward the war.

Although newspapers offered coverage that was much more widely differentiated than we found in television (discussed in detail in Chapter 6), battle coverage tended to be framed supportively by the press as well (see Table 5.8). Overall, almost two-thirds of newspaper battle stories presented military progress in this way, while only one-tenth of reports were oppositional. The vast majority of the pro-war, populist *Sun*'s battle coverage was framed supportively as was just over two-thirds of the conservative *Telegraph*'s. At the other end of the scale, although battle reporting attracted supportive framing in just less than half of its coverage in the anti-war *Mirror* and *Guardian*, these figures were still higher than for negotiated or oppositional coverage of battle. Only at the *Independent* was supportive coverage displaced by negotiated coverage as the largest category. In some newspapers, supportively-framed stories of British raids were written up by embedded journalists in the heroic language of boys-own fiction. In the *Sun*, Nick Parker wrote: 'Saddam's henchmen fled in terror as the Desert Rats closed in on Basra with tanks yesterday. Dozens of bloodthirsty thugs loyal to the tyrant were killed as warplanes blitzed three of their official buildings' ('Trapped by Rats', 27 March 2003: 8), while a report of a different raid by Gethin Chamberlain in the *Daily Mail* ended thus: 'A job well done, the CO said later. Now the Iraqis knew they were there and that they meant business' ('The Black Watch sniper fixed his moving target in his sights . . .', 26 March 2003: 6).[6]

Broadsheet reports tended to be more soberly written, but emphasis on the superior might of coalition forces was common, as in this *Daily*

Telegraph extract: 'The Iraqis, who were mostly on foot, fired rocket-propelled grenades and small arms at the Americans but were decimated by the firepower of 7th Cavalry's MI Abrams tanks and Bradley fighting vehicles' ('Hundreds of Iraqis killed in biggest battle so far', David Rennie and Stewart Payne, 26 March 2003: 4). For one reporter whom we spoke to, embedding, and the interdependence that it created between journalists and the military, helped to explain supportive coverage that benefited the objectives of both groups:

> I think it can be for both the military and the media, two groups who have traditionally eyed each other with great suspicion, I think it can be win-win because it's like intersecting circles . . . There is a huge area in the middle of mutual benefit . . . where we can get information out, they can showcase what they're doing. [7]

Overall then, an emphasis on successful coalition attack and ineffective Iraqi resistance represented a common pattern in many battle reports. As such, coverage tended to present the progress of coalition forces as inevitable and positive ('holding the military initiative', as Hallin (1986: 129) described a similar pattern in Vietnam war reporting), rather than remaining cautious in relation to the military situation and the outcome of the war. In doing so, it reflected the coalition's own media strategy which, as we have seen, involved 'giving out a very positive line' that was 'always very much about forward progress'.[8]

Justifying the war: reinforcing official WMD and humanitarian narratives
While we found that scant attention was paid to the 'war on terror' rationale across both television and press,[9] our findings for the framing of two official justifications for the invasion – Iraq's possession of WMD and the humanitarian case for war – show that these were also covered in a manner that was supportive of the coalition. Two-thirds of television news reports concerning Iraqi WMD implicitly or explicitly reaffirmed coalition claims about their existence, the threat that they posed and, in some cases, discussed 'evidence' of their discovery by coalition forces (see Figure 5.4). For example, ITV's second headline on 28 March claimed to 'uncover compelling evidence that Iraq is ready for chemical warfare'. Two stories followed: one in which James Mates reports on supposed finds of Iraqi WMD equipment; another showing an Iraqi television clip featuring Dr Huda Salih Mahdi Ammash ('Mrs Anthrax') at an Iraqi war cabinet meeting. According to ITV anchor Sir Trevor McDonald, this offered 'another sign today that if President Saddam Hussein is contemplating the use of biological weapons against coalition forces, he doesn't seem to care who knows it'. Stories concerning WMD in the press were not particularly common (only 119 in all, see Table 5.9).

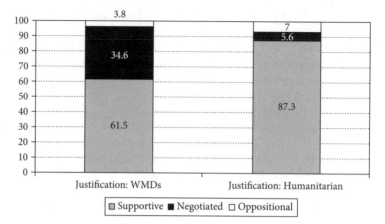

Figure 5.4 Framing of WMD and humanitarian justification themes (all TV channels; as percentages)

Table 5.9 Framing of WMD and humanitarian justification themes by newspaper (as percentages)

	Sun	Mirror	Mail	Indep-endent	Guard-ian	Times	Tele-graph	All
Supportive	100.0	40.0	81.8	33.3	47.1	72.7	87.5	64.7
Negotiated	0.0	26.7	9.1	47.6	41.2	27.3	12.5	25.2
Oppositional	0.0	33.3	9.1	19.0	11.8	0.0	0.0	10.1
No. of stories	17	15	11	21	17	22	16	119
			WMD justification					
Supportive	100.0	63.3	93.9	63.9	75.0	83.9	85.7	82.4
Negotiated	0.0	4.1	4.1	11.1	11.1	8.9	6.3	6.1
Oppositional	0.0	32.7	2.0	25.0	13.9	7.1	7.9	11.5
No. of stories	58	49	49	36	36	56	63	347
			Humanitarian justification					

Nevertheless, this was a successful justification for war in that two-thirds of such stories were framed supportively. The *Independent* was the only newspaper where negotiated stories about WMD outweighed supportive ones, while the *Sun*'s coverage of the issue was wholly supportive. One lengthy example from the *Sun*, reporting that 'military chiefs are now braced for a chemical assault in the next 72 hours', was based on the appearance on Iraqi TV of the same Dr Ammash. Naming her 'Dr Evil' and 'Chemical Sally' ('the petite 50-year-old is known to be one of the key architects of Iraq's chemical weapons programme'), it reported that 'US and British forces have found mounting evidence of a potential chemical or biological attack since the invasion nine days ago' (George Pascoe-Watson, 'Chemical Sally', 29 March 2003: 8). While his own reports remained agnostic on the question of WMD, Tim Butcher from the *Daily Telegraph* colourfully reflected the eagerness with which journalists became caught up in the WMD story:

> Of course, as journalists, we all wanted to find weapons of mass destruction. We wanted to be the first to find this stash of anthrax . . . And I got very excited in Umm Qsar when I went into this hangar at the port and there was this missile . . . I thought: 'here is my Pulitzer Prize', and I walked up to it and, unfortunately, it had an 'As viewed by the UN inspectors, 2001' sticker on it.[10]

The humanitarian justification proved even more successful for the coalition, and featured in many more stories. Such coverage took a number of forms. Some stories referred positively and overtly to the humanitarian case for war, but others did so more implicitly through phrases directed to the Iraqi people such as 'we won't fail you', emphasising the role of the coalition as saviours. Many stories reinforcing the humanitarian justification did so by calling attention to the past brutalities of the Iraqi regime and highlighting its dictatorial nature. In television news, almost nine-tenths of reports that referred to it supported the humanitarian argument for war – for example, reaffirming the case for regime change by reference to the nature and atrocities of the Iraqi regime (see Figure 5.4). In one example, on 3 April, ITV News presented an item on 'Iraq's Most Wanted', with a Wild West-themed graphics display in which Saddam's son Uday was described as an 'unstable psychopath'. The humanitarian justification for war was similarly successful in the press, where coverage was overwhelmingly supportive in every newspaper (see Table 5.9). A *Daily Telegraph* article about the capture of Basra by Patrick Bishop emphasised the reception of British troops as saviours and the atrocities of Saddam simultaneously, as neatly summarised by its headline: 'Kisses for the British and curses for Saddam' (4 April 2003: 5). In the *Sun*, a brief and vaguely-sourced article was among several that linked the WMD and humanitarian justifications, raising fears about the use of chemical weapons while presenting British troops as protecting the Iraqi people from Saddam's 'savagery':

> Saddam is planning to poison Iraq's water system as a last act of savagery, Allied commanders fear. British army chiefs are braced for a massive humanitarian effort to counteract any sabotage of the country's drinking water. They believe Saddam could slip nerve agent into reservoirs and pumping stations, killing thousands of his people. A military commander said: 'There is no telling what this man will do. Much of the water is contaminated already but the situation would be made far, far worse.' (no byline, 20 March 2003: 4)

Overall, both television and press gave substantial reinforcement to the two main official justifications for war and these findings represent a remarkable success for the coalition. They demonstrate the extent to which journalists absorbed, without question, official claims about the presence of WMD. They also show that journalists scarcely questioned the notion that troops would be accepted by Iraqis as liberators rather than invaders, as well demonstrating the power that tales of Saddam's past brutality exerted, as they had during the 1991 Gulf War. (Bennett & Paletz, 1994).

Visualising the war: reinforcing supportive coverage

Drawing on our analysis of television and press visuals, we turn now to an examination of the visual character of news coverage. Here we highlight some of the most common types of images through which the war was visualised and consider the extent to which the selection of visuals contributed to the supportive approach to coverage that we have identified so far.

Visualising battle and the anticipation of chemical attack

Our results showed a close correspondence between the subjects of visuals and our findings for story subjects (given in Figures 5.2 and 5.3). Battle was the predominant visual subject, depicted in 51.7 per cent of television news stories and 30.8 per cent of press photographs. Such stories contained images of airstrikes, explosions, guns and rockets being fired, military hardware and weaponry, armed soldiers patrolling, and armoured convoys 'charging through the desert' (BBC News, 21 March 2003). In television, only Channel 4 News, at 43.6 per cent, included battle-related visuals in fewer than half of its stories. The avidly pro-war *Sun* published the highest proportion of battle-related pictures (38.6%) of any press title.[11] From the perspective of the coalition, such images generally provided positive coverage of the conflict and helped contribute to the prevalence of supportively framed battle stories. Although problematic battlefield visuals, such as tanks breaking down, military setbacks or weapons malfunctioning, appeared from time to time, most visuals from the battlefield sent a message of coalition military superiority. As Michael Griffin remarked on the domination of battle and weaponry-related imagery found in US newsmagazines, the unquestioning adoption of the military 'push to Baghdad' narrative served to keep battle progress as the main focus and movement towards Baghdad as the central objective (2004: 398). Television, in particular, made use of cameras mounted on gun turrets, grainy green night vision, and aircraft shots that either originated with the Pentagon's own camera crews or were only possible with close military cooperation. Only occasionally were such dominant militaristic perspectives downplayed in the accompanying reporting: in one example, a camera mounted on a tank showed a radio mast being destroyed, while a somewhat unimpressed Channel 4 reporter mentioned that it took six shots to achieve its objective (30 March 2003)!

Besides the prominence of battle, however, television and press had slightly different priorities in visualising the conflict, reflecting the formal differences in representation between video and text. In television news, the next highest categories were domestic politics (23.7%), involving images of parliamentary debates, political press conferences and politicians, and 'graphics/maps/ polls' (21.5%), reflecting broadcasters' reliance on flashy graphics packages, often accompanying an analyst in the studio. Pictures of coalition military casualties (12.4%), the visualisation of which is discussed further in Chapter 6, and of Saddam (6.7%), were the second and third highest categories in the press. Images of Saddam served as an oft-repeated shorthand for the oppressive nature of his regime and their use reflects the themes of personalisation and vilification recognisable from 1991 Gulf War coverage. This category includes Saddam Hussein's personal appearances but also the destruction of his murals and statues, which represented 38 per cent of 'Saddam' images in newspapers. Created as symbols of idolatry, their symbolic resonances were effectively turned against Hussein as coalition forces and Iraqi citizens defaced and destroyed multiple likenesses of Saddam, most (in)famously in toppling his statue in Baghdad's Firdos Square, captured on film and hailed as signalling the destruction of the regime (Aday, Cluverius and Livingston, 2005; Fahmy, 2007; Major and Perlmutter, 2005).

While media pictures of Saddam's symbolic destruction and celebratory Iraqis generally provided support for the coalition's humanitarian rationale, the failure to find any concrete evidence of WMD, despite their status as the central justification for the invasion, is reflected in the near absence of relevant visuals across news media: only 1.2 per cent of television news stories and a much smaller proportion of press photographs (0.3%) contained any reference to WMD. Television pictures of journalists reporting with gas masks on were perhaps the most striking visuals of this kind. For example, on 20 March, Sky News interrupted other stories to cut live to its Kuwait correspondent in a gas mask as air raid sirens blared in the background. The value of such images in lending credibility to proponents of the invasion was not lost on one of the anchors in this Sky bulletin, who commented: 'One wonders . . . if Jacques Chirac is watching these pictures, of course, and what he makes when he sees coalition forces wearing respirators and full chemical suits.' Despite its scarcity, such imagery helped to reinforce the credibility of news stories that were supportive of the WMD case for war and Sky News, in particular, continued to report finds in a supportive manner, including possible nerve agents (7 April 2003) and 'a biolab on wheels' (10 April), even when other channels started to question the existence of WMD.

The 'British' perspective on the 'Arab' perspective: press visuals attributed to coalition, Iraqi and Arab sources

News media outlets, whether television or press, did not always acknowledge alternative sources for visuals. However, we coded for those occasions where other named media, military or agency sources were overtly credited. These results give some indication of the extent to which images provided by alternative news media, such as Al Jazeera, were assimilated in UK news media coverage, as emphasised by advocates of the media empowerment thesis, as well as where a military provenance for visuals was openly acknowledged. In the press, only the broadsheets routinely credited sources for visuals; wire agencies (such as Associated Press or Reuters) were the most commonly named source (as high as 46.4% for the *Independent*). Although we cannot be sure that *all* usage of alternatively sourced imagery was credited (especially in the red- and black-tops), *The Times* (pro-war) was most likely to credit the coalition (3.5%) while the *Mirror* (anti-war) printed the highest proportion of stills from Iraqi and Arab news media sources (4.8% combined).

The majority of coalition-supplied images came from the Ministry of Defence pool and, not surprisingly, they carried clearly supportive connotations. Among their themes were the successful delivery of aid, such as the arrival of the *Sir Galahad* at Umm Qasr ('Ship, ship hooray', *Sun*, 29 March 2003: 12–13), the heroism of British soldiers ('Marines defy hail of fire to lead assault', *Daily Telegraph*, 22 March 2003: 4; 'The sniper is king in patient battle of cat and mouse', *The Times*, 31 March: 6), and, later, the restoration of law and order ('Iraqi police return to the streets of Basra under British Army tutelage', *Independent*, 14 April: 3).

With the exception of the *Mirror*, there was a tendency among the newspapers to frame video stills from Arab and Iraqi news media as evidence that these news media represented the war differently from 'us'. Rather than the 'othering' (Said, 1997) of Iraqis, and of Arab peoples more generally, occurring through depiction alone, it also involved representing the perspective of their news media as savage and brutal (Parry, 2009). The intention behind these images appears to have been to distance 'us' from the enemy by insinuating that their conceptions of taste, decency and morality were 'inferior'. Indeed, the press themselves reported on cultural differences in the visual representation of the conflict, especially where depictions of casualties were concerned. Only rarely did the press recognise the journalistic integrity of Al Jazeera, rather than viewing it as a 'tool of the Iraqi regime' as described by Air Marshall Brian Burridge in response to the broadcast images of dead British soldiers. Not surprisingly, images relating to this incident were considered too shocking to print at all in the British press, even in condemnation ('War of words with Al Jazeera', *Mirror*, 28 March 2003: 16). In fact, newspapers used images from Arab television sources to depict civilian or military casualties only on a few occasions. Instead, the Arab footage that predominated included Saddam Hussein on walkabout, other Iraqi regime leaders, general Iraqi crowd hostility towards the coalition and images of American prisoners captured by Iraq. Although the veracity of such images in representing 'reality' was not directly questioned, accompanying text often emphasised their propagandist nature in an effort to condemn the Arab 'way of seeing' that they supposedly reflected.

Turning briefly to our television sample, while images taken from Arab media channels were employed on occasion to raise objections, for example towards their use as propaganda in displaying injured coalition PoWs or picturing Saddam Hussein on walkabout, for the most part, images from Arab and Iraqi news media were employed unselfconsciously in British television news. Abu Dhabi TV provided recurrent pictures of Baghdad under air attack while Al Jazeera was the most commonly credited Arab channel on the whole, providing images of US prisoners of war, downed coalition aircraft, hostile crowds and post-missile destruction. Despite being associated with unflinching depictions of the human cost of the war, Arab channels were not a source of many images of civilian casualties for UK television audiences.

For some advocates of the media empowerment thesis, the emergence of global news media means that sources for the supply of information have become so diffuse that national news media boundaries are increasingly irrelevant (e.g. Shaw, 2000: 33). However, despite the growing popularity of the Arab channels across Europe (Cozens, 2003a) and the availability of other new media sources at the time, the results presented here provide little support for a noticeable incursion of alternative image sources that, in turn, legitimated a genuinely alternative, or non-Western, way of seeing the war.

Coalition troops as 'humanitarian warriors': the Iraqi PoW photograph
On many occasions, a particular image was selected for publication by several newspapers on a single day. This was most likely to occur when the visuals relating to a certain key event or person were restricted to one main source, as with Jessica Lynch's rescue or the Al Jazeera video stills of American prisoners of war 'paraded' on television. More generalised themes were likely to be illustrated with multiple emblematic images – for example, a soldier firing his weapon, an airstrike, or refugees. However, in one notable instance, the same photograph was published in each title that we surveyed, despite its role as a thematic rather than specific illustration. The image – an Associated Press photograph by Itsuo Inouye – of an Iraqi prisoner receiving water from US marines (see Figure 5.5), appeared on 22 March 2003, accompanied by articles that were largely supportive of the coalition. Here, we subject this photograph to further analysis, asking what the photograph's subject matter and its various framings in our newspapers tell us about the way in which

Figure 5.5 The Iraqi PoW photograph (AP Photo/Itsuo Inouye). Original caption,
as filed in the AP archive: 'Cpl David Briggs from Broken Arrow, Oklahoma, right,
of the 15th Marine Expeditionary Unit, helps an Iraqi soldier with water from
a canteen in southern Iraq, on Friday, March 21, 2003. Some 200 Iraqi soldiers
surrendered to the US 15th Marine Expeditionary Unit just an hour after it crossed
the border into Iraq from northern Kuwait.'

this war was represented in the press. We also look at whether alternative interpretations that could potentially be attached to this image were omitted from its framing in the British press. Following a general description of its subject matter and form, we examine how newspapers placed the image in a lexical context and evaluate critically the associations and meanings that were offered for it. Primarily, we argue, the image served to underpin two of the dominant supportive narratives found across the British press: coalition military success and the 'humanitarianism' of the invading forces.

The photograph shows two US marines giving water to an Iraqi prisoner. A further, marginal marine figure is also present; only his hand and gun barrel enter the top-left corner of the frame. In accordance with good compositional practice, the background is simple and uncluttered, accentuating the outline of the three main figures and removing any distracting context. Reading from the left, the first main US marine figure has his back to us, with a raised knee and hand visible, and the side of his face obscured by the protruding gun. The Iraqi prisoner between the two marines is sitting with his legs in front of him, apparently raised a little off the floor, judging from the position of the other two figures. His hands appear tied behind his back and his head is positioned back, held in place by the third main figure. This third figure, another US marine, is facing the camera and positioned slightly behind and above the Iraqi. The marine's right hand is placed on top of the Iraqi's head, holding it back as he pours water into the prisoner's mouth from a canteen with his left hand, and he looks down at where the water is trickling into the Iraqi's mouth.

All the figures are in military uniforms, but the bulky, heavily-equipped body-wear of the US marines contrasts sharply with the saggy, oversized uniform on the Iraqi's emaciated body. Likewise, the marines' large helmets draw attention to the bare, unprotected head of the Iraqi, whose beret appears to be in his front shirt-pocket. The strangely bare background, without distinct markers of land or sky, emphasises the iconicity of the image. The three figures appear in an almost symmetrical composition, which has resonances of religious iconographical postures: the imprisoned man receiving succour from two enemy combatants connotes the Christian themes of charity and of the Good Samaritan. The marine's gaze is steady and paternal as the Iraqi's face is upturned towards him in response but with his eyes closed. The slightness of his neck is emphasised as he cranes to drink the (purifying) water. This submissive pose further highlights the disparity between the actors; the saviours coming to the aid of the subjugated prisoner. These are not invading, injuring forces but protective humanitarian guardians.

Although this description and interpretation is one of many possibilities, the identified themes are also evident in the newspapers' use and treatment of this image. That each newspaper published this photograph demonstrates its professionally accepted status as a 'good' image, particularly since its subject

Table 5.10 Captions and placement for the Iraqi PoW photograph

Newspaper	Caption	Page	Size
Sun	Compassion . . . US marines give water to an Iraqi soldier wounded near the border with Kuwait yesterday. Several injured Iraqis were airlifted to Allied ships for medical attention	8	Extra large
Mirror	Mercy: US Marines from the 15th Expeditionary Unit give water to a captured soldier in south Iraq an hour after crossing the border from Kuwait yesterday	10	Extra large
Mail	Drops of mercy: A US marine dispenses water to a surrendering Iraqi soldier as the 15th Marine Expeditionary Unit forges its way into Iraq yesterday	9	Extra large
Independent	US Marines from the 15th Expeditionary Unit trickle water from a canteen into the mouth of an Iraqi prisoner of war who had surrendered in southern Iraq yesterday	2	Medium
Guardian	US marines give an Iraqi soldier water	5	Small
Times	Arms and alms: under guard, an Iraqi soldier is given water from a canteen by US Marines	14	Small
Telegraph	A surrendering Iraqi soldier is given water by men of the US 15 Marine Expeditionary Unit yesterday hours after they crossed into Iraq	7	Large

matter is essentially thematic. Table 5.10 illustrates the contexts in which the picture was published, including caption, size and page number. Notably, it appeared in the top half of the page in each newspaper, occupying over half a page in the *Sun*, *Mirror* and *Mail*, and always accompanying headlines that were supportive of both the coalition's military advancement and its treatment of Iraqi prisoners, imbuing a sense of inevitable progress towards Baghdad, and even towards Saddam Hussein in person: 'Forward march: the Allied military machine rolls on towards Saddam' (*Independent*). The captions direct readers first and foremost towards moral evaluations – 'mercy', 'compassion', 'alms', 'giving water' – leaving no ambiguity in the pronounced appraisals of the kindness of the US marines' actions. Only the *Guardian* is concise and neutral: 'US marines give an Iraqi soldier water' being the most succinct caption, partly because the photograph's small size allows little space.[12] The *Sun* provides extra information, adding not only that this Iraqi soldier is injured, but that others have been airlifted to receive medical attention on 'Allied ships'. Other captions stress the rapid military progress achieved by the same unit as it 'forges its way' into Iraq. All seven newspapers, despite their varying editorial positions in relation to the war, print this photograph and caption within the context of unquestionably supportive coverage.

However, within this photograph's frame, which through its publication, reprinting and prominence came to symbolise the compassion of the coalition advance, a certain ambiguity exists, most clearly through the gun pointing directly at the Iraqi prisoner's head. The kindness in the act of offering water and positioning the bottle so that the captive can drink is pierced by the intrusion of the gun barrel. The impact of this intrusion is lessened to some degree by careful cropping in some newspapers, and by the lexical framing, which manages to promote both coalition military prowess and the incompetence of the enemy army at the same time. The fact that the gun is out of focus, and possibly not so much 'aimed' as accidentally positioned at such an angle, may also lessen its disruptive impact. Removed from the historical context of those first few days of the military advance into Iraq, at a time of high expectations and some patriotic fervour, the ambiguity of the image emerges more strongly.

Viewed several years later and with the practice of 'waterboarding' – condoned by the US administration – receiving critical news media treatment, the act of 'trickling' water becomes imbued with more sinister connotations. The photograph has not changed and it does not explicitly signify torture, yet our knowledge permeates our interpretation of the picture. The hand on top of the head starts to look more grasping and forceful, the marine's expression becomes disinterested and blank. Prisoner abuse scandals and the vivid amateur trophy pictures from Abu Ghraib now haunt this beautifully composed image. Next to those now-familiar snapshots, the symmetry appears false or conspicuous in its striking iconography of compassion.

In recognising the fluid nature of this photograph's meanings within a historical and political context, the uniformity of its supportive presentation in the news media at the time is brought even further into relief. There appears to have been no desire to give emphasis to the more ambiguous elements at work within it. At the time, this image was published to support two interconnected notions about this particular conflict: simultaneously, coalition soldiers are both humanised liberators and part of a militarily effective war machine – interpretations that resonate with the coalition discourses of humanitarianism and good soldiering. In contrast, Iraqi soldiers are shown as ineffective, weak, surrendering, or alternatively 'fanatical diehards' using immoral tactics. Interestingly, the enemy combatants are not simply demonised, as has been reported in past conflicts (Hallin, 1986). They are also disarmed through coalition 'compassion' towards an ill-equipped, starving and reluctant conscript army. The slight figure in the photograph with a long neck, closed eyes and submissive posture becomes the compliant accepter of American goodwill. The 'white man's burden' in this case encompasses not only the duty to rescue the native women and children from the savage ruling men as Dana Cloud (2004) identifies in the war in Afghanistan, but also to rescue the conscripted men who are not considered the 'real enemy'. It is this depiction, rather than that of the many dead or severely injured Iraqi soldiers, that newspapers chose, implicitly portraying the coalition military as a 'non-injuring' force (Scarry, 1985) and combining the unseen effects of military prowess with responsibility towards the Iraqi people.

Although this is only one visual out of the 3,949 analysed, its repetition seems to foreground the key role performed by images in the print media. Pictures may require words for their 'defining power' (Entman, 2004: 104) but in some cases a single photograph is deemed by editors to express something significant about a particular conflict at a particular time. Despite the diversity of editorial positions adopted by the press, particular themes promoted by coalition leaders also hold irresistible appeal for news editors. The righteousness of the soldiers fighting at the nation's behest is one that is promoted with ease and is only later opened to serious challenge when more disturbing photographic evidence – from Abu Ghraib prison, for example – emerges.

Explaining the predominance of supportive coverage

To a significant extent, the evidence presented so far indicates that both television and press reporting conformed to a pattern of supportive coverage, as predicted by the elite-driven model. As explained in Chapter 3, reliance on official sources, patriotism and ideology are regularly invoked in order to explain this mode of news media performance. In the final section of this chapter, we take a closer look at our findings so far in order to assess the extent to which they provide evidence for the importance of these explanatory variables.

Reliance on official sources and viewpoints

As described in Chapter 3, the tendency of journalists to rely upon, and defer to, official sources and viewpoints, or to index their reporting within the boundaries of official debate, is a common and widely accepted explanation for supportive news media coverage (e.g. Bennett, 1990; Hallin, 1986; Herman and Chomsky, 1988; Schlesinger and Tumber, 1994). Moreover, as Wolfsfeld's (1997) political contest model suggests, the conditions of war are likely to increase the dependence of journalists on official sources amid the dangers of the battlefield and the difficulty of accessing the 'enemy'.

What evidence is there from our study to support the significance of this factor in shaping coverage? Of course, our aggregate level finding that supportive coverage tended to dominate, coupled with the prominence of coalition sources across both press and television, is consistent with the idea that reliance on official sources and viewpoints is a powerful influence on news coverage. A more fine-grained analysis of inter-channel and inter-newspaper findings provides further indication of the impact of sources on news coverage. In television, Sky News and ITV ran the largest number of supportively-framed battle stories (76% and 60% respectively – see Table 5.7) while also being the biggest users of coalition sources. Sky News used coalition sources 70.3 per cent of the time and ITV 59.1 per cent of the time (see Table 5.2). In contrast, the BBC and Channel 4 News had a lower proportion of supportive battle stories (49% and 43% respectively – see Table 5.7) and were less likely to use coalition sources (56.9% of the time for the BBC; 52.5% for Channel 4 – see Table 5.2). The pattern, however, was more ambiguous in the press. Although the avidly pro-war *Sun* had the highest proportion of direct quotes attributable to the coalition and the anti-war *Guardian* the least (55.2% and 39.6% respectively – see Table 5.4), there was no clear association between editorial orientation and use of coalition sources at most of the other papers.

From another perspective, the policy of embedding journalists with frontline units reflected a coalition media strategy aimed, at least in part, at ensuring that journalists formed their reports from the perspective of the coalition (Cortell et al., 2009: 667). Here, our research provided further evidence of the influence of this information strategy on reporting. Sky News, the most supportive news programme, sourced 26 per cent of its stories from embeds whereas the figure for Channel 4 News, the least supportive, was only 19 per cent. So the most supportive TV news outlet was also the biggest user of reports from embeds. We also found a small but noticeable effect when comparing battle coverage from embeds with battle coverage from other sources: except at Channel 4, embedded reports were more often supportive of the coalition. For example, 82 per cent of Sky News reports from embedded journalists were supportive compared with only 72 per cent of its non-embedded battle coverage. Overall, although there is evidence that embedding led to some instances where journalists were critical of the coalition (Lewis et al., 2006) and that embedded reporters perceived themselves as free of censorship and self-censorship (Johnson and Fahmy, 2009), our study shows that greater use of coalition sources and the involvement of embedded reporters are both associated with increasing levels of supportive coverage. Consistent with research by Haigh et al. (2006), Lindner (2009) and Pfau et al. (2004), our findings serve to confirm the claim that the process of embedding helped to shape reporting of the war in favour of the coalition.

Finally, the importance of official sources and viewpoints is also supported by our findings for coverage of the presence of WMD, the British government's primary justification for invading Iraq. Considerable effort was expended on both sides of the Atlantic to promote the belief that Iraq possessed WMD or could quickly acquire them. As we now know, WMD were never found in Iraq and subsequent investigations in Britain and the United States indicated that the significance of intelligence about their presence was exaggerated in order to bolster claims about the 'threat' that they posed (see Chapter 4). The main sources for claims about Iraq's possession of WMD were the British and American governments while, elsewhere, the United Nations weapons inspection mission (UNMOVIC), headed by Hans Blix, remained scrupulously agnostic about the existence of Iraqi WMD, and Iraq itself denied that it possessed them. Faced with these different claims, British journalists followed the rules of indexing and tended to accept the viewpoint of their own government regarding WMD. ITV's Bill Neely commented on the extent to which he and other journalists had to accept the official attitude towards WMD:

> We could only report what had happened in the past. That was one of Rumsfeld's 'known unknowns' or whatever . . . We didn't know that he didn't have them . . . We ended up saying that Iraq had used these weapons, had had them in the past, had used them in the past . . . We were all sceptical about the 45 minutes claim and the dodgy dossier . . . but, at the same time, when Blair stood up in the House of Commons, argued for the war, . . . there was an element of doubt and you could not be certain that Iraq did not have these weapons and that they might not pose a threat if they fell in to the wrong hands.[13]

Consequently, most coverage of the WMD case (62% of television news reports and 65% of newspaper stories) implicitly or explicitly reinforced the idea of their presence in Iraq. Indeed, very few reports suggested that there were no WMD there.

However, although the evidence discussed here indicates the importance of sources in shaping news content, several outlets were able to generate significant proportions of negotiated and oppositional coverage despite relying heavily on coalition sources (see Chapter 6). So, while they are influential, the importance of sources should not be over-determined. In the conclusion, we return to the questions that our findings raise in relation to a theoretical understanding of sources and their impact on news coverage.

Patriotism

Our findings also support the importance of patriotism. On the one hand, significant levels of overt flag-waving and jingoism were found only in the *Sun* newspaper. In addition, most of the journalists interviewed showed clear resistance to the idea of patriotic or jingoistic reporting in wartime. For example, Bill Neely, for ITV News, suggested that patriotic reporting might be applicable during wars of national survival, such as the Second World War, but was certainly not appropriate in the case of Iraq: 'I am not there . . . as a patriot. I am very aware that I am there as a Brit . . . I am aware of the baggage that I bring to every story. But I am acutely aware of my responsibility to be objective.'[14] Alex Thomson of Channel 4 News dismissed patriotic reporting as 'advertising not journalism',[15] while Richard Sambrook, Director of BBC News at the time of the invasion, commented that 'the BBC, as an international broadcaster in particular, also feels it has to take a more neutral position than that, and that does slightly set us apart from the more jingoistic coverage'.[16] Indeed, when the occurrence of patriotic, supportive reporting was acknowledged by our interviewees, it was normally in the context of a description of the behaviour of other news media outlets. As Richard Sambrook put it:

> One of the tensions you always get when British troops are in conflict is the extent to which you simply support the British interests, and that's a particular dilemma for the BBC. So, obviously, the tabloid press and probably to a greater extent than the BBC Sky News, and possibly ITN – ITN are slightly closer to us, I think – have a fairly clear agenda of supporting our interests. It's the kind of 'our boys' coverage, if you like.[17]

In a similar vein, other journalists noted the tendency of American and Israeli journalists in particular to be more patriotic than their British counterparts.[18] So it seems that patriotic and supportive journalism was acknowledged only as something which 'other' news media outlets engaged in.

Nevertheless, coverage of the military campaign did present the conflict primarily from the perspective of coalition forces – 'our boys' – and, as we showed earlier, tended to report their operations positively, emphasising inevitable military victory. Our television news analysis illustrates this particularly well. Of the 1,063 stories analysed, only one – a Channel 4 report by journalists in Baghdad – actually presented the war from the perspective of those fighting against coalition forces (this example is discussed further in Chapter 6). Twenty television news stories included the subject of 'daily life of coalition troops', emphasising a human interest angle, but, of course, there were no equivalent stories for Iraqi troops and fighters. Similarly, deaths of coalition forces were reported and due attention given to the loss of British lives, but the deaths of Iraqi troops and fighters went unheeded. Finally, although the war was fought primarily by US forces, the activities and progress of British troops remained the primary concern for UK news media. As such, the British national perspective prefigured coverage – not in an overtly jingoistic fashion, but rather in the sense of Billig's (1995) notion of 'banal nationalism'. As he notes,

> nationhood provides a continual background for their political discourses, for cultural products, and even for the structuring of newspapers. In so many

little ways, the citizenry are daily reminded of their national place in a world
of nations. However, this reminding is so familiar, so continual, that it is not
consciously registered as reminding. (Billig, 1995: 8)

Journalists also acknowledged repeatedly the importance of the national perspective in shaping news reporting, while making a clear distinction between
patriotic journalism and reporting that focused in particular on the progress
of British troops. Even Alex Thomson from Channel 4 News, which paid less
attention to battle progress than its competitors, noted the inevitability of
such coverage, explaining: 'You are writing news ultimately for a British audience if you want people to watch . . . All politics is local.'[19] Several journalists
also noted the imbalance in the way in which the war was reported that was
caused by an adherence to the national perspective.[20] Most colourfully, Alex
Thomson commented: 'If you'd just come down from Mars, you'd think –
bloody hell, you know – the Brits and the Americans are fighting 50:50, or
possibly even the Brits were a bigger part of it.'[21] Others even noted the tendency to play off the perceived success of British troops in the south against
the different challenges faced by US troops in the remainder of Iraq.[22]

Patriotism, then, usually manifested itself in subtle ways – not through
crude and jingoistic reporting but by reflecting and reinforcing a British
national perspective. As Billig's idea of banal nationalism reveals, it is precisely this mundane and seemingly obvious reminding of our nation's place in
the world that underpins nationhood, nationalism and patriotism.

Ideology: the 'humanitarian warfare' narrative

Some scholars have identified the cold war, the 'war on terror' and humanitarian warfare as having had an ideological effect on the way in which Western
societies perceive and legitimise military action, as documented in Chapters 2
and 3. These mechanisms work by providing straightforward, widely 'acceptable' explanations for military action while working to limit more complex
and controversial explanations and justifications for war. The findings in this
chapter, which show high levels of support for the invasion of Iraq on humanitarian grounds, are suggestive of the importance of the humanitarian warfare
ideology in particular and are worthy of detailed discussion.

As noted in Chapter 2, the idea of humanitarian intervention gained cur-
rency during the 1990s and was associated with interventions during humanitarian crises in Northern Iraq (1991), Somalia (1992), Bosnia (1992–95) and
Kosovo (1999) (Ramsbotham and Woodhouse, 1996; Wheeler, 2000). Tony
Blair's 'Doctrine of the International Community' speech (Blair, 1999), setting
out his vision of a foreign policy committed to intervening when national
interests coincided with the need to prevent human rights violations, became
a prominent articulation of this idea. When the foreign policy agendas of

Western governments shifted to a focus on fighting terrorism following the attacks of 9/11, the Blair government sustained its humanitarian discourse. Although Iraqi possession of WMD remained the central justification for the 2003 invasion, the humanitarian case for regime change was a regular feature of the British government's rhetoric in promoting action against Iraq. Indeed, according to Bluth, 'the "moral" case appeared in practically every speech, starting in April 2002, and was exemplified in the "Human Rights Dossier"' (Bluth, 2005: 600) published by the UK government (Prime Minister's Office, 2002). Christopher Meyer, former British ambassador to the USA, confirms the linkage between the humanitarian intervention doctrine of the 1990s and the invasion of Iraq in his memoirs. Discussing Blair's 'Doctrine of the International Community' speech (Blair, 1999), he wrote:

> Against the background of Kosovo he promulgated a doctrine of international community and humanitarian intervention, almost pre-emption: that it was justified to violate the frontiers and sovereignty if within its borders genocide was about to be, or was being, carried out. This was not a million miles from one of the main arguments used to justify the attack on Iraq in 2003. (Meyer, 2005: 103)

The humanitarian rationale was also a prominent feature of coalition briefings during the invasion. Craig Copetas of Bloomberg News remarked on the pressure from the British government to present British forces in a humanitarian light:

> We were not allowed to take any pictures or describe British soldiers carrying guns. I was told that there was a decision made by Downing Street that the military minders of the journalists down there were to go to any lengths to not portray British, the British fighting man and woman, as fighters. They wanted them there to have them there as nation-builders, that they weren't going to be killing people. The media minders would get very, very upset with you very fast and threats were levelled that you would be disembedded.[23]

However, the problem with justifying the war in humanitarian terms was that the case did not meet the criteria by which humanitarian intervention is normally justified. The International Commission on Intervention and State Sovereignty report, *The Responsibility to Protect* (ICISS, 2001), makes clear that intervention can only be justified as a last resort when there is actual or imminent loss of life on a large scale that cannot be averted by any other means. There has been some subsequent debate over whether the threshold criteria could be argued to have existed in the case of Iraq,[24] but it remains unclear that any ongoing human rights abuses attributable to the Iraqi regime were sufficient to justify invading Iraq in 2003, or that the suffering of the Iraqi people could not be relieved by alternative means (e.g. by the lifting of sanctions). Of course, the post-invasion loss of life and suffering, with estimates starting at around 100,000 killed, makes the case for humanitarian intervention even more problematic.[25] Even at the time of the invasion, the British Attorney General made clear in his legal advice to the government that there were no humanitarian grounds by which invading Iraq could be justified: 'I know of no reason why it would be an appropriate basis for action in the present circumstances' (Goldsmith, 2003).

Yet despite the difficulty of associating the invasion of Iraq with the idea of humanitarian intervention, this narrative was strikingly successful in shaping the perceptions of journalists. As we have seen, 87 per cent of television news reports that referred, explicitly or implicitly, to the humanitarian rationale for war were supportive of it (see Figure 5.4). Even the relatively independent Channel 4 News gave it supportive coverage most of the time. Of the national newspapers, those that took an anti-war position still showed support for this rationale (*Mirror* 63.3%, *Independent* 63.9%, *Guardian* 75.0%) and support in the remaining papers was even greater – over 80 per cent in each case (see Table 5.9). The prevalence and consistent reproduction of this narrative in the news media suggests that it was operating at an ideological level, with journalists accepting it unquestioningly.

Overall, our evidence shows that the rationale for war upon which journalists were most likely to agree was that ousting Saddam by invading Iraq would benefit the Iraqi people and that this alone was a worthwhile cause for which to fight a war. And yet this position of substantive support for war on humanitarian grounds was arrived at with little sensitivity for or understanding of either the legal or academic arguments governing when it is appropriate to use force for humanitarian purposes. As such, the evidence from our study supports those (e.g. Chandler, 2005; Chomsky, 1999; Hammond, 2007a; Kampfner, 2003) who argue that the discourse of humanitarianism has an ideological effect, both in limiting journalists' critical engagement with the substance of the humanitarian warfare rationale and in discouraging consideration of alternative geo-strategic motives for the war, such as the projection of US power. We return to this issue in presenting conclusions from our study in the closing chapter.

Summary

In many ways, at least at an aggregate level, British news media coverage of the Iraq invasion conformed to the predictions of the elite-driven model. Press and television news relied heavily on coalition sources and supportive battle coverage prevailed even among newspapers that had opted to oppose the war. At the same time, there was substantial support for the WMD and humanitarian rationales for war. Battlefield visuals, the downgrading of Arab-based sources of alternative news and the 'humanitarian warrior' photograph offer further indications of the extent of supportive, pro-coalition coverage across much of the news media. A more detailed examination of news content emphasises the importance of sources, patriotism and the humanitarian warfare ideology in establishing the dominance of supportive coverage.

In spite of this, not all coverage conformed so readily to the contours of the elite-driven model. Among particular news media outlets and certain subject areas, a more nuanced and diverse picture emerges and it is to these pockets of resistance that we turn our attention in the next chapter.

Notes

1 There were so few cases of reinforcement that such figures must be treated with caution, but the BBC provided reinforcing treatment on one occasion each to UK political actors, US military and Iraqi opposition groups, ITV offered reinforcing treatment predominantly to UK military (six occasions) and Iraqi civilians (five occasions), while Sky News was more likely to reinforce the UK military (four occasions) and US political actors (twice). However, Channel 4 never produced reinforcing coverage towards coalition actors.

2 Telephone interview with Richard Beeston, 9 December 2008.

3 Telephone interview with Jon Snow, 19 December 2008.

4 Telephone interview with Richard Sambrook, 12 December 2008.

5 Telephone interview with James Meek, 19 December 2008.

6 This report, credited to Gethin Chamberlain of *The Scotsman*, appeared in several newspapers at varying lengths and on different dates. The *Sun* published it five days later on 31 March (p. 2) under the heading 'Snipers KO the vipers'. The style of language differed markedly in each, illustrating the way in which newspaper sub-editors routinely rewrite copy to match each newspaper's style.

7 Telephone interview with Bill Neely, 12 December 2008.

8 Telephone interview with Angus Taverner, 10 February 2009.

9 In television news, the 'war on terror' rationale was almost absent from coverage, generating only eight stories. Where it was mentioned, negotiated coverage was most common, but little can be read into such a small sample. It was also little reported in the press, where it was mentioned in 62 stories. Here it was framed supportively in 31 stories but received oppositional treatment in 26 stories. Three titles, the *Mirror*, *Independent* and *Guardian*, took an overwhelmingly oppositional line in referring to it. This minimal attention from the news media reflects the fact that the British government chose not to focus on promoting the war as part of a 'war on terror'.

10 Telephone interview with Tim Butcher, 11 December 2008.

11 The subject percentages that we give here for press visuals refer to the number of photographs in each category as a percentage of all photographs; each photograph could only be allotted one subject code and more than one photograph could appear connected to a single news story. These figures are not directly comparable with those given for our story subjects measure, for which stories could be given more than one subject code where appropriate.

12 The *Guardian* was also the only newspaper to obscure (pixellate) the face of the Iraqi man so that he could not be identified. There was some confusion in the beginning stages of the conflict as how to interpret the Geneva Convention with regard to the public display of prisoners of war as it applied to newspapers printing such photographs. This resulted in some inconsistency in the representations of both Iraqi and coalition prisoners, sometimes with obscured faces but not on all occasions.

13 Telephone interview with Bill Neely, 12 December 2008.

14 Telephone interview with Bill Neely, 12 December 2008.

15 Telephone interview with Alex Thomson, 10 December 2008.

16 Telephone interview with Richard Sambrook, 12 December 2008.

17 Telephone interview with Richard Sambrook, 12 December 2008.

18 Telephone interviews with Tim Butcher (*Daily Telegraph*), 11 December 2008, and Bill Neely (ITV News), 12 December 2008.

19 Telephone interview with Alex Thomson, 10 December 2008.

20 In our telephone interviews with Richard Beeston (*The Times*), 9 December 2008, and Ed Pilkington (*Guardian*), 10 December 2008, for example.

21 Telephone interview with Alex Thomson, 10 December 2008.

22 Telephone interview with Ed Pilkington (*Guardian*), 10 December 2008.

23 Speaking in the BBC2 *Correspondent* documentary 'War Spin', broadcast 18 May 2003. Transcript available at: http://news.bbc.co.uk/nol/shared/spl/hi/ programmes/correspondent/transcripts/18.5.031.txt (accessed 3 October 2008).

24 For a useful discussion of the various perspectives, see the 'Special issue on ethics and force after Iraq', *Ethics and International Affairs*, 19 (2), 2005.

25 According to Iraq Body Count, between 89,600 and 97,828 civilian deaths from violence had occurred between the start of the invasion and December 2008. This figure is based on mainly on deaths reported in news media. In July 2006, a study published in the *Lancet* (Burnham et al., 2006) estimated civilian deaths as a consequence of the invasion at between 392,979 and 942,636. For a discussion of the statistics behind these two studies, see Zeger and Johnson (2007).

6

'Independence, diversity and professional autonomy': Evidence for negotiated and oppositional coverage

Overview

This chapter is devoted to documenting and analysing evidence for negotiated and oppositional coverage. This is done in three ways: first, by examining critical coverage that emerged across specific subject areas; second, by describing patterns of coverage in particular media outlets; and third, by presenting time series data. The chapter begins by examining the representation of civilian casualties, military casualties and humanitarian operations across both television and press – three subject areas that generated a good deal of media criticism. Because of their particular importance with respect to the representation of casualties in television news coverage, we integrate our analysis of visuals with our discussion of negotiated and oppositional television reports. We then consider specific media outlets, starting with an examination of Channel 4 News which departed from the pattern set by other television news programmes in adopting a largely negotiated stance in its coverage of the war. Following this, we move to a close comparative analysis of the British press, where we found a diversity of approaches to reporting the war among different titles. We explore our evidence, which included the emergence of an unprecedented and surprisingly vociferous anti-war press and differential use of visuals, but we also show that there were limits to the anti-war stance adopted by some newspapers. Finally, we present further evidence of variability in news media performance in our analysis of time series data that compares reporting in different phases of the war. As in Chapter 5, we finish by relating these findings to the explanatory variables, set out in Chapter 3, associated with the independent and oppositional models.

Negotiated and oppositional subject areas: challenging the coalition over casualties and humanitarian operations

The invasion period was marked by successive reports of civilian deaths from missile attacks on markets, hospitals and homes, and at US checkpoints.

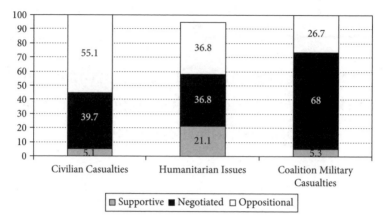

Figure 6.1 Framing of civilian and military casualties and humanitarian themes (all TV channels; as percentages)

Note: A small number of Humanitarian Issues stories coded as 'other' (2 stories in all) are excluded.

Despite coalition attempts to present these issues to their best advantage, emphasising precision targeting and the importance of humanitarian objectives in Iraq, for example, reporting departed from the official line more often than not.

In our findings for television news, only a fraction of stories (5.1%) about civilian casualties were supportive towards the coalition, while more than a third (39.7%) were coded as negotiated and the majority (55.1%) were oppositional (see Figure 6.1). Reporting on a Baghdad marketplace bomb in one example, Rageh Omaar interviewed the father of an injured child who sought vengeance on America. Omar ended his report by commenting on the feelings of civilians and questioning the terminology of the coalition: 'Many of them wonder how would-be liberators could impose such a toll on the people they want to set free' (BBC News, 29 March). Stories about civilian casualties were typically illustrated with pictures of angry crowds carrying coffins, pools of drying blood among the rubble of destroyed buildings, hospital scenes, and families in grief. Although these casualty images (present in 8.7% of news items) were problematic for the coalition it is also important to note that much available footage was not shown. We found that while there were images of the civilian wounded in our sample, and of coffins or body-bags, we never saw the dead themselves. Nevertheless, in this subject area, reports were largely negotiated or oppositional.

Similar patterns of coverage regarding casualties could be observed in the press. Across all newspapers, three-quarters of these stories were oppositional, as Table 6.1 shows. Most newspapers carried emotionally

Table 6.1 Framing of civilian and military casualties and humanitarian themes by newspaper (as percentages)

	Sun	Mirror	Mail	Indep- endent	Guard- ian	Times	Tele- graph	All
Supportive	36.4	8.3	23.5	0.0	3.6	5.0	25.0	11.1
Negotiated	9.1	16.7	11.8	6.2	14.3	10.0	20.8	13.3
Oppositional	54.5	75	64.7	93.8	82.1	85.0	54.2	75.6
No. of stories	11	48	17	32	28	20	24	180
				Civilian casualties				
Supportive	100.0	11.1	40.0	14.8	12.5	41.7	31.3	32.2
Negotiated	0.0	22.2	16.7	37.0	16.7	20.8	25.0	22.0
Oppositional	0.0	66.7	40.0	48.1	70.8	37.5	43.8	45.8
No. of stories	13	9	5	27	24	24	16	118
				Humanitarian issues				
Supportive	35.1	20.0	35.3	12.5	10.5	40.0	27.5	27.0
Negotiated	57.9	43.1	29.4	59.4	52.6	45.7	62.5	50.0
Oppositional	7.0	36.9	35.3	28.1	36.8	14.3	10.0	23.0
No. of stories	57	65	34	32	19	35	40	282
				Coalition military casualties				

Note: A small number of stories coded as 'other' (4 civilian casualties stories, 22 humanitarian issues stories, 6 military casualties stories) are excluded.

charged stories and photographs of Iraqi civilians, often children, under headlines such as 'Her name was Sarah . . . and whether she was killed by an American or Iraqi weapon, this insane war is to blame' (Brian Reade, *Daily Mirror*, 31 March 2003: 12–13) and 'Amid Allied jubilation, a child lies in agony, clothes soaked in blood' (Robert Fisk, *Independent*, 8 April 2003: 4). These reports placed considerable pressure on the British government: for example, the *Independent's* Robert Fisk had been singled out on 4 April by Geoff Hoon, Britain's Defence Secretary, for what the *Independent* described as a 'vitriolic attack', after Fisk's earlier reports of the marketplace bombs prompted anti-war MPs to launch a Commons motion criticising coalition bombing of civilians. Although Fisk claimed to have been handed a piece of US cruise missile after the attack, Hoon maintained that there was not 'a shred of corroborating evidence' for coalition responsibility (see Paul Waugh, 'Hoon: "No proof that Allied bombs hit marketplace"', *Independent*, 4 April 2003: 10). Even a majority of the few civilian casualty stories to appear in the *Sun*, the most pro-war paper in our sample, were oppositional.

Regarding humanitarian operations, over one-third (36.8%) of television reports were critical of the coalition and were coded as oppositional, with only one-fifth (21.1%) being supportive (see Figure 6.1). One example was a report from Safwan, a town where the water supply was apparently lost owing to coalition bombing. Here, an attempt to bring aid was met with some anger and confusion: 'A water tanker did arrive, supervised by British soldiers', explained Alex Thomson, 'but it was a humiliating and chaotic affair' (Channel 4 News, 29 March).

Criticism of humanitarian operations was reinforced by the visual representation of Iraqi civilians. Here, we found that encounters between Iraqi civilians and coalition forces were a prominent visual theme of television coverage of the invasion, occurring in 10.0 per cent of stories. Pictures of Iraqi civilians smiling or waving, or receiving humanitarian food and aid from coalition soldiers, would have been of significant value to the coalition. Overall, however, there were more images of Iraqi civilians exhibiting wariness, indifference or even hostility towards coalition forces (present in 48.2% of such stories) than of jubilant Iraqis celebrating or greeting the advancing coalition troops (33.2%). In meetings between civilians and the coalition, much of the meaning attributed to the images came from the reporter commentary. Reporter interpretations of the Iraqi mood included optimistic assessments but a common tendency was for journalists to emphasise suspicion or nervousness. Similarly, visuals of soldiers delivering aid were sometimes underscored by reporter voiceovers mentioning that aid had been seriously delayed or was insufficient, or criticising its disorganised and chaotic delivery. In some instances, civilians were filmed fighting each other for scraps (e.g. ITV News, 28 March).

With regard to press coverage, more stories received an oppositional framing than a supportive or negotiated one (see Table 6.1). In combination with the similar findings for television, this represents an interesting finding in comparison with our data showing overwhelmingly supportive (and much wider) coverage for the humanitarian justification for war discussed in Chapter 5. The picture revealed here is of abstract arguments for humanitarian-inspired warfare continuing to be supported by journalists, despite the persistence of practical problems with regard to the delivery of aid, shortages of water and power, and acute difficulties in hospitals. In keeping with the theoretical distinction between procedural and substantive-level criticism (e.g. Althaus, 2003; Hallin, 1986; Mermin, 1997), journalists showed far greater willingness to criticise tactical matters concerning the coalition's humanitarian performance than substantive claims about its humanitarian intentions. Several stories reported aid agencies' dismay at a mounting humanitarian crisis in Southern Iraq even after the coalition had apparently secured the area: 'The agencies contrasted public relations pictures of British soldiers engaged in relief work in Southern Iraq with horrendous conditions on the ground', wrote Ewen MacAskill and Burhan Wazir in the *Guardian* (5 April 2003: 6). In the *Observer*, Peter Beaumont used an interview with the unnamed head of the American Disaster Assistance and Response Team (DART) to highlight the inconsistencies in the coalition's humanitarian message:

> These are the men who usually rush to bring US aid to the victims of earth-quakes, hurricanes and floods. This time they have been asked to patch up the damage inflicted by their own government. No Name seemed uncomfortable with the contradictions inherent in this position. His voice seemed to quaver as he explained his budget so far expended $110 million, against the billions being spent on bombing Iraq. ('Food crisis in store for refugees', 23 March 2003: 7)

Finally, the subject of coalition military casualties was also a problematic area for the coalition. Here, a quarter (26.7%) of television news stories were coded as oppositional and most reporting (68.0%) was negotiated. One report reflected on the effect of 'bad news from the battlefield' on British public opinion and bereaved families. A father holds up a photograph and speaks to camera: 'I want President Bush to get a good look at this. Real good look here. This is the only son I had. Only son' (Robert Moore, ITV News, 24 March). In terms of their visual representation, coalition military casualties were rarely shown (5.0% of stories). Only two items depicted wounded British soldiers and the only images of coalition deaths involved footage of coffins being returned home. On the day when other channels' coverage was dominated by the fall of the Saddam statue in Baghdad, Channel 4 News pointedly recog-nised the contrast between the images felt to be acceptable for British news audiences and those broadcast by the Arab satellite channels:

> These were the scenes shown on British TV of US tanks entering Baghdad. Al Jazeera today showed what became of the coach of Iraqi troops apparently fired on by the tanks. The Arab world is seeing the war in all its graphic horror. (Channel 4 News, 10 April)

Overall, while coverage of this subject area was rarely supportive, a reluctance to show British casualties meant that coverage was more often negotiated, as opposed to oppositional. Across all newspapers, half of the stories concerning coalition military casualties were framed as negotiated, with the remainder spread fairly evenly between supportive and oppositional. Table 6.1 gives pro-portions for individual newspapers, showing that this pattern of negotiated coverage is repeated across most of them. Only in the *Mail*, which nonethe-less contained equal quantities of supportive and oppositional coverage, was 'negotiated' not the largest category. Coalition military casualty stories took several forms in the press, including reflecting the regret of loved ones (for example, 'Mum-to-be in mourning' (Geoffrey Lakeman, *Daily Mirror*, 25

March 2003: 4), which catalogued the grief of widows, fiancées and children of Royal Marines killed in a helicopter crash) and criticising equipment or tactical failures (such as an *Independent* story by Cahal Milmo and Charles Arthur headlined 'Allies order review after two die in tank blunder' (26 March 2003: 6)). However, despite the predominance of negotiated coverage among coalition casualty stories, caution is required in interpreting these findings: In some newspapers, more than a third of these stories were supportive, whereas in others more than a third were oppositional. This, then, was not a subject that the press reported in a uniform fashion and we return to the question of press diversity shortly. Nevertheless, the subject of military casualties was clearly one towards which journalists in both media were prepared to depart from supportive reporting.

Overall, whether as a consequence of a technology-driven 'chaotic, dense and fast-changing . . . information environment' (Tumber and Webster, 2006: 2), or simply because neither the occurrence nor the perception of all wartime events is ever completely under the control of those conducting war (Wolfsfeld, 1997), our results for casualties and humanitarian operations show these as areas where news coverage deviated from a supportive mode and generated a challenge to the coalition perspective. However, negotiated and oppositional coverage was not confined only to specific subject areas but was a feature of the broader output of some news organisations. We now examine those outlets which conformed to the independent and oppositional models.

Negotiated and oppositional media outlets: setting its own agenda and challenging existing assumptions – the case of Channel 4 News

Among television news programmes, Channel 4 News came closest to adopting a negotiated stance. It was the only channel for which the majority (51%) of its battle coverage was coded as negotiated, and it also had the lowest proportion of supportive battle stories (43%, compared with 49% (BBC), 60% (ITV) and 76% (Sky News) – see Table 5.7). In an interview, Channel 4 News anchor Jon Snow emphasised the importance of remaining detached from 'our troops' even when they were in combat:

> Our critical faculties were not suspended, although I can imagine a lot of peoples' were – what with our troops in the field, our brave boys on the ground, it was not the time to be questioning whether they were doing a good or a bad job. . . . I don't accept that at all, it's not our job.[1]

Indeed, Channel 4 News was responsible for the only occurrence we found of a news report showing the war from the perspective of those fighting the coalition forces. Introducing this remarkable report, broadcast on 8 April, Jon

Snow describes it as an 'exclusive insight into the fighting by the defenders, not the attackers – a desperate and chaotic attempt by one of Saddam's ultra loyal Fedayeen militia' to take back a bridge in Baghdad. At one stage, a young Iraqi (possibly a teenager) is shown in close-up angrily shouting 'fuck you, George Bush' at the camera, after the engagement with US forces ends in a failure to retake the bridge. The voiceover explains that the fighters are still 'defiant despite their losses', while the bodies of those who died are shown. Although it ultimately depicts the defeat of the fighters, this report gives a human face to the resistance and thus may have evoked some sympathy for their plight. At the very least, the report offers the perspective of those on the receiving end of coalition firepower.

More generally, the attitude of independence and detachment from 'our troops' was reflected in the behaviour of Channel 4 News reporters. Chief Correspondent Alex Thomson, embedded in Kuwait and Iraq, commonly introduced both his own field reports and those by others in the conflict zone. Unlike fellow journalists travelling with the same unit, Thomson often questioned the information he was receiving and frequently drew attention to the media-management strategies of his 'military minders' (19 March 2003). For example, on 21 March he directly challenged senior administration officials' claims about the taking of Umm Qasr:

> Not quite true what Donald Rumsfeld and Geoff Hoon were saying about it [Umm Qasr] being completely fallen and pacified, if you like. We were intending to go there late into this evening but we haven't been able to get there because there are still pockets of resistance. That's what we're being told on the ground.

He showed the same scepticism on 28 March:

> The British Army insists Iraqi militias fired upon their own people today to stop them from leaving the city. But there's no proof, and it has to be said the British Army here has made a series of claims about Basra, all of which have turned out to have no substance in recent days.

Interestingly, as an embedded journalist, it was Thomson's very closeness to the daily lives of the troops, where he was party to unofficial, if unnamed, sources and to local security information, that allowed him to counter claims made by distant politicians. On 23 March, he used his first-hand knowledge to refute official claims about the 'sabotage' of Iraq's oilfields:

> The [British] Army cares about its PR, and the story they wanted reported was the speed with which this oilfield was secured with very little damage. That's true, and it's impressive – except that all the evidence on the ground suggests that Saddam Hussein never had the slightest intention of sabotaging the Rumaila oilfields . . . So was it all just so much spin and propaganda? What the soldiers on the ground here are saying to us is that there is no evidence even of any attempt to lay mines or charges to blow up the Rumaila oil fields. Instead

what you've got is one or two isolated, and there are very few of them, isolated oil
wells dotted around which have been blown up, presumably to blind incoming
jets trying to bomb Iraq.

The following day, Thomson explicitly refuted Tony Blair's claims that Iraq
had mined its oilfields, saying that not only did he see no evidence of it, but
the military 'categorically denies it' (24 March).

Thomson was not alone among Channel 4's correspondents in offering a
sceptical and reflective account of events. Although Channel 4 News maintained quite a high reliance on coalition sources (if lower, at 52.5%, than
the other channels, which averaged 56.4% – see Table 5.2), a number of its
key reporters were careful to avoid aligning themselves too closely with the
coalition agenda. Correspondents such as Lindsey Hilsum in Baghdad and
David Smith in Washington showed similar detachment in their reporting of
events, sometimes drawing attention to what they had been directed to say or
show visually. In so doing, they were able to provide a meta-commentary on
the coalition's (and Iraq's) media-management strategies, as in the following
comment from Hilsum on 23 March:

> The Iraqis today have tried to give us a very clear indication of what they think
> is happening on the battlefield. Now of course, what they tell us isn't necessar-
> ily true – but then what the Americans and British tell us isn't necessarily true
> either: both sides try to give the best picture.

Similarly, reporting from Washington, Smith repeatedly referred to the 'rhetoric' coming out of Washington and drew attention to the manner in which
'the White House message machine had worked overtime at putting its man
in the best possible light' (26 March). Moreover, such observations, and much
of his narration generally, were commonly delivered in an incredulous, even
disdainful, tone of voice.

Finally, with regard to substantive issues, Channel 4 was uniquely sceptical towards the official justifications for the war. Its coverage of the WMD
justification was entirely negotiated and almost half of its coverage of the
humanitarian justification was either negotiated (19%) or oppositional (24%).
The few Channel 4 reports during the invasion phase that referred to the
'war on terror' justification were oppositional: indeed, Thomson stated that
Channel 4 'bent over backwards to explain to people . . . that this [the war] was
nothing to do with Al Qaeda'.[2] A good example of Channel 4 News' ability
to adopt a negotiated stance toward substantive-level issues can be seen in
the exchange between anchor Jon Snow and Paul Bremer, later to become US
Presidential Envoy in Iraq, following the parading of American prisoners
of war on Iraqi television on 23 March. In a follow-up piece discussing the
Iraqi footage, aired on 24 March, Snow started the interview by commenting:
'It is perhaps worth pointing out that Guantanamo Bay has given the whole

process of holding prisoners of war a very bad name'. Bremer rejected any 'moral equivalence' between the two cases, to which Snow retorted:

> You clearly didn't see, then, the scenes of blindfolded, deafened people being carted around on wagons, being brought all the way from Afghanistan, still denied legal rights, still holed up in Guantanamo eighteen months afterwards, no judicial process, totally illegal under all concepts of international law.

Although his claims were thoroughly rejected by Bremer, partly on the basis that he is not an attorney, Snow continued to talk about Guantanamo rather than the US PoWs held in Iraq: 'Well, if these people are not prisoners of war you ought perhaps to try them for crimes.' So although this interview provided Bremer with ample opportunity to put forward the US government case, it is marked by Snow's willingness to challenge the basic legitimacy of US conduct over Guantanamo Bay. Overall, even with respect to substantive-level issues surrounding the war, Channel 4 News showed a remarkable degree of independence from coalition perspectives.

Diversity and range of coverage: pro-war and anti-war press and differential use of visuals

While Channel 4 News was the only television news programme that could be classified as generating negotiated coverage, a comparative analysis of the British press reveals significant diversity of approach. Moreover, as shown in Chapter 4, some titles opposed the invasion altogether, while others publicly advocated it. The following analysis examines the extent to which these differing editorial positions helped to generate a range of press coverage, from supportive through to oppositional. We trace the evidence for this diversity in the subject framing to be found in each newspaper, looking first at subjects in all stories and then giving more detailed scrutiny to editorials.[3]

Story subjects and editorial subjects

Table 6.2 shows the subject framing measure and illustrates vividly the variety of positions taken by different newspapers and, in particular, the division of the press into pro-war and anti-war factions. By some distance, the *Sun*'s coverage was the most supportive of any newspaper and it reported scarcely any stories in a manner that challenged the coalition's position. More than half of the *Mail* and *Telegraph*'s coverage was also supportive, with *The Times* also more likely to be supportive than negotiated or oppositional. But the *Mirror* and *Independent* contained more oppositional than supportive coverage, with the *Guardian* giving most prominence overall to negotiated coverage.

Of course, a comparison of leader columns is likely to provide the most compelling evidence of diversity, since they can be taken to represent each

Table 6.2 Subject framing for all subjects by newspaper (as percentages)

	Sun	Mirror	Mail	Indep- endent	Guard- ian	Times	Tele- graph	All
Supportive	78.2	35.1	52.6	24.1	28.8	41.7	52.1	43.6
Negotiated	16.3	27.7	28.7	44.1	43.6	40.3	34.2	34.9
Oppositional	5.4	37.2	18.7	31.7	27.6	17.9	13.8	22.0
No. of stories	753	826	694	882	973	1,042	966	6,136

Note: 1,144 subjects coded as 'other' are excluded.

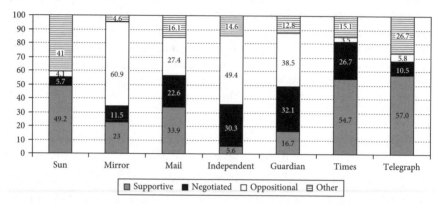

Figure 6.2 Subject framing in newspaper editorial subjects by newspaper (as percentages)

newspaper's 'voice'. Figure 6.2 shows results for subject framing solely for newspaper editorials. Here, the *Times* and *Telegraph* present similar pictures, with more than half of subjects coded as supportive and a minimal amount (3.5% and 5.8% respectively) of oppositional subjects. Although each acknowledged that there had been opposition to it, in editorials as the war began they chose to dismiss any doubts about the policy of war: 'The rights and wrongs of the campaign to oust Saddam will now be for historians to argue about' ('Master of the house', *Daily Telegraph*, 19 March 2003: 25); 'There has not been, despite what some critics charge, an unseemly rush to war on the part of the United States and the United Kingdom' ('War and after: A conflict that could not be avoided after September 11', *The Times*, 20 March 2003: 21). Both titles drew attention to Saddam's tyranny before urging support for British troops.

Editorials in the *Guardian* and *Independent* were also closely matched in their approach: Their framing is negotiated for just under a third of editorials (32.1% and 30.3% respectively) and oppositional for an even higher proportion (38.5% and 49.4%). Few editorial subjects in these papers could be coded as supportive (16.7% and 5.6%), reflecting their disagreement with the policy of war in Iraq. The *Independent* was quite restrained as the invasion was launched in calling for 'a swift conclusion with as few casualties on both sides as is possible in war', adding: 'But that does not mean we should not debate how the fighting is about to be conducted' ('When democracies do battle with a despot, they must hold on to their moral superiority', 20 March 2003: 18). By contrast, the *Guardian* was forthright: 'This war is wrong. It did not need to happen; it is unnecessary and was avoidable . . . This recourse to war is a substitute for thought and understanding, divisive in conception and enormously damaging to the international order' ('Hope against hope', 20 March 2003: 27).

The *Mirror*'s opposition to war is plain from these figures too. Although it admits more supportive subjects (23.0%) than the *Independent* or the *Guardian*, it is also the only example with more than half (60.9%) of its editorial subjects coded as oppositional. Its editorial attitude was unequivocal: 'The *Daily Mirror*'s view of this conflict could not be clearer – we believe it is wrong, wrong, wrong' ('Heroes led by man of real principle', 20 March 2003: 6).

The *Sun*'s leaders were ultra-supportive: there was minimal evidence of an oppositional tone (4.1%) and nearly half of its editorial subjects were supportive (49.2%). As war began, it declared: 'The *Sun*'s message to all Our Boys and Girls on land, at sea, and in the air is from the heart: Fight the good fight with all your might – and come home soon, safe, sound and successful', before urging those left behind to 'ignore the voices of those few misguided souls who refuse to support your loved ones' ('Safe home', 20 March 2003: 8). Notably, 41.0% of the *Sun*'s editorial subjects[4] were devoted to attacking the war's supposed opponents, including the BBC, prominent British anti-war politicians such as Robin Cook, and the UN ('The useless UN failed miserably to do anything to liberate the Iraqi people. The Security Council ratted on Britain and America and forced us to go it alone' ('Cut out UN's food racket', 27 March 2003: 10)). The *Sun*'s most fervent condemnation was reserved for Jacques Chirac, the French president:

> THAT slippery snake Jacques Chirac warns the war will have 'serious long-term consequences'. Too right. Serious for him. The French government has been exposed as cynical and mercenary. When Chirac says the UN must be in charge of rebuilding Iraq after the war, what he really means is this: He'll try every trick in the book to make sure France gets a big share of the contracts. He's off his chump . . . Chirac has shown he hates America and despises Britain. There can be no going back now. ('Back, Jacques', 21 March 2003: 8)

Finally, the *Mail*'s editorials prove not to have been as consistently supportive as its subject framing measure might have predicted: in fact, it is the only newspaper whose leaders did not seem to amplify its stance towards the war when compared with the other newspapers (see Table 6.2). Instead, only a third (33.9%) of the *Mail*'s editorial subjects proved to be supportive against 22.6 per cent negotiated and 27.4 per cent oppositional. Its leader columns made no mention of the invasion on 20 March, devoting themselves to domestic issues instead. However, a leader from 17 March – as the prospect of war was being debated in Parliament – not only set out the *Mail*'s position on the impending war but seemed to echo the scepticism of the anti-war titles:

> When the troops go into battle, they will – rightly – have overwhelming public support. That doesn't mean the doubts and concerns – so frequently expressed by this paper – have gone away. These are matters that will have to be addressed, once the fighting is done. ('Diplomacy given its last chance', 17 March 2003: 10)

So our analysis of the framing of its leader columns suggests that the *Mail*'s editorial orientation towards the war is ambiguous. The most likely explanation for the paper's behaviour is rooted in domestic politics. With its right-wing agenda, the *Mail* had long been known as a persistent and much-feared critic of Tony Blair and his Labour government. Temperamentally inclined to back the invasion of Iraq, it was nonetheless unimpressed by government behaviour in creating a *casus belli* and wary of the boost that a successful invasion could give to Blair's standing and the electoral chances of his party. Tellingly, the *Mail* newspapers reported the huge anti-war demonstration held in London on 14 February almost entirely in terms of its political damage to Tony Blair, and its coverage of the war contained more references to domestic issues than any other paper (9% compared with an average below 7% for the other titles).

To sum up, the *Sun*, *The Times* and *Telegraph* clearly emerge as newspapers in which a supportive line in relation to the coalition and the war predominated. In the *Sun*, this was overwhelmingly the case. So the pattern of coverage for these three newspapers was largely supportive, although even these titles tended to report casualties and the humanitarian situation in Iraq in a negotiated or oppositional fashion, in common with all of the news media surveyed. There is interesting evidence that the *Mail* had an ambiguous editorial stance and domestic political advantage seems to have been in play here. But despite this distinctive editorial position, the *Mail* still emerges as a newspaper that took a supportive line across most of its coverage. To varying degrees, however, the *Mirror*, *Independent* and *Guardian* took a more critical line in accordance with their anti-war editorial stance. Their coverage showed lower levels of support for the coalition and provided much more in the way of negotiated and oppositional coverage.

'In the eye of the beholder': evidence for press diversity in the differential use of visuals
An interesting feature that emerged from our analysis of press visuals was the scope for similar images to be used in contrasting ways by different

newspapers. Images of coalition prisoners of war provided a notable example. Particularly in the *Sun* and *Mail*, they were used to negotiate otherwise damaging coverage by drawing attention to the humiliation or ill-treatment meted out by Iraqi captors ('At mercy of savages', *Sun*, 24 March 2003: 1; 'Our disgust will make us stronger', *Mail*, 24 March: 4). Despite publishing the same frame-grab images from Iraqi television, the broadsheets were more likely to balance their 'disgust' toward the Iraqi authorities with reporting that was problematic for the coalition, while the *Mirror* took an oppositional stance on the subject. Despite berating the Iraqis for displaying their captives, the *Mirror*'s front page juxtaposed a PoW image with a photograph of a badly burnt Iraqi child and defiantly asserted: 'Still anti-war? Yes, bloody right we are' (24 March). The following day, it compared the Iraqis' actions directly with the US administration's release of prisoner images from Guantanamo Bay: 'Sickening: But what the hell does America expect when it treats PoWs like this?' (25 March: 1).

Images relating to the subject of coalition military casualties featured regularly in the press (12.4% of stories). Although images of actual casualties aroused sensitivity (the US Government prevented their publication in America, for example), they rarely appeared in a straightforwardly oppositional context. In fact, most coalition casualty images were family snapshots, posed military photographs or flag-draped coffins arriving home with military honours. The effect was to humanise coalition victims – something never done for Iraqi military casualties and rarely for civilians – or to emphasise ceremonial pride, rather than the brutality of the battlefield. Where wounded soldiers appeared, they were generally shown being helped by fellow soldiers or treated in hospital. Coalition deaths were principally characterised as honourable and heroic sacrifices, with soldiers named and praised for their bravery (e.g. 'Homecoming fit for a British hero', *Daily Mail*, 30 March: 1), even when they resulted from military blunders. Images such as these were most common in the red- and black-top titles, in keeping with their human interest focus, and in the *Telegraph* (present in 12.2% of stories), with the highest proportion (19.7%) in the oppositional *Mirror*. The *Guardian* (4.4%) printed the fewest, perhaps suggesting an aversion towards what could be considered a hyper-patriotic theme.

Different titles adopted contrasting positions on the picturing of civilian casualties and the acceptability of graphic images of them. For the *Sun*, Tony Blair's promise, as the conflict began, that civilian casualties would be minimised led to it proclaiming 'The first "clean" war' (David Wooding and Charles Rae, 20 March 2003: 6). For readers of the *Sun* this was certainly the case, with civilian casualties rarely being pictured (only 0.8% of stories). Where it did show them, the *Sun* tended to frame civilian casualty photos supportively ('PM: I'll do very best I can for Ali', *Sun*, 15 April: 7). Challenging this line, the *Mirror* used an editorial to attack the *Sun* for avoiding civilian casualty coverage (the 'repulsive newspaper that didn't cover the market bomb that killed 55 Iraqi civilians because it wasn't interested' ('Lies will not disguise the ugly face of war', 8 April 2003: 6)). The *Mirror* not only showed many such images (8.0% of stories) but made a conscious effort to reveal more explicitly the 'reality of war' ('After the TV war . . . the reality of war', *Sunday Mirror*, 23 March: 12). As Tom Newton Dunn, then its defence correspondent, explained: 'the *Mirror* . . . did get very excited about civilian casualties because it helped their stance on the war and what the paper believed was its moral position'.[5]

In keeping with its anti-war stance, the *Mirror* was even prepared to show full-page photographs of dead children alongside damning commentaries ('Her name was Sarah . . . and whether she was killed by an American or Iraqi missile, this insane war is to blame', *Daily Mirror*, 31 March: 5). There was a similar use of visuals in the other anti-war newspapers: 'This is the reality of war. We bomb. They suffer', *Independent on Sunday*, 23 March: 1; 'Children killed in US assault', *Guardian*, 2 April: 1). Indeed, Ed Pilkington, the *Guardian*'s Foreign Editor at the time, noted his newspaper's emphasis on civilian casualties: 'We were in difficult places, we saw difficult things . . . [we] did a lot on civilian casualties, . . . portrayed that fulsomely in a way that other papers shrank from doing'.[6]

The limits to anti-war reporting

The stance taken by the anti-war papers served to generate coverage that departed from a supportive line towards the coalition, and this pattern was readily detectable in our story and editorial subject framing measures. At the same time, there were discernible limits to their ability to oppose the war once battle was underway. As shown in Chapter 5, for example, even the anti-war newspapers produced significant quantities of supportive battle coverage (the dominant news subject) as well as reinforcing the humanitarian justification for war. Of course, reporting through the prism of the national perspective, the anti-war press also had to explain the actions of British troops, the circumstances in which they found themselves and the dangers that they faced, and it is this perceived need to support British troops in action that best explains their impulse towards supportive coverage.

Understandably, there was a consensus that the responsibility for the invasion of Iraq lay with politicians and not with those carrying out military orders, who were portrayed as highly skilled, efficient and, at times, heroic. James Meek, who was a *Guardian* foreign correspondent, puts this succinctly:

> In this newspaper, which in its opinion pages and in its editorials and in many of the stories has put out a message that the war, that the invasion from the very beginning was a very bad idea . . . it's also been carrying these reports . . . that presented a picture of good, honest, heroic fighting men.[7]

The *Guardian*'s Ed Pilkington emphasised the importance of the 'national perspective' to his newspaper:

> We do quite a lot of reporting about how British troops were coping better in the South than the Americans were in the North . . . a tiny vein of 'our boys do better'. . . . We are not averse to praising British soldiers in a really difficult situation who seem to be doing a good job. . . . And we would do that more than Americans because they *are* British soldiers . . . We are a British newspaper.[8]

Of course, any other stance would have appeared deeply unpatriotic. But this created a difficult balancing act for the three newspapers that opposed the invasion: how to express opposition to the policy of war without appearing to undermine support for those charged with prosecuting it. This caused particular difficulties at the *Daily Mirror*, whose anti-war position directly affected its circulation. Faced with sales having 'fallen off a cliff', the *Mirror*'s editor, Piers Morgan, recalls his circulation manager telling him: 'Piers, I know you're anti this war. But we just can't go on attacking it while our boys are under fire' (Morgan, 2005: 391). The *Mirror*'s coverage contains repeated attempts to clarify this awkward position to its readers. Two days before the invasion, it carried adjacent pages on which a picture of Blair was set against one of a soldier, under the heading: 'HE's let us down. HE never will' (18 March 2003: 2–3).

When the invasion was launched, the same sentiment recurred even more plainly in a leader headed: 'Troops are heroes, the war's insane' (21 March 2003: 8). The loss of sales suggests that, for some red-top readers at least, this attempt to distinguish the responsibility of politicians from that of service personnel was too subtle to be effective. Ultimately, the *Mirror* was forced to respond to falling sales by toning down its anti-war coverage somewhat (Morgan, 2005: 391). But opposition to the war does not seem to have had such a clear-cut effect on sales of the anti-war broadsheets. The *Independent* lost 1.1 per cent, but the *Guardian*'s circulation grew by 3.9 per cent (Cozens, 2003b).

The effects of this balancing act on the anti-war press can be identified quite readily in our data. The *Times*, *Telegraph* and, most notably, the *Sun* offered relatively little oppositional coverage of the coalition. In the framing that they adopted towards story subjects, the ratio of supportive to oppositional reporting in these newspapers ranged between 2.3:1 (*The Times*) and 14.5:1 (*Sun*) (see Table 6.2). Indeed, in its orientation towards coalition actors, the *Sun* was 40 times more likely to offer reinforcing than deflating coverage (Goddard et al., 2008: 23)! In contrast, even the newspaper with the most oppositional subject framing, the *Independent*, had only 1.3 times more oppositional than supportive reporting, whereas the *Guardian* actually had fractionally more supportive than oppositional reporting (see Table 6.2). And unlike the *Sun*, its chief red-top rival, the *Mirror*, was only 2.7 times more likely to deflate than to reinforce coalition actors (Goddard et al., 2008: 23). So, while it is accurate to describe the anti-war titles as offering coverage that was negotiated and, at times, oppositional, they were not *as* critical as the pro-war titles were supportive. Moreover, since their opposition was to the policy of war and not to British forces themselves, their coverage also necessarily contained elements that could be classified as supportive. Of course, those titles that supported the war faced no such impulse to incorporate elements of oppositional coverage. The likely effect of patriotism, then, is to introduce a form of structural pressure towards supportive reporting.

Before and after the major invasion phase: variations in coverage across time and circumstance

We now turn to the final area in which we found significant evidence for variation and diversity of approach – that of time series data. Examining this data allowed us to observe coverage before and after the major combat phase of the invasion and to consider how levels of supportive, negotiated and oppositional coverage varied between these periods. Here, evidence of variation in the orientation of coverage gives greater insight into the extent of diversity and independence. One important question concerns whether wartime news coverage should be understood as constituting an exception to the normal expectations with regard to independent journalism. For example, in *The Press, Presidents and Crises* (1990), Brigitte Nacos argues that during crisis phases such as war, news media coverage is characterised by a temporary narrowing of the range of sources used by journalists and a tendency to become more supportive of political authority – a claim that we label below as the 'exceptionality' argument. Another important issue concerns the 'rally effect' (Mueller, 1973) and the associated pressure to support troops in action, which was noted in our discussion of patriotism in Chapter 3. According to John Mueller, the outbreak of war normally witnesses a patriotic surge whereby a nation, including journalists and the public, rallies behind its government as both patriotism and accelerated government media-management efforts gather strength. As a consequence, government influence over the news agenda increases, so the rally effect predicts a significant upsurge in supportive coverage between these two periods.

We found that the shift from pre-war debate to military action led to dramatic changes in the news agenda. Our data for story subjects showed a rapid decline in the number of stories dealing with the rationale for war (10% – 0% for television and 18% – 6% for press), with battle-related subjects growing to dominate coverage (80% for television and 60% for press). Of most interest, however, is the clear shift in the framing of television news and press stories as the war got underway. In the days immediately prior to the war, overall story

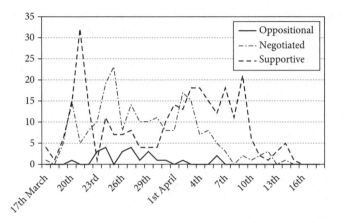

Figure 6.3 Quantity and framing of battle theme stories in television news as time series (17 March–18 April 2003)

framing was often negotiated. But as the invasion began on 21 March, supportive stories in television news dominated (70%) while oppositional stories in the press dropped significantly (from 24% on 18 March to under 10% on 22 March). The dramatic rise in supportive stories on television can be seen in Figure 6.3, which details the framing of battle stories (based on the thematic framing measure). This 'rally effect' (Mueller, 1973) mirrored the calls for national unity from politicians at the start of the invasion (see Chapter 4). There was also a patriotic rally in public backing for the war as polls showed a sizeable increase in support for it. Whereas a majority of the public had been opposed to the war, one poll on 21 March showed 54 per cent in favour and opposition as low as 30 per cent (see Travis, 2003).

Swiftly following the spike in supportive coverage, however, was a period of about six days during which battle coverage was largely negotiated. This period was the so-called 'week of wobble', when the coalition advance stalled in bad weather after an initial 'race to Baghdad' and early optimism about a quick victory, both among journalists and coalition officials, gave way to a realisation that there would be actual fighting and not just a chase across the desert. In particular, criticism was fuelled by public statements from US commanders such as Lt Gen. William S. Wallace who told journalists that: 'the enemy we're fighting is different from the one we'd war-gamed against' (quoted in Ricks, 2006: 124). In addition, embedded journalists began to report stories of actual conflict, the first coalition prisoners of war were shown on Iraqi TV and strategic doubts began to emerge, especially over the number and preparedness of troops. Optimism about the conflict soon returned, however, and supportive coverage increased again; by 4 April, negotiated and oppositional coverage had reverted to a low level and remained there.

By 9 April, the central military task of invading Iraq and removing Saddam Hussein's regime was nearly complete. For many, the now famous toppling of Saddam's statute in Firdos Square represented a symbolic endpoint to the coalition's invasion and Saddam's regime. Although this event was enthusiastically reported by some Western journalists at the time, inviting comparisons with the popular uprisings associated with the collapse of Communist regimes in Eastern Europe, it was also the subject of controversy. Some commentators pointed out that the statue was pulled down with practical help from US soldiers and, apart from those working with the US marines to pull it down, the Square was sparsely populated with Iraqi civilians who remained passive when the statue fell. Accordingly, the idea that the event was staged, a pseudo-event, has been widely discussed, as has been the accuracy of news media reporting that day (see Aday, Cluverius and Livingston, 2005; Fahmy, 2007; Major and Perlmutter, 2005).

Our data for story subjects showed a clear shift in the news media agenda during this period, with battle stories peaking on 9 April (60% for television and 45% for press), when the statue falls, and then rapidly being overtaken by law-and-order stories by 10 April (60% for television and 30% for press). As the statue fell, there was a clear spike in supportive coverage on 9/10 April (75% of television stories and 55% of press stories). This reflected a further manifestation of the rally effect (Mueller, 1973), occurring here when victory was perceived to have been achieved. However, the rise of post-war law- and-order problems represented the beginning of a rather problematic period for the coalition. Between the fall of the statue and 15 April, supportively-framed stories declined to around 30 per cent of television coverage and a low of 35 per cent for press; there was some increase in oppositional stories, although these remained below 20 per cent of all television stories and never higher than 24 per cent of press stories. So, with the rapid disappearance of supportively-framed battle stories, law-and-order stories overtook the news agenda. Most of these were negotiated or oppositional in orientation, with hardly any supportive of the coalition. However, the ambiguous and often negative coverage that emerged during this period did not have a measurable impact on journalists' assessment of the humanitarian case for war, which remained supportive even during this period.

Overall, analysis of pre and post-invasion phase coverage highlights the variability of news media performance, with supportive coverage replacing negotiated coverage as war started, as predicted by the rally effect (Mueller, 1973) and the exceptionality thesis (Nacos, 1990), but a brief period during the war when coverage became more problematic for the coalition (the 'week of wobble'). Interestingly, reporting of the 'week of wobble' corresponds closely to Entman's (2003) suggestion that journalists may have become more independent and questioning towards authority in reporting recent wars:

'even during popular and seemingly successful wars', he notes, 'the media now pounce upon any signs of failure or "quagmire" and . . . apply their own evaluative criteria' (Entman, 2003: 423). But our analysis also shows the return to a more independent and critical news media during the aftermath of the invasion (Nacos, 1990). The theoretical implications of these findings are discussed further in the concluding chapter.

Explaining patterns of negotiated and oppositional coverage

As outlined in Chapter 3, two explanations are frequently put forward to account for the negotiated coverage associated with the independent model and the oppositional coverage associated with the oppositional model. Emerging in part from strands of new institutionalist thinking, the professional autonomy thesis (e.g. Benson, 2004, 2006; Hallin, 1994; Hallin and Mancini, 2004) argues that journalists can and do think independently of elite power and are able to scrutinise and criticise government actions by virtue of their professional commitment to journalistic norms of independence. Field theory and new institutionalism also point toward distinctive features of different media systems ('system characteristics'), which also affect their levels of autonomy and patterns of news media performance. The event-driven news thesis argues that unexpected, dramatic and disturbing events that occur beyond the control of authorities can 'provide legitimizing pegs to support relatively independent and critical news narratives' (Bennett et al., 2006: 468; and see Lawrence, 2000; Wolfsfeld, 1997: 25). To what extent do our findings concerning the occurrence of negotiated and oppositional coverage connect with these explanations?

Event-driven news

Some of the findings in this chapter provide considerable support for the event-driven news thesis. It is significant, for example, that evidence for negotiated and oppositional coverage emerged much more strongly in relation to particular subject areas. Civilian and military casualties, humanitarian operations and law and order (particularly following the fall of Baghdad) all attracted such coverage, whereas battle coverage was relatively supportive of the coalition. In fact, in contexts where the coalition possessed considerable control and influence, such as the course of the military campaign, it was much more likely to command positive coverage. In most cases, the strategy of embedding journalists with coalition forces seems to have reinforced this effect still further. But difficulties in the shape of the accidental killing of civilians, the loss of its own troops and the humanitarian situation faced by local people are, by definition, beyond the immediate control of the coalition. When they occurred and journalists were able to report on them, coverage became far more critical of the coalition, as predicted by the event-driven news thesis.

Significantly, our findings also show that the impact of these uncontrolled events in generating coverage deemed problematic for the coalition was apparent for each of the news outlets examined, irrespective of their orientation in relation to the war. So these types of events had a consistent and pervasive effect in facilitating reporting that was largely negotiated or oppositional even at outlets that were otherwise strongly supportive. Comparing across news outlets, we found that where coverage was generally supportive, it tended to be pulled largely into the negotiated category by these events; where coverage was more often independent or oppositional, it was pulled even more strongly towards the oppositional category (see Table 6.1, and Tables 5.7, 5.8, 5.9). As such, our data provides strong support for the event-driven news thesis in indicating that such 'bad news' events create a uniform and pervasive effect upon the tone and slant of coverage across all news media.

In addition, as we showed in our analysis of news coverage of events following the fall of Baghdad, reporting of the ensuing law-and-order problems became distinctly critical of the coalition. Here, of course, the uncontrolled nature of the looting and chaos in Baghdad and elsewhere clearly fits the description of the event-driven news thesis. But additional dynamics came in to play at this stage in the conflict which were also consistent with it. Once major combat operations started to subside and troops were no longer exposed to the same degree of danger and threat, the wartime constraint of patriotism would have weakened. Similarly, the reliance on official sources and the effect of embedded journalism became less significant factors at this point in the conflict. Embedded journalists, whose main focus had been the progress of their accompanying troops during the major combat phase, suddenly found themselves freer to report on the unfolding events as the post-war looting and civil unrest took hold.

For those who advocate the effect of technological developments in increasing the occurrence of event-driven news (see Chapters 2 and 3), the findings here offer qualified support for this thesis. On the one hand, we found little evidence that the deployment of new technology (such as satellite phones, real-time reporting, and so on) was a major driver for these negotiated and oppositional reports. Information, particularly on coalition casualties, tended to come from coalition sources, while other stories were the result of journalists being in the right spot at the right time.[9] As in previous wars, information did filter back when 'bad' events occurred. On the other hand, the findings here offer evidence for the idea that official control over the information environment is far from total, even in conditions of war. The question of whether this lack of control has actually increased in recent years is considered in the concluding chapter.

Professional autonomy

The influence of professional autonomy on reporting is clearly indicated in the coverage provided by Channel 4 News. As shown, much of Channel 4 News coverage conformed to the independent model and its journalists were notable for the way in which they strove to distance themselves from their sources. Three factors combined to strengthen the professional autonomy of this news outlet: the regulatory context and Channel 4's 'alternative' remit, a culture of independent thinking among journalists attached to the programme, and particular editorial decisions made during the war. As documented in Chapter 4, in addition to the obligations of 'due impartiality' that are universal in British television, Channel 4 is required by statute to offer distinctiveness, innovation and diversity when compared to other channels. Accordingly, the self-declared aim of its flagship news programme is to 'provide a broadsheet news service which reflects Channel 4's own spirit of innovation and scepticism', with a commitment to 'set our own agenda', 'come up with a distinctive take on events' and 'challenge existing assumptions'.[10] To a considerable extent, our findings seem to show the effects of this pursuit of distinctiveness and independence. Jon Snow, the programme's anchor, confirmed that the programme was prepared to 'challenge existing assumptions': 'Obviously our job is to report facts, but I think that we certainly very strongly entertained the idea that [the invasion] was an illegal act and that it was wrong.'[11]

As well as the programme's remit, this attitude also reflects the culture of independent thinking among Channel 4 News journalists, which was evident in their unwillingness to accept official claims at face value. Alex Thomson suggested to us that there is a need for journalists to recognise that: 'officialdom lies, and they never tell bigger and more blatant, more obvious lies than during a time of war'. His rule of thumb was that journalists needed to 'assume everyone is lying to you'.[12] Snow explained his approach in similar terms: 'I think your job as a reporter is to use the residual knowledge you have, set it against what is happening, set it against what people are telling you, and come to some sort of conclusion.'[13] Speaking of the editorial process, he described the commitment of Channel 4 News to journalistic independence in the following terms:

> There are news organisations in which editors direct the way they want coverage done. That's not the way it's done here. Here it is a much more organic process: You put somebody in the field to find out what the hell is going on. You don't tell them what is going on and tell them to report that . . . That's a lot of what happens in other news organisations.[14]

Allied to this approach was the recognition of the value in ensuring that a broad range of sources and viewpoints were represented, including those of Iraqis themselves during the invasion phase, and this contributed to the extent of negotiated coverage that the programme was able to provide. Noting the limits of embedded journalism, Jon Snow explained: 'We had . . . small units of Iraqis who were dashing about the country filming; we'd set up with a private company called "Out There News" to ensure that we did have indigenous Iraqi material . . . We had about 30 people loosely associated [with us] . . .'.[15] When this decision is considered alongside the sceptical attitude of its reporters and the trust that editors were prepared to place in them, it does appear that the editorial process at Channel 4 News was an important factor in the form that its coverage took.

What is so significant about the case of Channel 4 News is that it demonstrates the potential of journalists to overcome the constraints that are predicted to limit news media autonomy in wartime, notably sources, patriotism and ideology. In our interview with him, Jon Snow emphasised this potential: 'There is so much material available on so many platforms from the Internet [and so on], I don't think it is possible to prevent people from doing a decent job.' What is ultimately required, according to Snow, is simply the 'will' to challenge authority in wartime, as opposed to merely 'going with the flow'.[16] However, journalistic 'will' is not enough on its own and it requires an enabling environment. Here, it is worth noting that Channel 4 News is produced by Independent Television News (ITN), the same organisation responsible for ITV News. The coverage of the war provided by ITV News was quite different – nearly as supportive in orientation as that of Sky News and conforming closely to the elite-driven model. What distinguishes these two news programmes is Channel 4's regulatory obligation to be 'alternative' and 'innovative', and the newsroom culture that the channel's remit appears to have created.

Considered more widely, our findings in the case of Channel 4 News indicate that norms of 'professional commitment to accuracy [and] balance' (Hallin, 1994: 5–6) can indeed create pockets of resistance to the kinds of pressures theorised by the elite-driven model. So factors such as patriotism, reliance on official sources and ideology do not inevitably structure and determine how journalists report war; as predicted by some strands of new institutionalism and field theory (in particular, Benson, 2004, 2006; Hallin, 1994; Hallin and Mancini, 2004: 33–41), under the right conditions, journalists can be enabled to overcome these pressures.

'System characteristics' of the British press

Drawing on a strong culture of critical and independent-minded journalism, Channel 4 News stood out from its competitors in television news in providing a large quantity of negotiated coverage. Our analysis of the British press has revealed, however, a more diverse picture marked most notably by the combination of negotiated and oppositional coverage found in the anti-war press – the *Mirror, Independent* and *Guardian* newspapers. Indeed, at an editorial level, these three newspapers chose to oppose the war. If journalistic 'fields' or 'institutions' possess particular 'system characteristics' (Benson, 2004: 284, Hallin and Mancini, 2004: 21–45) which, in turn, shape the behaviour and output of news media, are there characteristics particular to the British press which enabled such a degree of negotiated and oppositional reporting? Here, its nationally-based and highly competitive structure, commercial calculations and its historically partisan and opinionated nature (see Chapter 4) are relevant to understanding our findings.

First, as a nationally-based press drawing readers from across the social spectrum, the British press is highly competitive in economic terms. This creates economic pressures for titles to differentiate themselves from one another. As we have seen, rival newspapers operating in the same segment of the market approached the war very differently (the *Sun* and the *Mirror* in the red-top market; *The Times* and *Telegraph* as against the *Guardian* and *Independent* in the broadsheet market). In markets elsewhere in the world that contain little direct competition, there is much less rivalry between newspapers and, consequently, much less pressure for them to differentiate themselves from one another. Following on from this structural feature are commercial calculations: the extent of opposition to the policy of war among the newspaper-buying public and, indeed, among opinion formers such as politicians (but not, notably, the two main parties' front benches) created a market opportunity for a negotiated and oppositional stance. The three anti-war titles have reputations as the most left-of-centre and liberal-minded national newspapers, and it was clearly felt that an anti-war stance was commercially viable – representing a position that would not alienate a significant number of readers and would indeed find favour among many. As it turns out, and as already discussed, the difficulty of opposing the policy of war but giving support to British troops does seem to have affected sales of the *Mirror*, some of whose readers may have interpreted its stance as unpatriotic. But the *Guardian* and *Independent* seemed to suffer no undue commercial consequences.

Finally, the nature of the British press as both partisan and opinionated, facilitated by the absence of regulatory requirements for impartiality (as discussed in Chapter 4), is important. Although the party-political orientation of the British press is less significant (both main parties supported the war while some of the press opposed it), this feature did appear to affect the behaviour of the *Mail* as it became caught between its pro-war stance and an instinctive hostility towards the Labour government. But the opinionated culture clearly enabled newspapers to adopt distinctive and vocal positions on the war, as seen in our analysis of editorials. Here the pro- and anti-war positions, seen most clearly in the vocal and passionate stances of the two major red-tops, the *Sun* and the *Mirror*, are a manifestation of this feature of the British press.

Linking this back to the professional autonomy of journalists, the conditions of partiality enabled anti-war journalists and editorial staff on the anti-war newspapers to follow their consciences and professional training in maintaining a sceptical stance, seeking perspectives beyond those of the coalition and attempting to scrutinise the actions and explanations of those in authority. Of course, by the same token, it also enabled pro-war newspaper editors and journalists openly to support the war.

Overall, as much as new technology and uncontrolled events might have enabled greater levels of independence and autonomy (an issue that we return to in Chapter 8), the combination of professional autonomy and the distinctive features of the British press was also important in terms of shaping an impressively diverse pattern of wartime news media performance.

Concluding comments

We have found that British news media representation of the 2003 invasion of Iraq was not uniformly consistent with the elite-driven model. Rather, in specific subject areas where the coalition had little control over events – notably civilian and military casualties and humanitarian operations – coverage became more negotiated and oppositional as predicted by the event-driven news thesis. More importantly, several news media outlets succeeded in generating coverage more generally that deviated significantly from the predictions of the elite-driven model. Channel 4 News was able to produce coverage of the war that was largely negotiated, in part, through a strong culture that emphasised commitment to professional autonomy. At the same time, coverage in the British press displayed a wide range that included a strongly anti-war element. Of itself, this diversity of coverage is a significant indicator of specific system characteristics which enabled relatively high levels of pluralism and independence across the UK press, even in wartime. Indeed, to a significant extent, the British press lived up to its reputation for being 'opinionated, partial and imbalanced' (Gavin, 2007: 13) and 'a useful troublemaker'.[17] Finally, time series data provides further evidence of the variability of news media performance, with higher levels of negotiated and oppositional coverage occurring before and after the main combat phase.

Before consolidating our findings from this chapter and the preceding one, we turn to a detailed examination of three case studies from the war: the case of Jessica Lynch and the news media circus surrounding her rescue, the case of Ali Abbas who became a *cause célèbre* after being seriously maimed in a coalition airstrike, and the case of British news media representation of the anti-war movement. Each of these case studies provides a more in-depth analysis of particular events that formed part of the broader patterns of supportive, negotiated and oppositional coverage documented so far.

Notes

1 Telephone interview with Jon Snow, 19 December 2008.

2 Telephone interview with Alex Thomson, 10 December 2008.

3 Further evidence for newspaper diversity, based on our main thematic framing measures, can be readily seen in Tables 6.1, 5.8 and 5.9.

4 In Figure 6.2, these are coded as 'other'.

5 Telephone interview with Tom Newton Dunn, 19 December 2008.

6 Telephone interview with Ed Pilkington, 10 December 2008.

7 Telephone interview with James Meek, 19 December 2008.

8 Telephone interview with Ed Pilkington, 10 December 2008.

9 For British viewers, one of the most notorious of such cases during the Iraq invasion concerned John Simpson, the BBC's World Affairs Editor, on 6 April 2003. Simpson was part of a group of US and Kurdish forces in Northern Iraq who were mistakenly attacked by an American fighter plane. The attack, killing Simpson's Kurdish translator and several others, and leaving Simpson deaf in one ear, was captured on video. With blood still on the camera lens, Simpson broadcast the story moments later on the BBC's 24-hour news service. See BBC News, 'This is just a scene from hell', 6 April 2003: http://news.bbc.co.uk/1/hi/world/middle_east/2921807.stm (accessed 14 September 2009).

10 Taken from the Channel 4 News website: www.channel4.com/news/about/programmes/c4news.html (accessed 21 September 2007).

11 Telephone interview with Jon Snow, 19 December 2008.

12 Telephone interview with Alex Thomson, 10 December 2008.

13 Telephone interview with Jon Snow, 19 December 2008.

14 Telephone interview with Jon Snow, 19 December 2008.

15 Telephone interview with Jon Snow, 19 December 2008.

16 Telephone interview with Jon Snow, 19 December 2008.

17 Lionel Barber, editor, *Financial Times*, and former managing editor of its US edition, speaking on *The Media Show*, BBC Radio 4, 12 November 2008.

7

Case studies from the invasion of Iraq: Jessica Lynch, Ali Abbas and the anti-war movement

Introduction

Here we provide a focused analysis of three case studies, which serve to represent the three differing modes of news media performance in wartime, as well as shedding more light on the news-making process. The Jessica Lynch case study, involving the 'dramatic' rescue of a US 'prisoner of war', highlights just how compliant and deferential news media can be in wartime and can be viewed as an 'ideal type' example of supportive coverage. The case of Ali Abbas, an Iraqi child maimed in a coalition strike, provides a poignant illustration of the opportunities for more negotiated and oppositional reporting in wartime. Finally, an analysis of how effectively the anti-war movement maintained positive news media representation during the invasion helps to delineate the 'outer limits' of political dissent when British troops are in action. For each case study, we offer an account of the background to the relevant events, provide a detailed review of British news media coverage and, finally, assess its implications for our understanding of news media performance during war.

Case study 1: 'Saving Private Lynch'

Overview

The case of Jessica Lynch has, over time, become one of the seminal news media events of the 2003 invasion of Iraq. Although her detention by Iraqi soldiers and subsequent retrieval by coalition forces generated a powerful 'good news' story for the coalition, controversy subsequently developed over the extent to which aspects of the story were exaggerated or falsified. For those most critical of the coalition's handling of these events, the Lynch story was seen almost as a pseudo-event (Boorstin, 1962), with the details of her capture being deliberately exaggerated and her retrieval by coalition forces being, in effect, a stage-managed affair designed to achieve maximum publicity. For example, in an article published in the *Guardian* on 15 May 2003,

John Kampfner described the rescue as 'one of the most stunning pieces of news management yet conceived', quoting an Iraqi doctor who said: 'It was like a Hollywood film. They cried "Go, go, go", with guns and blanks and the sound of explosions. They made a show – an action movie like Sylvester Stallone or Jackie Chan – with jumping and shouting, breaking down doors.'[1] For many commentators, the story of her capture and rescue was understood as important for its broader political importance and meaning. For example, Pin-Fat and Stern (2005) use the Jessica Lynch story to explore the relationship between gender, war and military sacrifice, while Kumar (2004) analyses how the gendered representation of Lynch as a female in distress functioned to aid US war propaganda. Kumar writes that:

> this is not a step forward for women. Instead, the Lynch rescue narrative, I argue, served to forward the aims of war propaganda. The story of the 'dramatic' rescue of a young, vulnerable woman, at a time when the war was not going well for the US, acted as the means by which a controversial war could be talked about in emotional rather than rational terms. Furthermore, constructed as hero, Lynch became a symbol of the West's 'enlightened' attitude towards women, justifying the argument that the US was 'liberating' the people of Iraq. In short, the Lynch story, far from putting forward an image of women's strength and autonomy, reveals yet another mechanism by which they are strategically used to win support for war. (Kumar, 2004: 297)

From the perspective of our research focus on news media autonomy in wartime, the case is worthy of close attention because it is a paradigmatic example of a 'good news' story, promoted by both news media and the coalition, which shows authorities at their most manipulative (or exploitative) and news media at their least independent and critical. The case was the subject of congressional hearings in April 2007, and the evidence generated there helps us to distil fact from fiction in the events as reported. As we ultimately show, this case is instructive for the insights that it offers into the relationship between the coalition's news-management strategy and the assumptions by which journalists select and edit 'the news'.

Events and controversies: was Lynch 'fighting to the last bullet'?

On 23 March 2003, Private Jessica Lynch, serving with the 507th Maintenance Company, was 'last in a march column of 600 vehicles' when, owing to 'the combined effects of the operational pace, acute fatigue, isolation and the harsh environmental conditions' (US Army, 2003), her company took a wrong turn and drove into Nasiriyah (Ricks, 2004: 119). At this point they were ambushed by Iraqi forces and 11 of the 33 US soldiers in the convoy were killed, while 7, including Lynch, were captured by Iraqi forces (US Army, 2003). Having received serious injuries when her Humvee vehicle crashed, Lynch was transported first to a military hospital and then to the Saddam Hussein General

Hospital in Nasiriyah (US House of Representatives, 2008: 41–2). Following the capture and interrogation of four Iraqi intelligence officers on 26 March 2003, it was established that an American from the 507th Maintenance Company was at the Saddam Hospital (Gordon and Trainor, 2007: 345) and, on the night of 1 April, a Special Forces operation was conducted which successfully retrieved Lynch and the bodies of nine US soldiers from the hospital (US House of Representatives, 2008: 41–2).

From this point onward, the reporting and representation of Jessica Lynch's capture and rescue began to diverge from these established facts and the 'story' became embellished in two key ways.[2] First, the false claim emerged that she had initially resisted capture when ambushed on 23 March and had received bullet wounds in doing so. The Congressional Oversight Committee investigating this event identifies a *Washington Post* article published on 3 April as the starting point for this claim,[3] which it sourced to US officials (US House of Representatives, 2008: 43). From that point on, the idea of Jessica Lynch as bravely resisting, and being shot in the process, was widely adopted in the US news media.[4] Lynch's testimony to the Congressional Oversight Committee made clear that this was false:

> Tales of great heroism were being told. My parents' home in Wirt County was under siege of the media all repeating the story of the little girl Rambo from the hills who went down fighting. It was not true. (Lynch, 2007)

Second, the story of the Special Forces operation gave the impression of a daring and dangerous night-time rescue in which Lynch was snatched back from the Iraqi regime. Informing journalists about the rescue, General Vincent Brooks said:

> Some brave souls put their lives on the line to make this happen. Loyal to a creed that they know; that they'll never leave a fallen comrade . . . At this point she is safe. She's been retrieved. I asked her who was holding her – the regime was holding her.[5]

The impression of a daring rescue was further reinforced by the release of film of the operation, captured by green-tinted night-vision cameras, showing US forces arriving by helicopter and ground vehicle, securing the hospital grounds and then carrying Lynch out by stretcher. The reality was somewhat different. Iraqi forces had already left the hospital and Lynch was actually being looked after by Iraqi medical staff who had already attempted to return her to US forces. Interviewed by the *Toronto Star*, Dr Harith Houssona explained:

> The most important thing to know is that the Iraqi soldiers and commanders had left the hospital almost two days earlier . . . The night they left, a few of the senior medical staff tried to give Jessica back. We carefully moved her out of intensive care and into an ambulance and began to drive to the Americans, who

were just one kilometre away. But when the ambulance got within 300 metres, they began to shoot (quoted in Potter, 2003).[6]

There was little evidence of any serious resistance to US Special Forces despite General Brooks's statement that there had been 'fire fights outside of the building, getting in and getting out'.[7] An Iraqi waiter, Hassam Mamoud (quoted in Potter, 2003), claims to have told US Special Forces prior to the raid that Iraqi soldiers had left the hospital, while a *Washington Post* article published two months later also confirmed that Lynch had been rescued without significant opposition (Priest et al., 2003). But in the short term, the impression of a daring and dramatic rescue came to dominate US perceptions of the rescue as well as those in Britain, as we shall see.

The impact on UK news media reporting: reproducing a fictional account of the rescue

The Jessica Lynch story broke at the end of what had been a difficult week for the coalition. During the so-called 'week of wobble' between 24 March and early April (see Chapter 6), coverage of the war had become largely negotiated as the coalition encountered higher levels of resistance than expected and journalists adopted a more questioning line towards the progress of the war. Although not oppositional, this was not the kind of supportive and upbeat reporting that the coalition would have wanted so early on in the invasion. But the Lynch story contributed to a turnaround in early April when supportive coverage returned to dominate media representation of the war. We look first at television news coverage of the Lynch story, before turning to its coverage in the press.

In television, twelve news stories, involving all four of the news programmes surveyed, featured Jessica Lynch as either a main or subsidiary subject, with the majority of these reports airing on 2 April 2003. The great majority of coverage (85%) adhered to norms of straight reporting with journalists avoiding the use of explicitly reinforcing or deflating language. However, the discussion of Lynch and US prisoners of war was always supportive of the coalition and these news stories were largely supportive overall except at Channel 4 News, where two of its three stories were negotiated. Within these news reports, family sources were prevalent, with over 60 per cent of BBC, ITV and Sky News quotes attributable to them, although, again, Channel 4 News departed from this tendency to offer a much wider selection of sources. As such, the news story was largely constructed around the relief and joy of Lynch's family. Initial coverage also reflected what we now know to be the fictional narrative of events. For example, BBC News correspondent Matt Frei, cautiously introducing his report as 'finally some news that everyone could agree was good', still relayed the idea of a daring rescue:

And this was her dramatic rescue filmed by the Special Forces. It's shortly after midnight at a hospital compound in Nasiriyah. The place is still held by Iraqi troops but they've been distracted by battles on the front . . . She has two bullet wounds. (BBC News, 2 April 2003)

Although the story of Lynch's rescue appeared in newspapers on 3 April, several titles had already run articles offering a human interest angle and reporting the fears of her family and others regarding her safety.[8] To some degree, therefore, the British public were primed for Lynch's 'dramatic' rescue. Between 3 and 16 April, the story became major news, with 38 articles involving Lynch either as a main or subsidiary subject. Thirty of these were coded as supportive of the coalition while seven were negotiated.[9] Only one report, published in *The Times* on 16 April (13 days after her rescue), was oppositional in nature. This article, headlined 'The real story of saving Private Lynch', reported that US soldiers terrified doctors and patients as they rampaged through the wards, looking for Iraqi soldiers who had left a day earlier. Dr Harith Houssona related how he tried to return Lynch to the US soldiers only to be fired upon. Besides this article, however, the bulk of reporting was extremely positive for the coalition. As with television coverage, the normal pattern of coalition domination of sources was displaced in these reports by the friends and family of Lynch describing their relief and joy. And, similarly, reporting was overwhelmingly straight (91%), with only the *Sun* departing from this in giving reinforcing treatment to the coalition and deflating the Iraqi regime. Table 7.1 lists the stories from the first three days, together with their headlines: Both the pro-war *Sun* and the anti-war *Mirror* invoked the image of Spielberg's film *Saving Private Ryan* in their headlines – 'Saving Private Lynch' and 'Saving Private Jessica' respectively – while the *Mail* referred to 'America's Joy for Jessica'.

As with television coverage, the articles relayed the fictional narrative regarding Lynch's 'rescue'. For example, *The Times* referred to her retrieval as 'daring', describing her as suffering from 'gunshot wounds' (A. Hamilton and D. Charter, 'Saving Private Jessica', 3 April 2003: 3). Moreover, even the 'quality' broadsheet papers provided dramatic and colourful details of the rescue, supplemented with a British angle on events in the role of Royal Marine Commando Major Mike Tanner who 'arranged a decoy assault in Nasiriyah to aid the rescue' (P. Smucker, 'Decoy raid opened way for rescuers', *Daily Telegraph*, 3 April 2003: 3). For example, in the *Guardian*, Rory McCarthy wrote:

Minutes before the operation began, heavily armoured troops led by a British officer launched a decoy attack near a bridge over the river Euphrates in Nassiriya. British Royal Marine Major Mike Tanner, who was on attachment with the US forces, led the decoy force, while on the other side of the town,

Table 7.1 Headlines linked to 'Jessica Lynch' stories (3–5 April 2003)

Date	Newspaper	Headline
3 April	*Sun*	Saving Private Lynch
3 April	*Sun*	Teamwork
3 April	*Daily Mirror*	Saving Private Jessica
3 April	*Daily Mail*	America's joy for Jessica
3 April	*Independent*	Allies: Dagger is pointed at heart of Baghdad regime
3 April	*Independent*	Words that Palestine, West Virginia, dared not hope for: Your Private Jessica is safe
3 April	*Guardian*	Saving Private Lynch: how special forces rescued captured colleague
3 April	*Times*	Saving Private Jessica
3 April	*Daily Telegraph*	'Prayer and our boys brought Jessica to safety'
3 April	*Daily Telegraph*	Decoy raid opened way for rescuers
4 April	*Sun*	Jess 'fighting to death'
4 April	*Daily Mirror*	Jessica battled like a lion
5 April	*Sun*	Local hero
5 April	*Sun*	Iraqi who risked all for Jessica
5 April	*Daily Mirror*	Hero risked life for Jessica
5 April	*Independent*	Iraqi lawyer turns out to be Jessica's saviour
5 April	*Independent*	Camp reveals dark secrets of Saddam's notorious Fedayeen
5 April	*Guardian*	Iraqi lawyer risked life to help rescue of PoW Jessica Lynch
5 April	*Times*	Iraqi risks all to save life of US captive

operating in total darkness, a Black Hawk helicopter loaded with special forces commandos flew in and landed next to the Saddam hospital. They came under fire from Iraqi soldiers but fought their way into the hospital unhurt. ('Saving Private Lynch: how special forces rescued captured colleague', 3 April 2003: 5)

So, in both television and press, UK coverage of the Lynch 'rescue' was initially overwhelmingly positive for the coalition, relaying, without exception, a fictional tale about the daring midnight rescue of a young female soldier who had fought heroically before being captured.

Analysing the case: coalition 'spin' vs. media news values
What does the Jessica Lynch affair tell us about news media and war? For one thing, the case points towards the significant ability of the coalition to engender positive news media coverage, even at a difficult time in its military campaign. This, of course, raises the question of the extent to which the story was stage managed or deliberately exaggerated; was the entire event, as John Kampfner described, 'one of the most stunning pieces of news management

yet conceived'?[10] On the matter of intentionality, the Congressional Oversight Committee, while confirming that official sources were the source for the false claims that (a) Lynch had received gun shot wounds, and (b) she had been captured fighting, was unable to establish who was responsible for the false information or the degree to which events were part of a deliberate attempt to mislead. Henry A. Waxman, who chaired the enquiry, explained:

> As the Committee investigated the Tillman and Lynch cases, it encountered a striking lack of recollection. In Private Lynch's case, Jim Wilkinson, who was the Director for Strategic Communications for the CENTCOM Commander and attended CENTCOM operational briefings, told the Committee he did not know where the false information originated or who disseminated it . . . The pervasive lack of recollection and absence of specific information makes it impossible for the Committee to assign responsibility for the misinformation in Corporal Tillman's and Private Lynch's cases. (US House of Representatives, 2008: 49)

Despite its failure to establish the truth behind the circulation of false information, in concluding its report, the Congressional Oversight Committee was highly critical of the US military:

> Our nation also has an inviolate obligation to share truthful information with a soldier's family and the American people should injury or death occur . . . That standard was not met in either Corporal Tillman's or Private Lynch's cases . . . [T]he Defense Department did not meet its most basic obligations in sharing accurate information with the families and with the American public. (US House of Representatives, 2008: 49)

At the same time, there are plenty of indications that this was a story that the coalition actively sought to promote to the news media, and little effort was made to correct the emerging media interpretation in which the details of her capture and her rescue were exaggerated. For example, Jim Wilkinson, Director of Strategic Communications at CENTCOM, confirmed that he had been alerted to the incoming story prior to the rescue: 'I stayed up all night. I got a call that this was happening, I knew it was going to happen in advance and we had a situation where there was a lot of hot news.'[11] A CENTCOM spokesperson, Lt Colonel Robinson, confirmed at the congressional hearings that media operations had requested the dramatic filming of the rescue:

> The visuals would have come from an officer who was assigned to the SOF unit who had an additional duty of providing visuals back to the press center . . . And so, these visuals that we received would have been visuals that we would have requested as soon as we found out there was a potential rescue. (Robinson, 2007)

The rescue itself was then presented to journalists at a CENTCOM briefing, complete with the dramatic visuals and proud, patriotic language which, as described earlier, gave the impression of a much riskier operation than had actually taken place. At the briefing, Jim Wilkinson asserted that: 'America doesn't leave its heroes behind . . . Never has. Never Will' (quoted in US House of Representatives, 2008: 42), while General Brooks stated: 'It was a classical joint operation done by some of our nation's finest warriors, who are dedicated to never leaving a comrade behind' (quoted in US House of Representatives, 2008: 42).

In the Congressional Oversight Committee report, Waxman makes clear that while initial reports of Lynch's rescue were accurate, later stories 'invented new facts' (US House of Representatives, 2008: 44) and raised serious questions about the behaviour of the coalition. The reluctance of the coalition even to explain that the initial news media reporting and narrative surrounding the Lynch story was at odds with reality is shown by the response of Bryan Whitman (US Deputy Assistant Secretary of Defence) to John Kampfner's questions: Asked if there was any Iraqi resistance to the rescue, he replies: 'I think that I will leave that story to be told in great detail when the time is right.' Later, when Kampfner asks about the actual injuries sustained by Lynch, Whitman states: 'Well I'm not going to get into the specific injuries that she received. That's up to her doctor to discuss at the appropriate time.'[12]

In sum, the balance of evidence would suggest, at the very least, that the coalition were actively promoting the Jessica Lynch story as a piece of good news, as well as bearing partial responsibility for creating and sustaining an exaggerated and false impression of the events in question. As the Congressional Oversight Committee report states:

> The misinformation was not caused by overlooking or misunderstanding relevant facts. Instead . . . affirmative acts created new facts that were significantly different than what the soldiers in the field knew to be true. And . . . the fictional accounts proved to be compelling public narratives at difficult times in the war. (US House of Representatives, 2008: 48)

Meanwhile, our analysis of British coverage highlights the extent to which the UK news media *wanted* the Jessica Lynch story, especially in its more colourful form. It seems that the tale of an exciting night-time rescue of a young woman from a brutal enemy, complete with helicopters, gunfire and the involvement of a British Marine, was too good a story to question. The extensive, prolonged positive news media attention, involving dramatic headlines, detailed accounts of the rescue and repeated reference to British involvement, indicates that this was perceived as such a 'good news' story that few UK news outlets thought it appropriate to adopt a more sceptical, negotiated stance. As much as the coalition may have sought to promote and exaggerate the Jessica Lynch story, news media – even in the UK – were also implicated in its spread.

Its drama, human interest and patriotic inflection had such news appeal that, in effect, the coalition was pushing at an open door.

A final, broader point emerges from this case study concerning the way wartime media management works in practice. To understand coalition media-management operations as activities that function primarily through deception or lying to journalists and the public[13] is to misunderstand a more subtle process that is at work. John Kampfner paints the Lynch rescue as a fabrication,[14] an attempt by the coalition to lie. Calculated misinformation or exaggeration may well have occurred in the case of Jessica Lynch, but what made it so successful was the conjunction of coalition aims to promote a good news story and news media imperatives for an exciting story that would appeal to readers and viewers. In this sense, media management involved channelling the 'right' kind of information – not only good news for the coalition, but also good copy for journalists – towards an attentive and 'hungry' media. In practice, coalition briefers had only to suggest the possibility of a dramatic and daring rescue, while off-the-record conversations indicated (although never confirmed beyond doubt) that Lynch had been shot while resisting capture. Directed in this way, journalists could then be relied upon to fill in the gaps and present, ultimately, a dramatically distorted account to the public which, in turn, benefited the coalition.

As such, the case of 'saving Private Lynch' represents an 'ideal type' example of media management. By carefully directing a flow of news information (with some level of embellishment along the way) that could dovetail with journalistic values of drama, human interest and patriotism, media briefers and news organisations, between them, created a news event that served the interests of each perfectly. In these circumstances, journalistic scepticism and detachment evaporated. As a consequence, the relatively unproblematic retrieval of an injured US soldier from the care of Iraqi medical staff was transformed for public consumption into a tale about a young female soldier fighting valiantly, being shot and captured, and then being 'saved' in a daring and dangerous midnight helicopter rescue.

Case study 2: Ali Ismaeel Abbas

Overview

The story of Ali Abbas, a young Iraqi boy who lost both arms and much of his family as a result of US bombing, represents one of the most significant and memorable British media interventions of the war. As shown in Chapter 6, civilian casualty stories were one of the areas of coverage that tended to attract negotiated or oppositional reporting throughout the news media, even from outlets whose reporting of the war was otherwise predominantly supportive. Ali's story was the most prominent civilian casualty story of the war. But the process by which this story was broken and then developed is also illuminating in its own right, showing how news media were able to frame the consequences of war in ways that, arguably, both particularised and universalised them, while also divorcing them, in part, from their context. Here too is an example which shows the extent of the media's power to influence both its audience and elite decision-makers, and the limits of this power. Furthermore, although numerous pictures of Ali appeared in the British news media, the first published photograph of him (reproduced as Figure 7.1) has repeatedly been thought of as iconic, symbolising, for much of the world, the suffering of Iraq. Only a few days after the story broke, the *Daily Telegraph* was already comparing this image of Ali to iconic pictures from earlier wars (Ryan, 2003; see also Konstantinidou, 2008: 149). There have been countless examples of similar comparisons since. Taking all these aspects into account, the news media's treatment of Ali, and the story behind it, offers a remarkable yet contradictory instance of news media coverage of the impact of the war on Iraqi civilians.

The horror of war: Ali's rise to the status of an icon

As the coalition invaded Iraq, Ali Ismaeel Abbas was a 12-year-old boy[15] from a large Shia family of subsistence farmers living in a rural location 21 kilometres from Baghdad. Shortly after midnight on 31 March 2003, a US missile – probably intended for nearby factories (Warren, 2004: 11–12) – destroyed the village of Arab Al-Khrsa, home to Ali's family, killing his father, pregnant mother, brother and 13 other family members. His arms and torso very severely burned. Ali was rescued from the ruins by a family member and taken to Al-Kindi hospital in Baghdad, where his arms had to be amputated. Ali's case came to the attention of journalists immediately. Within a day, he was visited by Jon Lee Anderson of the *New Yorker* and by Francisco Peregil of the Spanish daily, *El Pais*, which ran Peregil's report about Ali on its 1 April front page (Addley, 2003). But Anderson filed nothing at the time, no other news outlets picked up the *El Pais* report, and the story lapsed.

A week after the missile attack, Samia Nakhoul, Reuters' bureau chief for the Gulf, arrived at the hospital accompanied by a photographer and asked to be shown its worst case. She was taken to meet Ali and was shocked by his injuries: 'When I came out I started sobbing like I have never sobbed in my life. I couldn't file the story for hours, I just sat and cried' (quoted in Addley, 2003). Among the pictures taken by the Reuters photographer, Faleh Kheiber, was the endlessly repeated image of Ali lying in bed under a metal hoop with peeling paint, the remaining part of an upper arm swathed in bandages, his face suggesting both pain and fortitude (see Figure 7.1). Reuters circulated the story worldwide on 6 April as one of the many Iraq War stories made available to the world's news media. A single newspaper, *Metro*, the London

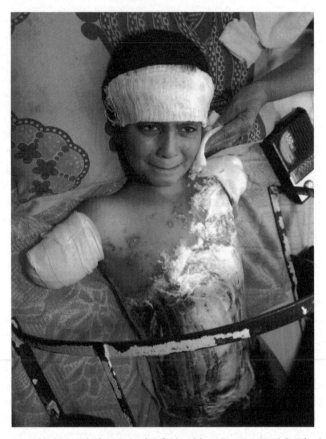

Figure 7.1 The 'iconic' photograph of Ali Abbas (Reuters/Faleh Kheiber)

free-sheet, picked it up, using Nakhoul's story and Kheiber's picture on its 7 April front page under the headline: 'The boy who lost everything – including hope.' Nakhoul quoted Ali saying: 'If I do not get a pair of hands, I will commit suicide.'

The response to the story was instant and overwhelming. Readers inundated *Metro* with offers of money and assistance, and it quickly became necessary to identify a charity to which such offers could be directed. By the afternoon, *Metro* had contacted the Limbless Association, which agreed to establish a fund for Ali and children like him (Warren, 2004: 56–7). The following morning, 8 April, much of the national press published the picture of Ali. The *Mirror* gave it the most prominence, devoting a two-page spread to the picture and an article whose headline reproduced Ali's 'suicide' quote, accompanied by an editorial that used the image to justify the paper's anti-war stance. By evening, footage of Ali had also appeared on ITV News. On the same day, however, the Palestine Hotel, which formed the Baghdad base for the world's news media, was attacked by US missiles, injuring Kheiber and Nakhoul, the latter severely.

This pattern of press coverage of the Ali story continued long beyond 18 April, when our survey period ended. Every day from 8 April, Ali appeared as a main story subject in at least two of the newspapers we surveyed, yielding 45 stories altogether in 11 days, with further references to him in more general Iraq stories. Day by day, fresh twists and tensions created a continuing narrative, enabling newspapers to offer their readers 'the latest on Ali'. On 9 April, looting and lawlessness at Al-Kindi hospital in the wake of the American capture of Baghdad forced it to close, and Ali was transferred to Qadissiyah (also known as Chawader, Saddam or Al-Sadr), the only remaining hospital in the city. In a dirty room with few medicines or facilities, medical staff could do little to treat Ali and it seemed likely that he would soon succumb to fatal septicaemia. By now, coverage had become focused on the need to 'save' Ali, which could only be accomplished by evacuating him from Iraq. On 13 April, the *Sunday Telegraph* carried a front page story in which Ali's doctor said:

> To be honest, it is probably better if he dies. I don't want it, but that's the awful truth. He has no arms and terrible burns. His physical suffering is enormous and the psychological damage will be immense ('"It would be better if poor Ali died", says boy's doctor').

Ali had only featured in a single television news story until this point, but on 13 April ITV News led its bulletin with a report on his condition, accompanied by emotional footage of its reporter, Andrea Catherwood, at his bedside. Catherwood showed the dreadful state of hospital facilities and interviewed Ali's doctor, who repeated his prognosis that Ali's survival was unlikely. Among the programmes we surveyed, Ali was the main subject of 11 more television news stories over the next four days.

The following day, the *Mirror*'s front page contained an 'open letter' to Tony Blair and George Bush from Ali's nurse, Fatin Sharhah:

> The situation is desperate. He will die if he stays. Please send one of your helicopters or planes . . . You have all this technology to bomb us, to make the missile that burned Ali's house. But you cannot spare one aircraft for one day to save a life? (S. Martin, 'Dear Mr Blair and Mr Bush.. get Ali out', 14 April 2003).

The news media fascination with Ali had already begun to attract the interest of politicians. As early as 9 April, Llew Smith MP had proposed an Early Day Motion in the House of Commons congratulating 'the *Daily Mirror* of 8th April for printing the horrific picture of Ali Ismaeel Abbas', and calling for generous compensation for injured Iraqi civilians (Hansard, 2003b).

On the day of the 'open letter' from Ali's nurse, Conservative leader Iain Duncan Smith raised the issue with the Prime Minister, announcing: 'The whole House will have been moved by the pictures of the plight and tragic case of Ali.' In response, Blair told the House: 'We will do whatever we can to help him and others in a similar situation', saying that the government was working with American forces to that end (Hansard, 2003c).

Not surprisingly, Blair's 'pledge to help Ali', as a *Mail* headline described it (15 April 2003: 11), became the focus of the next day's stories. At last, on 16 April, the news media could report that Ali had been stretchered from his hospital (amid 'cheering crowds', said the *Daily Mirror* (S. Martin, 'He's out': 1)) and airlifted by US Marines to a well-equipped hospital in Kuwait where he could receive appropriate treatment. Nevertheless, newspapers continued to publish even trivial stories about him, such as 'Ali orders a kebab for dinner' (A. Williams, *Daily Mirror*, 18 April 2003: 5).

Stories about Ali appeared in every newspaper we surveyed and on every television news service, generally acting as a significant vehicle for negotiated and oppositional coverage. We coded the subjects of the majority of these stories as negotiated (38%) or oppositional (36%). Only four stories (9%), all from the day on which Ali was airlifted to Kuwait, had a supportive tone. Of all media outlets we surveyed, the *Mirror*'s coverage far outdid that of its competitors, as Table 7.2 shows. That Ali provided a graphic illustration of the suffering and unfairness that the war brought with it, in keeping with the *Mirror*'s opposition to it, might explain this in part, although it is noteworthy that the next greatest quantity of coverage was in *The Times* and *Telegraph*, both of which covered the war supportively.

But the popularity of this human interest story is also likely to have appealed to the *Mirror*. When it first published Ali's picture, the response from readers was enormous – so much so that it republished the picture on its

Table 7.2 Stories in which Ali Abbas was a subject, by newspaper and television channel (8–18 April 2003)

	Sun	Mirror	Mail	Indep-endent	Guard-ian	Times	Tele-graph	Total
No. of stories	4	20	3	3	3	5	7	45
No. of front page stories	-	5	-	-	-	1	2	8

	BBC	ITV	C4	Sky				Total
No. of stories	2	7	1	3				13
No. of lead stories	-	2	-	-				2

front page the next day under the headline 'Help him' and launched an appeal, describing him as the 'Iraqi boy who captured the hearts of *Mirror* readers' (9 April 2003; see also Morgan, 2005: 395) – so it is clear that the *Mirror* regarded Ali as engaging readers and selling papers. Although television gave much less space to Ali than the press, ITV's coverage took the lead – perhaps a sign of a stronger populist, human interest agenda than on other channels. On the day on which he was airlifted to Kuwait, ITV chose to devote its first two reports to Ali, one of them a live two-way with a reporter on the spot. Ali's airlift featured in each news programme that we analysed on that day, but only ITV presented it as the day's most prominent story.

For journalists prevented by time and logistics from giving more than a snapshot of the distress of Iraqi civilians, Ali served another valuable purpose, becoming a device to signify much wider suffering:

> Not that many others haven't suffered in Iraq during this war, but sometimes the sheer enormity of suffering in a war is so great that it becomes, if you like, concentrated on the particular plight of an individual. (M. Draper, ITV News, 15 April 2003)

Indeed, much reporting was at pains to stress that Ali was only one of many similar casualties and various stories repeated his doctor's words: 'There are hundreds of Alis here.' Furthermore, stories with Ali as their focus enabled reporters to illustrate numerous other consequences of the war, including conditions in and the collapse of Baghdad hospitals, looting and the breakdown of law and order, power blackouts and a decision to withdraw British medical aid from Southern Iraq. In this respect, Ali's personification of civilian suffering had a considerable effect in drawing attention to the consequences of war and compelling news media to report it widely. As Richard Sambrook (BBC) explained: 'Human interest stories of that kind do crystallise some of the issues [of war] in terms of the impact on the civilian population.'[16]

However, although the story became a vehicle for negotiated and oppositional coverage, highlighting the suffering of the Iraqi people, some aspects of its telling were much more problematic and self-serving: a fundraising 'bandwagon' founded largely on misrepresentation, 'improvements' to or omissions from the narrative, and the selective presentation of Ali's views. Below, we deal with each in turn.

Managing the coverage: the fundraising focus, 'improving' the story and moderating the voice of Ali

Much reporting in the British news media after the initial story broke was organised around the need to 'save' Ali. This first manifested itself in fundraising. We have seen how the response to *Metro*'s initial publication of Ali's picture led the paper to identify the Limbless Association (LA) as a UK charity that could help. LA announced an appeal on 8 April and launched it formally as the ALI fund ('Ali's fund for the Limbless of Iraq') two days later. Both events gave rise to stories with Ali as their focus and to newspapers claiming credit for the campaign and encouraging readers to donate. *The Times*, for example, suggested that the LA appeal came '[a]fter a "deluge" of telephone calls from the public who saw the photograph in *The Times*' (H. Rumbelow, 'Appeal launched to save injured Ali', 9 April 2003: 6). The *Guardian* and ITV News also published the address for donations. In parallel, the London *Evening Standard* launched an appeal for the Red Cross, again predicated on reader's reactions to Ali's picture (B. Graham and J. Murphy, 'Suffering children who cannot wait long for the aid they need', 9 April 2003: 1). A fundraising campaign in the *Sun* – 'Give a quid for an Iraqi kid' – was already running, with proceeds going to Save The Children, but it was quick to use Ali's story and image to promote it (M. Bowness, '100,000 quids for Iraqi kids', 10 April 2003: 8).

As we have seen, the most prominent press appeal linked to Ali was the *Mirror*'s, launched on its front page on 9 April under the headline 'Help him'. 'Many readers were so moved they phoned, faxed and emailed the *Daily Mirror* offering to help the brave lad', explained the accompanying article, while a two-page spread reproduced quotes from readers all over the world. 'The British don't just have the best fighting forces in the world. They have the greatest compassion, too', maintained an editorial about the appeal in the same edition of the *Mirror* ('We owe the child victims a real future': 6). Following the pattern of the *Sun*'s 'Give a quid' campaign, the *Mirror* gave regular updates as the appeal total grew and organised celebrities to endorse it. In addition, the press coverage gave rise to offers from several wealthy individuals to fund Ali's treatment, including the Maharani Gayatri Devi, wife of a former ruler of Jaipur, for whose concern the *Mirror*, rather incongruously, claimed credit (J. Palmer, R. Parry and A. Rudd, '"I saw the picture of Ali lying there so helplessly and burst into tears"', *Daily Mirror*, 9 April 2003: 8). Another much-publicised offer, promising to supply Ali's prosthetic needs at cost, came from Dorset Orthopaedic Company; here the *Daily Telegraph* claimed credit for publishing the photo of Ali that alerted the company (G. Tibbetts, 'British company offers to make artificial arms for orphan Ali', *Daily Telegraph*, 9 April 2003: 8).

These charitable appeals raised well over £1m (Addley, 2003), and there is no question that news media claims about the public's desire to help Ali were genuine. No matter how admirable such fundraising might be, however, for Ryan (2003) they represented 'a story of competing agendas and some dishonesty', which verged on 'blatant deceit'. Although most newspapers added the rider 'and other children like him' in appealing for funds, 'the public ... could be forgiven for thinking that all that stood between Ali and a new pair of arms was money – their money' (Ryan, 2003). In fact, there was little likelihood that any of these appeals would benefit Ali, who was in a part of Baghdad only loosely under US control.[17] None of the charities concerned was operating in Baghdad at the time, nor had any means to provide an airlift. In practice, only the US military could 'save' Ali and here British news media pressure could have little effect since, at this stage, Ali's story had failed to register in the USA despite blanket exposure in the Western and Arab worlds. Nonetheless, when the USA did airlift Ali to Kuwait, the *Mirror* was quick to claim credit: 'Tony Blair asked the US to provide a mercy airlift after reading a heartrending appeal for help from Ali's nurse in Monday's *Mirror*', it explained (S. Martin, 'He's out', 16 April 2003: 1).

The *Mirror*'s claim is one of the more striking examples of the tendency of news media outlets to adjust or omit aspects of the story to make it more palatable to readers or, as in this case, to claim a greater share of credit. The letter from Ali's nurse, which it published on its front page was written 'with the help of a *Daily Mirror* journalist' (Warren, 2004: 76) although the paper never acknowledged this. And neither Downing Street nor Blair, who was responding to the Leader of the Opposition and not directly to the *Mirror* story, actually had any involvement in the US decision to provide an airlift, as Alistair Campbell, the Prime Minister's official spokesman, later confirmed (Warren, 2004: 90–1). Instead, the airlift was facilitated by Peter Wilson, a journalist with *The Australian*, and his fixer, Stewart Innes, who managed to win over both the Kuwaiti government and a Baghdad-based US Marine officer (Warren, 2004: 86–8; Addley, 2003). However, only a single news story in our corpus mentioned their involvement (B. Graham, 'A mercy flight brings hope for little Ali', *Daily Mail*, 16 April 2003: 19). In fact, the only British news report that may have assisted in providing an airlift for Ali seems to have been Catherwood's ITV story on 13 April, which was picked up by CNN and seen both in the USA (where it finally broke Ali's story to the American public) and by the Kuwaiti Ministry of Health (Warren, 2004: 70–1). The 'cheering crowds' which, the *Mirror* claimed, greeted Ali's departure from hospital actually represented a protest by the Shia militia in charge of hospital security, who 'objected to the child being evacuated by Americans who could then claim that they were rescuing him' (J. di Giovanni, 'Ali manages his first smile as he is flown to new hospital and hope', *The Times*, 16 April 2003: 1; see also Warren, 2004: 92–5).[18]

In another example of adjustment, it is worth noting that Kheiber's iconic photograph of Ali was not the first image of him available to journalists. The hospital took photos of his wounds immediately before surgery and these were made available to journalists including Anderson but never published. 'The truth', suggests Warren (2003: 43) 'is that if Ali had been found by journalists before surgery – and the tidy application of cream and bandages – his image would have been judged too upsetting for publication'. In contrast, the published photos of Ali followed established journalistic ethics 'where injury

is never explicit or bloody and fresh wounding is almost never recorded'
(Konstantinidou, 2008: 155).

At a more general level, Ali's repositioning by the media from being a sig-
nifier of dreadful civilian suffering to become the focus of a story of fundraising and rescue can itself be viewed as problematic. As Holland (2004: 186–8)
notes, the presentation of a story such as his relies on simplification and the
appeal to emotion, encouraging responses based on straightforward notions
of good or evil, which obscure the complexity of actual circumstances – in
this case, leading to crude demands that he be 'saved'. It also encourages
a focus on victimhood and vulnerability: 'In the simplified narrative with
instant appeal, it is easier to deal with childhood when children are helpless'
(Holland, 2004: 187). Konstantinidou (2008: 144) goes further, suggesting
that visual representations of children such as Ali construct objectified,
infantilised subject positions for Iraqis as 'speechless, helpless, vulnerable,
innocent victims', while readers, in contrast, were addressed as 'socially
powerful'. For readers, it is possible to argue that this focus on a single victim
serves another purpose: 'Now that we are observers of wars, rather than active
participants, our overriding emotion is guilt. Seizing on a single innocent
casualty allows us to reclaim our humanity and absolve our guilt' (psycholo-
gist Susan Quilliam, quoted in Warren, 2004: 66). In other words, the value of
Ali's 'salvation' in seemingly purging guilt about the war may deflect readers'
attention from, and guilt towards, the suffering of other Iraqis. Similarly, such
concern for the tragic consequences of war may have the effect of distancing
readers from a full appreciation of the responsibility for causing them.

Even more problematic was the news media's selective presentation of
Ali's own views and attitudes. In the various quotes attributed to him, Ali
was chiefly presented as a helpless victim lamenting the effect of the loss of
his arms on his desire to be a soldier or a doctor, even to go fishing, and
threatening suicide as a result. In fact, he was also highly critical of the war.
To Jon Lee Anderson, the first reporter to speak to him, Ali said: 'Bush is
a criminal and the war is about oil' (quoted in Warren, 2004: 53). In an
unusually revealing article in the *Independent* on 12 April, illustrated with
Ali's picture, we hear that he is unwilling to travel to Britain for treatment
because of UK involvement in the invasion, and that other child victims are
forthright in criticising Britain and the USA. Meanwhile his doctor asks:
'Why do you all want to talk to Ali? There are hundreds of children suffering like him' (Kim Sengupta, 'Frenzy over Ali, but there are thousands
of children like him': 6). Ali also seems to have been critical of journalists.
Nakhoul claims that he became fed up with their constant visits: 'Everyone
was asking the same questions, and he had to tell the same stories over and
over again' (quoted in Addley, 2003). And the *Telegraph*, alone among British
papers, reported him demanding:

to know why numerous promises that he would be treated in the West had not been kept: 'The journalists always promise to evacuate me – why don't they do it now?' he asked. (D. Blair, 'You've broken your word, says Baghdad boy who lost his arms', 15 April 2003: 1)

Peter Wilson, the Australian who organised the airlift, supports Ali's criticisms:

> The British press were just disgraceful, to be honest. Ali's room was meant to be a sterile environment – his body was just an open sore – but you had all these publicity-seeking English journalists leaning over him, putting his head next to their heads, dropping their hairs on to his body. Eventually he was saying in Arabic, 'Keep them away from me, keep them away.' (quoted in Addley, 2003)

Furthermore, while many news reports were quick to reproduce poignant things that Ali said, none of them acknowledged that he spoke no English and that his words were translations. Speaking later, Ali claimed to have had little understanding of what was happening at the time: 'I was in another world when I was in the hospital in Iraq . . . With all the pain I had, I preferred to die. It was when they took me to Kuwait that I realised I didn't have arms' (BBC News, 2007). Keen as they were to present Ali as an 'international symbol of the horror wreaked by war' (H. Rumbelow, '"I wanted to become an officer, but not now"', *Times*, 8 April 2003: 9), Ali's poignant quotes were a gift to journalists, even if their reporting overlooked the likelihood that they were the product of a 12-year-old's trauma.

Ali Abbas: A contradictory story from war?

Outwardly, our analysis shows that the story of Ali Abbas represented a negative development for the coalition, yielding coverage that was largely negotiated or oppositional. Certainly, for the anti-war *Mirror*, the story became a major subject for the paper, symbolising the suffering of the Iraqi people and reflecting its anti-war stance. At the same time, we have shown how aspects of this coverage were highly misleading, ensuring, in turn, that the tale of Ali was made more engaging and palatable for British audiences: money could be raised to save a boy whose anti-war sentiments were played down. Can these two strands of analysis be reconciled?

To a large extent, early coverage of the story and the basic facts concerning the dreadful plight of this Iraqi boy were deeply problematic for the coalition and succeeded in bringing the suffering of the Iraqi people to the attention of the British public. However, the success of the story in capturing the attention of the British news media and public created a media circus in which the focus shifted to the question of how this one boy could be 'saved'. Coverage of this aspect of the story then became sanitised, misleading and, at worst, a method by which responsibility for the war might be alleviated. In short, although the quantity of supportive coverage generated was relatively small, this shift does demonstrate how the focus of such a story on generalised civilian suffering in war could swiftly be subverted to create what was, in some interpretations, a particularised feel-good exercise in charity and salvation that had more to do with how 'we' feel than with the suffering of civilians.

Case study 3: UK news media and the anti-war movement

Overview

The 2003 Iraq invasion was a hard sell for the Blair government. Polls taken in the period leading up to war emphasised the large numbers of British people who opposed military intervention. As late as 14–16 March 2003, less than a week before the invasion, Ipsos-MORI found that 63 per cent opposed war if it were to go ahead without either specific UN approval or evidence from UN inspectors that Iraq was hiding WMD: two conditions that were, ultimately, never met.[19] Opposition had been as high as 77 per cent in January 2003.[20] Despite a sharp swing in favour of war as it was getting underway – *Guardian*-ICM polls showed a jump in support from 38 per cent to 54 per cent between 14 and 21 March (Travis, 2003) – anti-war sentiment still remained substantial for the duration of the conflict. Ongoing polling by YouGov showed that 30–40 per cent continued to believe that the invasion was wrong, with one poll two weeks into the war revealing that 26 per cent thought British troops should be withdrawn.[21] Lewis et al. have suggested that these figures may even underestimate the extent of anti-war feeling, arguing that: 'Many people who expressed support during the war may *still* have opposed the decision to go to war, but felt obliged to show support for British troops once war began' (Lewis et al., 2005: 52; original emphasis).

Channelling and directing the groundswell of popular opposition was the grass-roots political movement, the Stop the War Coalition (StWC), formed in September 2001 in response to the Bush administration's newly declared 'war on terror'. The group's most prominent spokespersons, such as former Labour MPs Tony Benn and George Galloway and activist Andrew Murray, were from the left of the political spectrum. During their campaign against the Iraq invasion in early 2003, StWC (together with the Campaign for Nuclear Disarmament and the Muslim Association of Britain) organised large public protest rallies across the United Kingdom. These included Britain's largest ever demonstration on 15 February 2003, in which it is estimated that between 750,000 and 2 million people participated; and the UK's largest ever war-time protest rally on 22 March (in response to the opening of hostilities on 20 March), which involved perhaps 200,000 people despite being organised at very short notice. In their book *Stop the War* (2005), StWC leaders

Andrew Murray and Lindsay German described the anti-Iraq War movement as 'Britain's biggest mass movement'. In addition to this large grassroots opposition, various elite actors in British society challenged the push for war. Besides Benn and Galloway, these included the Liberal Democrats, Britain's third largest political party, and a large number of Labour MPs. At the 17 March House of Commons debate on the war, 139 Labour MPs staged the largest rebellion in Commons history when they voted against their own government's war policy. The government nonetheless prevailed, with the remaining Labour MPs (the majority of the party) and most Conservative MPs voting for war.

As our final case study, our analysis of news media and the anti-war movement enables us to examine closely the evolution of the British news media's treatment of anti-war dissent over the course of the conflict and assess the limits of 'acceptable' public and political debate in wartime.

'The protest paradigm': media and the limits of dissent in wartime
Past research into the coverage of protest movements has shown that dissenters tend to receive unenthusiastic or dismissive news media treatment. This is commonly explained by the fact that most protest movements campaign for minority causes. As McLeod and Detenber (1999: 6) argue, 'the more a protest group challenges the status quo, the more closely the news media will adhere to the characteristics of the protest paradigm'. Within this 'protest paradigm', coverage of demonstrations will often focus on phenomena that distinguish dissenters from 'ordinary' people, such as involvement by 'extremist' elements, unusual appearance, or violence and disruption. Coupled with an emphasis on 'spectacle' that often drowns out the activists' message, this frequently leads to coverage that 'marginalises', 'delegitimises' or even 'demonises' those involved (Gitlin, 1980; Glasgow University Media Group, 1985; Hall, 1973; Hallin, 1986; Luther and Miller, 2005; Murdock, 1973; Smith et al., 2001).

Yet the anti-Iraq war movement in Britain was clearly untypical of dissenting groups. In the prelude to war, it was not only massive in scale but represented the sentiments of most Britons, including sections of the social and political 'elite'. It would be reasonable to expect, therefore, that anti-war dissenters might receive fairer, perhaps sympathetic, coverage on this occasion. Moreover, recent academic work has suggested that protest generally has become more 'mainstream' and that this has made the protest paradigm less applicable now than in preceding decades. According to Cottle:

> Much has changed since earlier studies documented how the mainstream news media invariably report protests and demonstrations through a dominant law and (dis)order frame, labelling protesters as deviant and de-legitimising their aims and politics by emphasizing drama, spectacle and violence. (Cottle, 2008: 855)

Representing dissent during the 2003 Iraq war
Despite the strength of opposition to war in Iraq and the notion that protest generally has received a kinder media profile of late, our analysis found that anti-war actors had a difficult time in gaining access to the British news media and winning sympathetic coverage. In line with other studies (e.g. Cushion, 2007), we found that although coverage was relatively widespread and sympathetic up to the eve of battle, thereafter it became both sparse and increasingly negative. Across our entire survey period (17 March–18 April), domestic and international anti-war protest was a significant feature in only about one Iraq-related story in twenty (6.1% of newspaper stories and 5.1% of TV reports), and dissenting voices comprised only 5 per cent of press quotations and 3.5 per cent of those accessed by television. Figures 7.2 and 7.3 display the spread of supportive, negotiated and oppositional protest subjects for newspapers and television news respectively across this period. Below we discuss the early, more positive coverage first, before considering the pattern of coverage that emerged as the war progressed.

Pre-war and early war coverage: 17–23 March
Anti-war protest subjects were quite prominent, and coverage relatively positive for anti-war actors, in the seven days between 17 and 23 March. This period corresponded to the pre-war Commons debate and vote (reported 17–19 March), the start of hostilities, and the various large protest demonstrations that followed this (reported 20–23 March). Between 17 and 23 March, subjects with a supportive (i.e. pro-coalition) framing were greatly outnumbered by those that were oppositional or negotiated. Most of the oppositional coverage related to the pre-war Commons debate and the Labour rebellion. Anti-war MPs were quoted extensively in many of these stories and often the size of the rebellion was framed as a problem for the Blair government.

Coverage of the street demonstrations organised by StWC between 20 and 23 March also produced more oppositional than supportive coverage, although negotiated coverage of these was most common. Many of these stories quoted anti-war activists, and the size of the demonstrations, when reported, also encouraged oppositional framing. However, such tendencies were often counterbalanced by 'delegitimisation cues' (Gitlin, 1980) including headlines and photographs with negative connotations and deflating or implicitly patronising reporter commentary. The result of these was often to produce a negotiated framing overall. Among such negative cues were an emphasis on disruption ('Schoolchildren bring city to a halt', *Times*, 20 March 2003), on decline in turnout ('Poor show on marches', *News of the World*, 23 March 2003) or on other delegitimising themes ('Hard left agitators behind school demos', *Daily Mail*, 23 March 2003: 18; 'Council pays its workers to

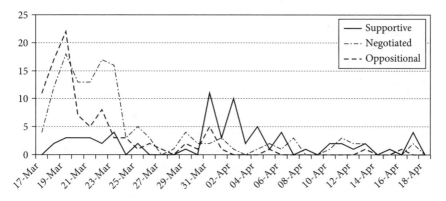

Figure 7.2 Quantity and framing of stories with protest as subject in newspapers (17 March–18 April 2003)

Note: Consistent with our analytical framework, coverage that played positively for the anti-war lobby is denoted as 'oppositional' coverage, that which played negatively as 'supportive', and that which was mixed as 'negotiated'.

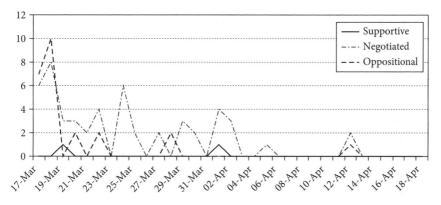

Figure 7.3 Quantity and framing of stories with protest as subject in television news (17 March–18 April 2003)

Note: Consistent with our analytical framework, coverage that played positively for the anti-war lobby is denoted as 'oppositional' coverage, that which played negatively as 'supportive', and that which was mixed as 'negotiated'.

attend demos', *Daily Telegraph*, 21 March 2003: 11; 'Terror fears as marchers jam the capital again', *Mail on Sunday*, 23 March 2003: 18).

As some of these headlines indicate, the most prominent sub-theme was a focus on participation by students, and particularly schoolchildren.[22] In the pro-war press, this involvement was often framed patronisingly, with headlines such as 'The truants take to the streets' (*Daily Mail*, 20 March 2003: 8) and 'Adults stay away but pupils on march again' (*The Times*, 22 March 2003: 10). Although the anti-war press also emphasised youth participation, here it was framed more ambiguously or encouragingly (e.g. 'Fighting for peace: children in countrywide protests', *Guardian*, 20 March 2003: 10). The *Daily Mirror* even used images of children and youths grappling with police to imply official authoritarianism ('Law of the fist', *Daily Mirror*, 21 March 2003: 11). Anti-war newspapers such as the *Guardian*, *Independent* and *Mirror* were also more likely to emphasise other positive aspects of these protests, such as the large turnout ('100,000 expected at London peace march', *Guardian*, 22 March 2003: 9; '200,000 marchers join "very British demonstration"', *Independent*, 23 March 2003: 8).

Elite and non-elite dissent

As noted above, most of the oppositional protest subjects appeared in connection with the Commons vote and Labour rebellion. By contrast, we found coverage of grass-roots protest action, such as the large public demonstrations that were organised by StWC shortly after the beginning of the war, to be predominantly negotiated. Arguably, one cause of these differences in framing was the pre-war timing of the Commons debate. Another likely explanation lies in the identity of the dissenters involved. Past research has found that elite protesters, such as high profile politicians, tend to receive more favourable news media treatment than non-elite or 'grass-roots' activists campaigning for the same cause.

In his analysis of anti-war dissent during the Vietnam War, Hallin (1986) found that elite dissenters such as anti-war politicians had more success in affecting news coverage than non-elites, although he concluded that the anti-war movement as a whole fell into a 'sphere of deviance'. The difference in framing between the reporting of the Commons debate and of the demonstrations seems to mirror this conclusion. Grass-roots protest also received significantly less attention than elite dissent. Of 200 newspaper stories focusing on specifically British anti-war activism, 127 covered elite protest and 74 non-elite (with one story covering both). Similarly, of 48 TV news stories about British protest, 31 were about elite dissent and 18 non-elite (one story covered both). Elite dissenters also received three times as many lines of quotations as non-elites in the press (3,134 to 913) and twice as much speaking time in television news (663 seconds to 329).[23] In the press, at least, elite protest stories were also more likely to contain substantive discussion of the reasons for war. This occurred nearly three times as frequently in reports of elite dissent (38%; 48 stories) as in those covering non-elite protests (14%; 10 stories). There was not such a clear trend in the small sample of television news stories, however, which showed little variation.[24] Overall, our results in this area support the findings of past research (e.g. Bennett, 1990; Entman and

Page, 1994; Hallin, 1986) that news media tend to favour elite protagonists over non-elites.

Later war coverage: 24 March–18 April

Following coverage of the public demonstrations, the level of reporting on anti-war activity declined markedly. In part, this simply reflected the fact that there was less activity to cover. With British troops in the field and majority public opinion having swung behind them, anti-war politicians and other public figures became less vocal. Nor were there any comparably large street demonstrations in the UK after the first week of the conflict. Yet decreased protest activity was not the only factor involved. From this point on, the news media itself also became less accommodating to dissent. Although protest activity declined in scale, it did not cease, continuing for much of the period between the invasion and the fall of Baghdad. In the UK, this included demonstrations involving thousands on 27 March in Manchester and on 28 March in Edinburgh. There were also large demonstrations internationally.[25] None of these received significant coverage in the UK news media.

Protest subjects did return to prominence briefly around 31 March to 1 April, however, following reporting of strong statements by former Foreign Secretary Robin Cook and fellow Labour MP George Galloway, as well as news of two conscientious objectors facing punitive action from the British military at about the same time. Among the few other protest events in the latter weeks of the sample were the desecration of Allied war graves in France[26] (early April) and an anti-war 'riot' in Athens staged to coincide with a European summit on 17 April. Otherwise, dissent after the war began was given a low profile, meaning that the first seven days of our sample contained 59 per cent of all newspaper stories (161 stories in all) and 64 per cent of all television news stories (42 stories) about protest.

A notable feature of the protest coverage after the war started was that the subject became a less significant topic in the anti-war newspapers (*Mirror, Guardian, Independent*) compared to its coverage in the pro-war press. Until protest subjects re-emerged on 31 March, for example, the three anti-war papers had published more protest stories than the four pro-war papers. From 1 April onwards, the pro-war press carried almost twice as many. This could signify that the anti-war newspapers had begun to distance themselves somewhat from dissent while the war was in progress. Indeed, the *Independent* attempted explicitly to move away from arguments about the war's validity in editorials at the time the invasion was launched. On 20 March, it noted that:

> The debate about the rights and wrongs of this war is over. The House of Commons has voted overwhelmingly in favour and the tanks have begun to roll towards the Iraqi border. Politicians across the political spectrum are united in

the conviction that the time has come 'to support our troops'. This newspaper
agrees and fervently hopes for a swift conclusion with as few casualties on both
sides as is possible in war. ('When democracies do battle with a despot, they
must hold on to their moral superiority': 18)

Rather than continuing to debate the legitimacy of military action, this
Independent leader called instead for a debate about the methods of fighting,
their proportionality and their consequences.

With the balance of protest stories increasingly shifting towards pro-war
papers, the proportion of negative stories about anti-war protest increased
markedly in the latter part of the conflict. Between 17 and 30 March, there
were four times as many oppositional subjects as supportive (83 to 20), but
thereafter (31 March to 18 April) supportive protest subjects outweighed
oppositional ones by five to one (49 to 9). There was no comparable trend in
television news, which featured very few supportive protest subjects at any
time. This was perhaps a reflection of the greater interest in anti-war protest
shown by Channel 4 News, which was responsible for over half of all TV
protest stories. Nonetheless, there was a marked decrease in oppositional
protest subjects in both news media once the war was properly underway,
with 79 per cent of all oppositional subjects in the press and 88 per cent in TV
news appearing in the first seven days of the sample.

Voices of dissent: MPs Robin Cook and George Galloway

The decline in the media's openness to dissent was perhaps most clearly shown
in the treatment of anti-war MPs Robin Cook and George Galloway. Cook
became a prominent figure among elite anti-war actors, largely because of his
high-profile status within the Blair Government, serving as Foreign Secretary
from 1997 to 2001 and then as Leader of the Commons until his resignation on
the eve of the war. Cook was also noted for his fine oratorical skills, a quality
highlighted in news media coverage of his dramatic resignation speech. The
eloquence of his criticisms was undoubtedly one of the principal reasons that
he received broadly positive treatment from most news media outlets following his resignation, including from some pro-war papers. The only notable
exception was the avidly pro-war *Sun*, in which he was deflated as a 'war
wobbler' and 'gnome-like' ('War wobbler Cook resigns', 18 March: 1; 'Cook:
I quit: Gnome won't back PM', 18 March: 8).

News media treatment of Cook changed markedly almost two weeks into
hostilities, however, when he restated his opposition to war in a *Sunday Mirror*
opinion piece and seemingly called for British troops to be withdrawn. This
time the press reaction was overwhelmingly negative. Editorials in six of the
seven newspapers in our survey criticised Cook's stand, with only the *Daily
Mirror* defending the statement. Cook's attempts to clarify his position were

labelled a 'humiliating somersault' in the *Daily Mail* (31 March: 11) with Simon Heffer branding his ambition 'obscene' ('Ambition so naked as to be obscene', *Daily Mail*, 31 March: 10). *The Times'* first leader characterised Cook's intervention as 'bizarre' and 'disastrous', sensing a plot against Tony Blair: 'That the "conscience" of the party should resort to pointless point-scoring suggests that he has mistaken a flimsy soapbox for the moral high ground' ('Overcooked', *The Times*, 31 March: 19). The anti-war *Independent*'s editorial called Cook's article 'cheap', fearing that his 'outburst' risked 'under-mining the cause of proper scepticism about the course of the war' ('Cheap sniping undermines Mr Cook's noble cause', *Independent*, 31 March: 18). Altogether Cook received explicitly deflating reporter treatment in 39 per cent of the newspaper stories in which he appeared from 31 March onwards.

Reporting on 'renegade MP' George Galloway resembled the treatment given to Cook but was even more scornful. Galloway was also a Labour MP at the time but was later expelled from the party because of statements he made in a 28 March 2003 interview on Abu Dhabi TV, where he asserted that George Bush and Tony Blair had attacked Iraq 'like wolves' and said that 'the best thing British troops can do is to refuse to obey illegal orders'. Although he was usually a marginal figure within his own party, his talent for oration and his provocative views had ensured that he tended to appear quite frequently in the press. However, like most other so-called 'Old Labour' voices, he was often treated with disdain within most of Britain's mainstream or 'establishment' media. Galloway received little attention in the first two weeks of our study period. This changed on 1 April when the *Sun* brought him to prominence with the large front-page headline, 'TRAITOR'. The article attacked his statements on Abu Dhabi TV and claimed that he had compared coalition soldiers to 'wolves'. From this point onwards, he received deflating coverage in 54 per cent of his press appearances. This negative treatment was not confined only to the pro-war press either. A common focus in reportage of Galloway was his much-publicised sympathy – sometimes interpreted as admiration – for Saddam Hussein. This point was emphasised in an ITV News story from 1 April, for instance. Here Galloway was at least shown giving his views early in the report, although a string of quotations from critical sources followed, includ-ing another Labour MP who called his remarks 'too ridiculous for words', and vox-pops from 'ordinary Glaswegians' who suggested that he had gone too far. The reporter contributed as well, describing Galloway as 'controversial as ever' and someone the government is 'used to tolerating', before noting how other anti-war MPs had opted for silence during such 'sensitive times'.

Protest in wartime: beyond 'legitimate controversy'
Overall then, the case of British news coverage of the anti-war movement tells two stories. Prior to military action and for a brief period after the start of the

war, coverage of protest activity played more positively than negatively for the anti-war movement. Although coverage was to become more negative over time, this finding reflects an unusual and probably unprecedented degree of reporting favourable to a wartime protest movement. It also provides some support to recent notions that news media framing of protest has become less negative (Cottle, 2008). The data here suggest that, prior to military action, the UK anti-war movement operated within a sphere of 'legitimated controversy' (Hallin, 1986) and that much of the UK press functioned as an 'advocate of the underdog' (Wolfsfeld, 1997), producing negotiated and oppositional coverage. However, although the anti-war movement was able to achieve sympathetic news media attention (albeit mostly early on), it was less successful in its attempts to generate substantive debate concerning the rationale for war (McLeod and Detenber, 1999: 3). The one notable exception to this was coverage of the pre-war Commons debate. Here, however, it was 'elite' dissenters who were most successful at influencing news media debate about the rationale for war.

Crucially, though, after this brief initial period, coverage came to conform more to the expectations of the research literature (Glasgow University Media Group, 1985; Gitlin, 1980; Hall, 1973; Hallin, 1986; Luther and Miller, 2005; Murdock, 1973; Smith et al., 2001). With the war in progress, even the interjections of prominent politicians were deemed unacceptable by most news media outlets, as reflected in the treatment of Robin Cook and George Galloway. Consistent with our findings in Chapter 5 regarding news media support for the humanitarian and WMD justifications for war, the marginalisation of the anti-war movement highlights how reluctant news media were to challenge fundamentally the substantive reasons for the war in Iraq once conflict got underway.

In short, despite the level of controversy surrounding the Iraq war, the presence of a powerful and popular anti-war movement, elite political dissent and an anti-war faction among newspapers, such political opposition to the war was beyond the bounds of acceptable mainstream debate. As with all other wars to date, protest and opposition remained a marginal and difficult task to pursue.

Summary

Taken together, our three case studies highlight the extremes or limits of news media performance in wartime. From the eager complicity of media with coalition media-management goals in the case of Jessica Lynch, through the focused and traumatic representation of the suffering of one Iraqi child and the marginalisation of the biggest anti-war movement in British history, the case studies are indicative of our broader findings regarding supportive battle coverage, negotiated and oppositional casualty coverage and the failure of news media to provide an adequate platform for substantive criticism of war.

In our concluding chapter, we draw upon our analyses of TV and press coverage in Chapters 5 and 6, as well as these case study findings, in order to assess overall patterns of news media performance and their implications for our theoretical understanding of war-time media-state relations.

Notes

1 'The truth about Jessica', *Guardian*, 15 May 2003. The material used in this article formed the basis for the BBC2 *Correspondent* documentary 'War Spin', broadcast 18 May 2003. Kampfner does not repeat his claim that the rescue was a 'stunning piece of news management' in the BBC transcript of this documentary: http://news.bbc.co.uk/nol/shared/spl/hi/programmes/correspondent/transcripts/18.5.031.txt (accessed 3 October 2008).

2 An Iraqi lawyer, Mohammed Odeh Al-Rehaief, is claimed to have helped the Americans rescue Lynch. Much was made of his involvement both by the coalition and the media and yet, subsequently, there has been no clear evidence for his participation. In Bragg's (2003) authorised account of Lynch's experience, there is no reference to Al-Rehaief. In the absence of verification for Al-Rehaief's claims, we have avoided discussion of this aspect of the case.

3 The article was by Schmidt and Loeb, 2003.

4 For an overview of how the story developed, see Chinni, 2003.

5 Shown speaking in the BBC2 *Correspondent* documentary 'War Spin', broadcast 18 May 2003. Transcript available at: http://news.bbc.co.uk/nol/shared/spl/hi/programmes/correspondent/transcripts/18.5.031.txt (accessed 3 October 2008).

6 Lynch also confirmed that the Iraqi doctors had attempted to return her to US forces in her testimony to the Congressional Oversight Committee (Lynch, 2007).

7 Shown speaking on PBS online News Hour on 2 April 2003. Available at www.pbs.org/newshour/bb/middle_east/jan-june03/lynch_04-02.html (accessed 6 November 2008).

8 'Fears grow for missing Jess', *Daily Mirror*, 25 March 2003; 'Family losing hope for GI Jessica', *Daily Mail*, 26 March; 'Dear Mrs Davies, it's cool to go travelling with the Army but I hope to get back alive', *Sunday Mirror*, 30 March.

9 Under the more specific subject code of 'Coalition PoW', 34 of the 38 were supportive and four negotiated. None were oppositional.

10 'The truth about Jessica', *Guardian*, 15 May 2003.

11 Speaking in the BBC2 *Correspondent* documentary 'War Spin', broadcast 18 May 2003. Transcript available at: http://news.bbc.co.uk/nol/shared/spl/hi/programmes/correspondent/transcripts/18.5.031.txt (accessed 3 October 2008).

12 Speaking in the BBC2 *Correspondent* documentary 'War Spin', broadcast 18 May 2003. Transcript available at: http://news.bbc.co.uk/nol/shared/spl/hi/programmes/correspondent/transcripts/18.5.031.txt (accessed 3 October 2008).

13 See Miller (2004), for example.

14 In 'The truth about Jessica', *Guardian*, 15 May 2003.
15 Although news reports gave Ali's age as 12, Addley (2003) suggests that he was actually 11.
16 Telephone interview with Richard Sambrook, 12 December 2009.
17 In fact, the Limbless Association was able to provide treatment and prosthetic limbs for Ali in London, paid for by donations to its fund, but this was only agreed in August 2003 after similar offers from numerous sources throughout the world had been considered.
18 According the *Daily Mirror*, 'A crowd of 100 well-wishers surrounded the vehicle, joined hands and chanted "God is good! God is great! God bless this child!"' (S. Martin, 'God bless this child', 16 April 2003: 4). In the same article, the *Mirror* also tried to claim credit for the involvement of Kuwait: 'Kuwait's government agreed to treat the boy after hearing of an appeal for help in the *Mirror* by Ali's nurse.'
19 Ipsos-MORI, 'War with Iraq: The ides of March', 17 March 2003: http://ipsos-mori.co.uk/content/polls-03/war-with-iraq-the-ides-of-march-poll.ashx (accessed 12 February 2009).
20 Ipsos-MORI, 'Blair losing public support on Iraq', 21 January 2003, http://ipsos-mori.co.uk/content/polls-03/blair-losing-public-support-on-iraq.ashx (accessed 12 February 2009).
21 YouGov, 'Part 6 of War Tracker', 31 March 2003, and 'Iraq War Right or Wrong', 15 June 2007, www.yougov.co.uk/corporate/archives/press-archives-pol-Main.asp?iID=1 (accessed 12 February 2009).
22 Altogether, 17 of 43 newspaper stories covering these demonstrations emphasised 'schoolchildren', 'pupils' or 'truants' in their headlines. Student involvement was also the subject of 21 of the 38 photographs accompanying these stories.
23 These results exclude some groups and individuals who may have spoken against the war but who were not defined primarily as 'anti-war' actors, owing to their other roles. These included religious leaders, humanitarian groups, UN inspectors and international leaders.
24 Substantive debate was present in 29 per cent of 'elite' protest stories (9 stories in all) and 22 per cent of non-elite (four stories).
25 For a list of demonstrations between the invasion and the fall of Baghdad, including estimates for turnout, see Wikipedia: http://en.wikipedia.org/wiki/Protests_against_the_Iraq_War#Invasion_to_the_fall_of_Baghdad (accessed 12 February 2009).
26 Although, arguably, the desecration of war graves should not be associated with anti-war dissent, coverage of this event tended to link the vandalism to anti-war protesters.

8

Conclusion: Patterns of support, negotiation and opposition

Overview

The conclusion starts by drawing together our multi-channel, multi-newspaper analysis, reviewing our aggregate-level findings from each chapter and summarising the overall performance of UK news media. In so doing, we provide a substantive assessment both of British news media performance during the 2003 Iraq invasion and of the implications of these findings for general claims regarding the elite-driven, independent and oppositional models. In particular, we discuss the implications of our results for key debates, set out in Chapters 2 and 3, concerning government sources and media-management operations, the impact of new technology (the media empowerment thesis), ideological shifts since the end of the cold war and theoretical debates concerning media-state relations. Also, we highlight the utility of new institutionalism and field theory in providing a more nuanced understanding of media–state relations, one that is compatible with the findings of this study. We then consider key research questions which should be pursued in conducting further analyses of different stages of the Iraq conflict. We conclude by considering the normative question of how journalists *should* report war. Here we discuss whether journalists can achieve 'better' or 'higher' standards of wartime reporting.

Patterns of continuity: findings consistent with the elite-driven model

At an aggregate level, many of the findings described in the preceding chapters are consistent with the predictions of the elite-driven model, as Table 8.1 shows. Among most news media outlets, coverage was largely supportive of the coalition with military progress reported positively, particular reinforcement given to the humanitarian rationale for war and heavy reliance on coalition sources. Dramatic battlefield visuals contributed to this supportive framing, along with the visual representation of coalition forces as humanitarian warriors and, albeit rarely, pictures that suggested the presence of WMD. The

Table 8.1 Principal findings: evidence for the elite-driven, independent and oppositional models

	Elite-driven model	Independent model	Oppositional model
TV channels	Sky, ITV, BBC	Channel 4	
Newspapers	*Sun, Mail, Times, Telegraph*	*Mirror, Independent, Guardian*	*Mirror, Independent, Guardian*
News subjects	Battle, justifications for war (esp. humanitarian)	Civilian casualties, military casualties, humanitarian operations, law and order	Civilian casualties, military casualties, humanitarian operations, law and order
Case study	Jessica Lynch, anti-war movement	Ali Abbas	Ali Abbas

Jessica Lynch case study provides an 'ideal type' example of the propensity of news media to champion 'good news' stories from the battlefront; moreover, it highlights the eagerness with which the news media snapped up a morale-boosting story in the midst of war. Meanwhile, our case study of the British anti-war movement highlights the boundaries of acceptable dissent at a time when British forces were in action. This marginalisation of anti-war sentiment in media coverage is very much as predicted by the elite-driven model.

In television news, three of the four news programmes surveyed produced coverage that was largely supportive of the coalition, with only Channel 4 News adopting a negotiated stance, largely in keeping with the independent model. Four of our seven national newspapers also offered coverage that was consistent with the elite-driven model. It is worth noting that the newspapers adopting a supportive stance had higher circulation and readership figures than the three papers categorised as independent or oppositional (see Table 4.1), so the coverage that the majority of people read and watched was supportive of the coalition and consistent with the elite-driven model. If we consider the regulatory expectations regarding balance and impartiality to which it is subject (see Chapter 4), our aggregate-level finding of supportive coverage makes it impossible to sustain a claim that the majority of British television news succeeded in achieving balance once war was underway. Indeed, only Channel 4 News appears to have come close to approximating balanced or impartial coverage.

With respect to the recent studies of the 2003 Iraq War reviewed in Chapter 2, our aggregate level findings support Lewis et al. (2006) and their claim that coverage generally supported the coalition, while challenging Tumber and Palmer's (2004) claim that coverage on balance was critical. Tumber and Palmer (2004) are correct in their identification of news media criticism, but this criticism tended to occur only within specific subject categories and among particular news outlets rather than at an aggregate level. Moreover, much of the criticism occurred at a procedural rather than a substantive level. Our findings here offer a bigger challenge to the US-based study by Aday, Livingston and Hebert (2005). On the basis of a reporter approach measure, they concluded that coverage was largely objective in the US news media (besides that of Fox News). Like them, we found that most reporting was straight, but this did not mean that news reports could be described as negotiated or objective. The question raised here is whether Aday, Livingston and Hebert would have found the US news media to be considerably less objective if they had employed a wider range of measures (including the framing of news reports) as we were able to.

Our findings are also consistent with other recent systematic content and framing analyses, all of which highlight the lack of news media independence: Dimitrova and Strömbäck (2005) found US coverage, compared with Swedish coverage, was heavily reliant on official sources and offered a supportive tone and framing toward the US government. Robertson's (2004) study demonstrates the dominance of stories about military achievement at the expense of information about death and destruction; in their analysis of US, British, Czech, German, South African and Al-Jazeera news, Kolmer and Semetko (2009: 654) find that 'the reporting of the war was conditioned by the national contexts in which it was produced . . . [raising] . . . serious questions about the credibility and impartiality of TV news in the reporting of war'. All of these studies highlight how journalists, when their country goes to war, lack independence. Overall, the patterns of deference that are indicated in the work of Hallin (1986), Glasgow University Media Group (1985), Morrison (1992) and Bennett and Paletz (1994), reviewed in Chapter 2, are reflected in our findings for the 2003 Iraq War. In addition, it is worth pondering for a moment the relationship of this scholarly orthodoxy to the politicians and commentators who perceive the role of news media as far more adversarial during war. Clearly, the accusations of anti-war bias that came from some British politicians, discussed in Chapters 4 and 5, were largely unfounded. And yet, these criticisms, and similar ones from other commentators and journalists, are a mechanism by which the elite-driven coverage is maintained. As Herman and Chomsky (1988) describe in their critical analysis of US news media, these criticisms, or 'flak' as they label them, become a powerful disciplining mechanism which serves to keep news media criticism and opposition in check.

What are our findings able to tell us more generally about the elite-driven model? As discussed in Chapter 3, when set within the domain of cases that fit into the category of media-and-war, the 2003 invasion of Iraq can be considered a relatively hard case (or critical case) for the elite-driven model because of the unprecedented levels of political and popular dissent surrounding the conflict. Our discovery that the elite-driven model is still applicable, even in this case, provides strong support for the model and suggests that it is likely to be even more relevant as we move to easier (less critical) cases of news media and war. For example, we might reasonably expect British news media performance during relatively uncontroversial wars such as the 1991 Gulf War and the 1982 Falklands conflict to have been even more consistent with the predictions of the elite-driven model. With respect to the broader domain of media-and-foreign-policy cases, the 2003 Iraq invasion – and indeed any case of news media and war in which the host country is involved – can be considered an easy one for the elite-driven model given the existing state of knowledge about news media deference in wartime. Accordingly, we can expect that the applicability of the elite-driven model will possibly reduce as we move to low intensity conflict, such as that experience following the invasion of Iraq, and non-war situations. Indeed, our evidence for the exceptionality argument (Nacos, 1990) presented in Chapter 6, showing lower levels of supportive and more oppositional and negotiated coverage before and after the invasion phase, gives further support to the idea that the elite-driven model becomes less applicable as we move away from major war fighting circumstances.

With respect to the explanatory variables associated with the elite-driven model – patriotism, the ideology of humanitarianism and, to a lesser extent, reliance upon official sources – these were all found to be relevant in helping to explain why so much coverage was supportive. Here, emerging from our findings are important implications for the importance of news sources and media management relative to patriotism, the impact of new technology (the media empowerment thesis) and the role of ideological factors, namely that of Western humanitarian warfare. We deal with each in turn below.

Sources and government spin vs. patriotism

As discussed in Chapter 3, the indexing hypothesis (Bennett, 1990) and equivalent arguments regarding the pervasiveness of officials among news sources (e.g. Gans, 1979; Sigal, 1973) are a central explanatory component of the elite-driven model. In wartime, the deployment of sophisticated media-management techniques, discussed in Chapter 2, serves to strengthen further the influence of official sources on news reporting. For some scholars, this influence, both during this war and in wars generally, is little short of total. Miller's (2004) edited collection *Tell Me Lies* documents at length the propaganda activities of the UK and US governments and their striking success at shaping news media coverage; Philip Knightley's (2003: 944) updated *The First Casualty* describes the end of any meaningful autonomy for journalists, owing to the combination of sophisticated news media management, embedding and the unprecedented dangers faced by independent reporters. The results from our study, however, suggest that there are more significant determinants of coverage than official sources and news media management.

On the one hand, we found some evidence that official sources and government media-management operations played a significant role in shaping media coverage of the war. Our study identified correlations between the use of official sources and supportive coverage and between embedded journalists and supportive coverage, as well as a largely uncritical acceptance of official claims regarding Iraqi possession of WMD. Each of these trends supports the idea that media-management operations exert an influence on coverage. The case of Jessica Lynch documented in detail one particularly successful instance of news media management. However, as briefly noted in Chapter 5, the importance of sources should not be overstated. Although we found an association between official sources and supportive coverage, we also found that every news media outlet surveyed relied on official sources to a substantial degree, even though some of them produced significant levels of negotiated and oppositional reporting.

For example, even on Channel 4 News, coalition sources represented more than half of those quoted, while no other category of source provided more than 15 per cent (see Table 5.2). Similarly, 43.3 per cent of quotes used by the anti-war *Mirror* came from the coalition, with the next most significant category – Iraqi civilians – reaching only 14 per cent (see Table 5.4). So despite the dominance of coalition sources in the reporting of each news media outlet, we found significant variations between them in the extent of their negotiated and supportive coverage. It follows, therefore, that reliance on official sources and opinions (i.e. the indexing hypothesis) is a variable that is not capable of explaining these variations in coverage by itself. In addition, the presence of three newspapers (*Mirror*, *Guardian* and *Independent*) whose publicly expressed opposition to the war had a measurable impact on the framing and content of their reports poses a further challenge to the indexing hypothesis, which predicts that news media will follow closely the contours of official debate.

Zaller and Chiu's (1999) study of indexing and the co-variation between the US press and political elite (as represented by congressional debate) also raises the possibility that the process of indexing may be more complicated than is generally thought. In their discussion, they note the possibility that a third exogenous factor might be acting on both political elites and the news media, causing each of them to adopt a similar perspective on events:

> Our interpretation of the co-variation between press and congressional opinion is that, in Bennett's terms, reporters 'index' coverage to the range of opinion

that exists in government . . . As far as our data alone are concerned, there is nothing that either supports or refutes this interpretation. The empirical results are equally consistent with the thesis of press dependence on Congress, with a thesis of congressional dependence on the press, and with a thesis that some 'third factor' causes both press slant and congressional opinion, thereby induc- ing a spurious correlation between them. (Zaller and Chiu, 1999: 10)

Zaller and Chiu go on to suggest that this 'third factor' might be a common culture which leads both public officials and journalists to perceive events in the same manner. In our study, the evidence that has emerged for the explana- tory relevance of patriotism is significant here. The role of patriotism could be identified in the positive focus on the progress of British troops and in the rally effect (Mueller, 1973) that we observed as troops went into action and again, briefly, when Baghdad fell to the coalition. At both of these points, cov- erage was overwhelmingly supportive of the coalition with very few instances of oppositional battle coverage (see Figure 6.3). Another notable example of the pre-eminence of the national perspective was the Jessica Lynch rescue in which much of the British news media highlighted the role played by a single British marine commando during the rescue, even though the operation was otherwise wholly conducted by the US military.

Tumber and Webster (2006: 163) may be correct in claiming that 'heroic nationalism holds less of an appeal' today, but any decline in 'blind', jingoistic patriotism did not undermine the primacy of the British perspective or the prevalence of 'banal nationalism' (Billig, 1995) in the reporting of the Iraq invasion. But perhaps the most telling evidence regarding the influence of patriotism lies in the behaviour of the anti-war newspapers – particularly our finding that the anti-war press felt obliged to provide support to British troops once the war got underway. In this unprecedented case, where several national news media outlets chose to oppose a major war that had gained the approval of the British Parliament, the newspapers that opposed the decision to go to war remained committed to expressing support for the troops ('our boys') in their coverage despite their challenge to the policy of war. As a con- sequence of this patriotic support for British troops, the anti-war press still generated a considerable proportion of supportive coverage (we found that the anti-war press was not as critical as the pro-war press was supportive).

The logical inference from this is that, in the context of war, patriotism acts as a more fundamental driver of supportive coverage than does the indexing hypothesis and reliance on official sources. So even when a newspaper adopts an overtly oppositional stance toward government war policy (a situation that is itself at odds with the predictions of the indexing hypothesis), the need to show patriotic support for the nation's troops in action overrides this. We suggest here, then, that our findings provide support for Zaller and Chiu's claim that there is more to the explanation of news media support for political elites than simply journalists' reliance on official sources: culture, and in this case patriotism, appear to be more important.

In weighing up the importance of media management in influencing coverage, a historical comparison is worthwhile: Long before the evolution of the sophisticated approaches to government media management that we witnessed in relation to the Iraq invasion (e.g. coordinated information strategies, embedding, and so on), news media reporting followed similar patterns of deference and support in Vietnam, which was a relatively uncensored and un-'managed' news media war (see Hallin, 1986). So while the arrival of such approaches has had an impact on wartime media–state relations, it remains a limited impact, which stops short of wholesale change.

New technology

Advocates of the media empowerment thesis, discussed in Chapter 2, emphasise the pluralising and empowering consequences of technological advances, including the ascendancy of 24-hour news, 'global' news media such as CNN and Al Jazeera, the Internet and new real-time reporting technology (e.g. video-phones). A key consequence of these developments is that the influence of officials and elites over the news is argued either to be significantly reduced (e.g. Deibert, 2000; Kellner, 1998; Volkmer, 1999), or, according to a more radical interpretation, fundamentally transformed (e.g. Castells, 2009; Hoskins and O'Loughlin, 2010).

Taking the more radical claim first, none of our findings suggest that there has been a paradigm shift in the way that news media cover war, at least during high intensity conflict. However applicable the media empowerment thesis may be to other spheres of media–state relations, claims for the pluralising and empowering impact of new technology are difficult to sustain with regard to news media and war. States may find greater difficulty today in controlling information flows (Brown, 2003: 88; Shaw, 2000; Tumber and Palmer 2006: 17) but reliance on official sources remains paramount in war, as shown in Chapter 5: across news media, including television, press, pro-war papers and anti-war papers, official sources were prevalent. The Internet and related technology may well empower non-elite groups to some extent and perhaps even facilitate anti-war protest (see Cottle, 2008; Gillan et al., 2008) but when British troops are in action dissent remains largely marginalised in mainstream news media. Overall, our findings regarding the extent of supportive coverage and the continued relevance of the elite-driven model caution against any claim that there has been a technology-driven paradigm shift in terms of wartime media–state relations.

The question of whether there has been at least some degree of pluralisation is more difficult to answer, as this study is based on one case. Perhaps the levels of oppositional and negotiated coverage found in this study represent a break from the past, driven in part by technological shifts. In particular, evidence in support of the event-driven news thesis, which came from our findings of negotiated and oppositional coverage of casualties and humanitarian operations (see Chapter 6), could be used to support the idea that new technology has increased the amount of such reportage. But it could also be the case that studies from earlier eras have simply been insensitive to these areas of news media criticism. Further comparative research is needed: by applying the framework established in this study to earlier wars, evidence can be collected that sheds light on whether there has been any increase in negotiated and oppositional reporting and whether this can be linked to developments in communication technology.[1] But, even here, professional autonomy and the particular characteristics of the British news media system are likely to be more important in terms of influencing negotiated and oppositional reporting. Certainly, there is no evidence, and indeed no reason, to suppose that either Channel 4 News or the anti-war press utilised more new communication technology than the ultra-supportive *Sun* or the relatively supportive Sky and ITV News bulletins. In other words, variation in levels of negotiated and oppositional coverage is not explicable through variation in the use of new communication technology.

Overall, a healthy dose of scepticism is called for with respect to the media empowerment thesis and it is worth noting four issues that have led advocates of this thesis to reach exaggerated conclusions. First, if we consider all the comments cited throughout this book which refer to the importance of advances in communication technology, it is clear that such claims are easy to make especially when supported by carefully selected and provocative examples. And yet, when systematic and structured analysis is undertaken, of the type contained here, the impact of such changes appears of much less significance. Livingston and Bennett (2003: 376), in their systematic content analysis of technology-driven news on CNN (between 1994 and 2001) were also led to a much more sober conclusion about the impact of technology: 'When an unpredicted, non-scripted, spontaneous event is covered in the news, the one predictable component of coverage is the presence of official sources' (see also Bennett et al., 2007). In other words, selection bias readily creeps into research and this is arguably a problem with a good proportion of non-systematic analyses that assert the importance of technological changes on news reporting. Second, the media empowerment thesis is often articulated without due regard to the 'disempowering' effect of technological developments. Perceptively, Tumber and Palmer (2006: 82–88) set out the tension between the potential empowering consequences of new technology and the potential for reducing the quality and depth of reporting. Although they do not resolve this tension, their interviews yield insightful comments regarding the downside of new technology. Uwe Kroeger of Germany's ZDF explains:

> Speed is an advantage no doubt, but it can also be a disadvantage when the demand for instant news gets so overpowering that you don't get a chance to do your own work . . . The worst situation is that you are chained to your hotel room with your editor, your picture editors, and your live shot is on the roof of the hotel and that's where you operate from – your hotel room. (quoted in Tumber and Webster, 2006: 85)

In a study of Australian journalists which included 37 interviews and a further 80 survey responses, Faye Anderson (2009: 14–15) is more forthright and concludes:

> Although advanced technologies have liberated contemporary correspondents, they remain captive to new pressures caused by the imperatives of infotainment and the speed of technology. Instant deadlines, 24-hour news, increased syndication and editorial expectations beset the reporters in the field and affect newsgathering, quality reporting and content. . . . In theory the audience receives far more information but much of it is duplicated, repetitive and flawed.

Third, and more broadly, scholars have witnessed previous points in history when technological developments have been heralded as introducing a new era of empowerment and pluralism: The proliferation of TV throughout US society in the 1960s was one driver for the claim, debunked by Hallin (1986), that an adversarial news media 'lost' the Vietnam war; the arrival of 24-hour news and real-time satellite reporting underpinned the CNN effect debate of the 1990s (discussed in Chapter 2) until more detailed research challenged the scope of this effect; finally, the emergence of the Internet during the 1990s drove many to believe that it would radically democratise Western societies only to be significantly moderated by more sober assessments of exactly what the Internet can do. More broadly, the Internet has underpinned a much wider cultural obsession with computer technology and its empowering potential (Golumbia, 2009). What appears to drive these claims is a media-centricism that leads researchers to reach exaggerated conclusions with regard to the independent influence of media. This, in turn, leads to a technological determinism that privileges communication processes to the exclusion of political processes. For example, it is this technological determinism that led much research into humanitarian intervention and the CNN effect to claim that it was media causing governments to intervene during humanitarian emergencies, while ignoring other, more significant, political factors.[2] This takes us directly to the fourth and final point. Claims about a paradigm shift in media–state relations being due to technology are, ultimately, undermined because they rely on the reification of communication technology and sideline the importance of political and social structures within which this technology is situated.

None of this is to say that technological developments have no significance or are not important. What it does suggest is that media-centric biases, and perhaps a desire to 'see' positive and transformative change, lead to a degree of selective use of evidence which overplays the extent to which technologies might drive more autonomous reporting. Ultimately, broader forces are at work, and this could be seen quite clearly in this study regarding the humanitarian justification for the invasion of Iraq. This brings us to the question of new ideological imperatives.

New wars, new ideologies

As discussed in Chapters 2 and 3, ideological processes, whether 'anti-communism' during the cold war or the 'war on terror' since 9/11, are cited by some scholars (Chandler, 2005; Domke, 2004; Hallin, 1986; Hammond, 2007a; Herman and Chomsky, 1988; Jackson, 2005) as key determinants of coverage. Here, ideological or political meta-narratives provide a broad and limiting structure that determines how most people view particular wars. In this study, the influence of a humanitarian warfare ideology could be seen in the near-uniform reinforcement given to the problematic humanitarian rationale for war by all of the outlets examined. Even though there was very little reason to understand the invasion as a principally humanitarian act, the majority of the reports produced by each of the newspaper and TV outlets surveyed were supportive of this official rationale for war.[3] The image of the Iraqi PoW, analysed in Chapter 5, was a powerful symbol of this humanitarian discourse.

Our analysis cautions against claims that the post-Cold War era has witnessed a more independent and adversarial news media because of the decline of ideological imperatives, as suggested by scholars such as Entman (2004) and Hallin (1994) (see Chapter 2). The international spectre of communism may have departed, but it appears to have been replaced by fresh ways to simplify the world which, in turn, generate an ideological bond between policy-makers and journalists. Military action in Vietnam was perceived as self-evidently justifiable by the USA because it was fighting communists, regardless of the consequences in terms of lives lost; in Iraq, most British journalists produced reporting that reinforced the idea, whether explicitly or implicitly, that the invasion was justifiable because Saddam Hussein was a dictator and abuser of human rights. As with Vietnam, the fact that many ordinary people would suffer or be killed in such an operation could be set aside as the regrettable consequence of achieving a 'greater good'. Accordingly, our findings here support the claims made by scholars such as Chandler (2005), Hammond (2007a) and Chomsky (1999) concerning the significance of the humanitarian warfare narrative in shaping post-cold war perceptions.

There are two important implications flowing from the humanitarian discourse, which dominated the coverage we examined. First, despite their problematic legitimacy, the combination of a claimed threat of Iraqi WMD coupled with the appeal to humanitarianism was a powerful political message for British audiences. For the more conservatively orientated sections of British society, following a realist outlook, British forces should be sent into action only when a threat exists to the UK. For these people, government claims regarding the WMD capability of Iraq and the suggestion that it could target UK interests in Cyprus ticked the 'threat to the UK' box. For more liberal and left-leaning sections of British society, following a more liberal and internationalist outlook, the idea that the war could be interpreted as an act of humanitarian intervention courted their support for it. The idea of justifying the war as an act of altruism ensured that anti-war opposition was blunted. In other words, the existence of multiple justifications for war ensured that there was 'something in it for everyone'. Given the outcome (no WMD and over 100,000 dead), it seems difficult not to conclude that the combination of aggressive perception management (or marketing) by the UK government, and the uncritical acceptance of dubious justifications by much of the news media and political establishment, made for a particularly dismal event in British democratic history.

The second issue concerning the prevalence of the humanitarian discourse relates to debate about humanitarian intervention. Whatever the merits are of the CNN effect debate regarding humanitarian intervention during the 1990s, our evidence here is suggestive of a shift in the locus of the humanitarian discourse. Whereas in the 1990s news media themselves might at times have directed calls for humanitarian intervention (Bahador, 2007; Robinson, 2002), by the twenty-first century this narrative – as adopted by Tony Blair, for example – had become a powerful device for politicians seeking to justify and promote interventions that have been conducted for many reasons other than humanitarianism. As discussed in Chapters 2 and 5, the origins of this shift, at least from the British perspective, could be observed in Tony Blair's problematic promotion of the 1999 Kosovo conflict as a humanitarian intervention. With the Iraq War, humanitarianism became a central theme in promoting a war that was not being driven by humanitarian imperatives (see Chapter 5).

Such a transformation in the relationship between humanitarianism, news media and governments is consistent with two major critiques of humanitarian intervention. First, the realist critique maintains that the existence of such a norm ultimately leads powerful states to abuse it by employing it as a convenient excuse to invade and intervene in other states (see Ramsbotham and Woodhouse, 1996). Second, critical realists such as Chomsky (1999) advance a similar criticism although they emphasise class interest, not state interests, as driving intervention.[4] In short, the case of British media and the

2003 invasion of Iraq highlight the extent to which the idea of humanitarian intervention can be exploited and abused by governments.

Reflecting on the media empowerment-ideology debate, our study serves as a reminder that political processes have a bigger impact on media than the other way round. News media reporting, and whatever effect technological developments might have upon that reporting, is created in a context where dominant narratives or master messages shape the overall limits of coverage. Coupled with the overpowering desire of journalists and the public to feel good about themselves, the actions of 'their' soldiers and of their country, comfortable stories about humanitarianism become easily accepted master narratives. In Vietnam, the story was one of saving the Vietnamese people from communism; in Iraq, it was one of saving the Iraqi people from Saddam. Currently, one would presume that a master narrative of 'saving the Afghan people from the Taliban' might be one that informs news media representation of this ongoing conflict.

But our study, as much as it documents many of the shortcomings of news media representation, also provides important new insights into wartime media–state dynamics, and ones which point towards a much richer and more diverse relationship than is often argued to be the case by the existing literature. It is to these important 'exceptions to the rules' that we now turn.

Towards a more nuanced understanding of news media and war: findings consistent with the independent and oppositional models

In the introduction to their *Political Communication* symposium on media–state relations, Bennett and Livingston (2003: 360–1) argue:

> There is no inherent contradiction in the idea that press-government relations are characterized by potentially extreme variations from independence to dependence. Rather than continuing to debate the extremes of [media] autonomy or dependence, it makes more sense to explore the uneasy and often disjointed combinations of the two. Thus, we may find that coverage of the Iraq war of 2003 contained moments of greater independence (for example, questions about government misjudgement regarding the Iraqi embrace of liberation . . .) and greater journalistic compliance with the news management strategies of officials (for example, the near universal celebration of being embedded in – or as Michael Moore put it, "in bed with" – the army . . .).

In turn, they call for a deeper understanding of the mix 'of the two modes of autonomy and dependence' (Bennett and Livingston, 2003: 361). Adding flesh to the bone of these comments, our findings provide precise empirical and theoretical support for the idea of a 'semi-independent' news media (Bennett and Livingston 2003). As documented in Chapter 6, we found a significant quantity of negotiated and oppositional coverage, suggesting that the independent and oppositional models were also relevant to understanding some aspects of news media performance in the case of the Iraq War. In specific subject areas negotiated and oppositional coverage dominated (see Table 8.1).

On television, the coverage provided by Channel 4 News conformed largely to the independent model. Among newspapers, a majority of coverage in the *Guardian, Independent* and *Mirror* could be categorised as consistent with both the independent and oppositional models, and each of these titles adopted an anti-war, oppositional editorial stance. Indeed, the diversity of newspaper coverage that we were able to identify represents one of our most remarkable findings: the 2003 invasion of Iraq was certainly not reported in a uniform fashion by Britain's press. Overall findings for negotiated and oppositional coverage suggest that news media performance is, at the very least, more nuanced and varied than is argued in the major works, discussed in Chapter 2 (Bennett and Paletz, 1994 Hallin, 1986; GUMG, 1985; Morrison, 1992), and in the prevailing elite-driven orthodoxy that exists among scholars. More specific issues concerning the negotiated and oppositional models are raised with respect to the generalisability of our findings, methodology and media–state relations outside the US context.

First, and by comparison with other cases of media-and-war, the 2003 invasion of Iraq can be considered a relatively easy case for these models given the high levels of controversy over the war, which might plausibly have created the conditions for journalists to challenge the coalition. So it is likely, as we move to less controversial wars, that levels of negotiated and oppositional coverage would decrease. Conversely, the invasion of Iraq can be considered a hard case for these models when contextualised within the broader domain of news media-and-foreign-policy cases. In other words, given the prevailing view that the elite-driven model is highly applicable in wartime, we are less likely to find evidence for the independent and oppositional models at times of war than at other times. Our case is, therefore, a critical one for these two models, and finding evidence for them is highly significant: As we move to easier cases (e.g. low intensity conflict and non-wartime), it is likely that we will find that these models hold even greater relevance. Our time series data and evidence for the exceptionality argument (Nacos, 1990) supports this claim in indicating that higher levels of negotiated and oppositional coverage occurred prior to and after the invasion phase. In sum, the fact that we have found evidence for the independent and oppositional models even in the unlikely circumstances of war offers strong support for the relevance of these models.

Second, with regard to methodology, many studies of news media performance have employed aggregate-level measures of news media criticism and limited their analysis to a few news media outlets, and also do not differentiate between news subjects. As Timothy Cook (2006: 164) admits: 'Most studies – including some I have done – assume a bit too blithely that we can judge news media coverage from the prestige press or from outlets with the largest audiences' (see also Goddard et al., 2008). Just as Althaus (2003) found evidence for journalists acting as an important independent source of criticism by differentiating between different types of news discourse (see Chapter 3), our study has also found that a fine-grain analysis revealed greater evidence of criticism than commonly indicated by the elite-driven model: that is, evidence for negotiated and oppositional coverage was established by disaggregating data according to both subject areas and a wide range of news outlets. The possibility raised both by our study and that of Althaus (2003) is that many existing studies in support of the elite-driven paradigm have under-measured news media criticism, by employing aggregate level data and analysing only a few news media outlets. The tantalising question raised is whether much higher levels of independence, both now and in the past, might be revealed in the US context by analysing more news media outlets and subject areas than has usually been the case. Future research in the US context should pay closer attention both to a wider range of news outlets and to specific subject areas.

Third, concerning non-US media–state relations, our results raise the possibility that the elite-driven model is less readily applied outside the US context. The great majority of media–state relations theory, particularly those models associated with elite-driven theory, has been developed and tested in a US context. Within that context at least, the elite-driven model is still considered to hold the greatest explanatory power (see Bennett et al., 2007, for example). However, our evidence for Channel 4 News' conformity to the independent model, and for the editorial opposition to the war maintained by the anti-war press, raises questions about the extent to which it can readily be applied outside the US context without important qualifications.

A brief comparison with the study of US TV news coverage conducted by Aday, Livingston and Hebert (2005) is instructive here. Whereas our study identifies Channel 4 News as an exception to the elite-driven model, conforming instead to the independent model (with oppositional coverage sometimes offered by the newspapers), the Aday study highlights Fox News for its even stronger conformity to the elite-driven model, offering coverage that was patriotic and jingoistic. These findings suggest that there are important differences between British and American television news coverage with the elite-driven model being more applicable to the US context and the independent and oppositional models also applicable in the British context. Further comparative research is warranted to explore these differences.

Moving on to explanatory and theoretical concerns, how do we account for the presence of negotiated and oppositional coverage? Much of the literature discussing news media in wartime, and media–state relations in general, emphasises the importance of structural constraints including the political economy of the news media (Herman and Chomsky, 1988) and the indexing norm (Bennett, 1990). But the evidence here for the negotiated and oppositional coverage provided by a number of outlets gives important support to the hypotheses and theories that underpin the independent and oppositional models: the event-driven news and professional autonomy theses and media system characteristics, the latter two both associated with new institutionalism and field theory. These hypotheses and theories provide much greater scope for understanding journalists and news media as being capable, at least to a degree, of acting independently of elite power.

The influence of uncontrolled events

There were particular subject areas in which negotiated and oppositional coverage dominated – civilian and military casualties, humanitarian operations and law and order (following the fall of Baghdad). Coverage here was often reinforced by visual imagery of destroyed homes, suffering Iraqi people and scenes of chaotic aid delivery. The case of Ali Abbas provides more detailed evidence for the extent of negotiated and oppositional coverage that occurred in response to this particular, widely-publicised civilian casualty story. As discussed in Chapter 6, these findings provide considerable support for the event-driven news thesis (Lawrence, 2000).

However, two qualifications need to be made. First, although such events generated negotiated and oppositional coverage, our data also indicates that this did not translate into more substantive criticism of the war itself. As shown, with regard to the humanitarian and WMD justifications for the war, most outlets produced reports that were largely supportive of the coalition line, and our analysis of coverage following the fall of Baghdad (see Chapter 6) showed little evidence of substantive criticism of the war taking hold. So, in the context of the invasion, event-driven news facilitated a good deal of procedural criticism, which offered a clear challenge to the coalition line, but failed to generate oppositional coverage of the substantive justifications for war. Second, as in the case study of Ali Abbas, despite the criticism that this event generated, the extended and selective coverage of his suffering and 'salvation' came close to becoming a feel-good exercise in charity and compassion, which seemed more directly concerned with how 'we' feel than with taking practical steps to alleviate the suffering of civilians. In this respect, while the impact of event-driven news is significant, it remains a relatively ephemeral and sometimes superficial phenomenon.

Regarding the media empowerment thesis, whether the data here can be taken to support this is not clear cut, as suggested earlier: evidence for the event-driven news thesis could be linked to technological developments, or it might be that earlier research has simply been insensitive to the occurrence of event-driven news. At this stage, and acknowledging the need for further comparative research, we contend that information regarding, for example, casualties is likely to get back to editors and newsrooms with or without the aid of new media technologies. Indeed, news media coverage of earlier wars has been influenced at times by terrible stories of suffering and death from the battlefield. At the same time, just because footage of casualties is available, this does not mean that editors will allow it to be shown (see Chapter 6 and the discussion of visuals). New technologies are not the driving force that many people think they are.

Most importantly, however, the fact that events tend to drive procedural-level criticism, as well as readily being turned around into good news stories, indicates caution regarding the *relative* importance of event-driven news. Here, our findings chime with the analysis by Bennett et al. (2006) of the Abu Ghraib scandal in the USA, in which they assess the relative cogency of the indexing hypothesis, Entman's cascading activation model and the event-driven news thesis. They conclude that critical reporting, which was initially driven by the emergence of the images of Iraqi detainees, was rapidly reigned in as the White House promoted the narrative that the abuses could be attributable to the independent actions of a few 'bad apples'. A story of 'torture' became merely one of 'abuse' (Bennett et al., 2006). In short, event-driven news, while significant, should not be over-emphasised.

Expanding the way we think about news media and war: the professional autonomy thesis, media system characteristics, new institutionalism and field theory

In contrast, more sustained, and therefore arguably more significant, determinants of negotiated and oppositional coverage emerged from evidence pertaining to the professional autonomy thesis and media system characteristics. Here, negotiated and oppositional reporting was not restricted only to uncontrolled events, but expanded beyond these events to encompass patterns of news media reporting across entire news media outlets. Consistent with arguments developed by scholars such as Benson (2004, 2006), Hallin (1986, 1994) and Hallin and Mancini (2004), the field (or institution) of journalism does contain at least some scope for the existence of journalistic professional autonomy. In our case, it was Channel 4 News that offered the clearest example of this: underpinned by its 'alternative' remit, a culture of independent thinking and editorial decisions to use a broad range of sources, it demonstrated a remarkable degree of independent reporting and professional autonomy.

Evidence for professional autonomy could also be found across the British national press and manifested itself in both anti- and pro-war stances. But professional autonomy also interacted with the 'system characteristics' particular to the UK context: that is, a nationally-based, commercial and highly competitive press with a partisan and opinionated culture. Consistent with the assessments made by those strands of new institutionalism and field theory that emphasise the significance of features particular to national media systems (e.g. Benson, 2004; Hallin and Mancini, 2004), the combination of these variables enabled a diverse and relatively plural pattern of war reporting. Also, the comparison described above between our results and those of Aday et al. (2005), which indicated differences between US and UK media coverage, also supports the relevance of the particularities of national media systems.

These findings have important implications for how we understand and theorise news media and war. Primarily, greater attention needs to be paid to professional autonomy and media system characteristics, and the way these act as a countervailing factor to those constraining forces identified by the elite-driven model. At present, most models and hypotheses associated with the elite-driven model pay little attention to this variable and, as discussed in Chapter 3, even those accounts which theorise variability in levels of dependence/ independence (e.g. Wolfsfeld's (1997) 'political contest' model, Entman's (2004) 'cascading activation' model and Robinson's (2002) 'policy-media interaction' model), do so with the qualification that elite dissent must be present before greater journalistic independence and autonomy is exercised. The results here show that, even under the circumstances of war, some journalists and news media challenge governments and political elites. As the war got underway, and when the major political parties closed ranks in support of military action, some news media outlets continued to produce reports and stories that both negotiated and opposed the coalition perspective (although bounded by the need to support British troops) despite the existence of elite consensus. To be sure, there were limits (i.e. patriotism, the humanitarian ideology/narrative) to the degree of independence that could be exercised, but these were not total and, as we have documented, did not prevent coverage that, at times, both condemned the war and graphically highlighted its human consequences. Accordingly, theoretical accounts need, at the very least, to explore professional autonomy and system characteristics as variables that modify the impact of constraining influences such as patriotism and indexing.

More generally, examined in overall terms, the evidence emerging from this study highlights the significance of a variety of factors that act to increase independence, specifically uncontrolled events, professional autonomy and media-system characteristics. But it has also identified important continuities in terms of the applicability of the elite-driven model and the influence of sources, ideology and patriotism. The elite-driven model continues to explain most of what we have observed, but important and significant exceptions provide support to the independent and oppositional models. For those committed to the liberal and critical perspectives on what media *should* do (see

Chapter 3), it is mostly, but not all, 'bad' news. In light of this, when theorising about news media and war (as well as media–state relations more generally), we need to develop ways of understanding the nuances and variations in coverage in a way that does not throw the baby out with the bath water.

In the first instance, new institutionalism (Benson, 2006; Cook, 1998; Sparrow, 1999), associated work on media systems (Hallin and Mancini, 2004) and professional autonomy provide ways of restoring analytical significance to journalists and media as independent actors. In addition, field theory provides a starting point for thinking about both the nuances and variations in wartime reporting and the competing influences (factors/variables) that shape that coverage. Returning to the description provided in Chapter 3, field theory visualises the field or institution of journalism as partially autonomous, with its own rules and structures, but also as being influenced and largely dependent on broader political and economic fields. In doing so, field theory provides a productive and holistic approach to the analysis of the media–state relationship. In wartime, the influence of ideology, patriotism and political elites, understood either as emanating from fields external to news media (such as the 'political' field) or from macro-level influences such as the nation-state, exact a powerful influence on coverage. At the same time, the field of journalism, possessing some level of autonomy, creates pockets of resistance to those forces which 'refract rather than simply reflect the play of external forces' (Benson, 2006: 196). In this study, we found that the degree of refraction was great enough to create, in some areas, outlets and instances, outright opposition to a war that had been supported by the two major political parties in Britain. This study, therefore, provides substantial empirical evidence in support of this holistic approach to understanding the forces that shape news coverage.

Indeed, given that the realm of foreign affairs, and even more so war, is widely believed to be one in which 'news media are most likely to rely uncritically upon the "indexing" provided by official sources' (Cook, 2006: 163), this study offers important 'hard case' support for these strands of new institutionalist thinking and field theory, especially with regard to their predictions with regard to media system characteristics and professional autonomy. Further theory building and empirical analysis, which draws upon, and develop these theoretical positions, promises a productive and insightful approach to exploring Bennett and Livingston's call for a deeper understanding of the mix between modes of 'autonomy and dependence' (Bennett and Livingston 2003: 361).

Further research into the 2003–09 Iraq conflict

In creating a systematic and theoretically-grounded approach to the study of news media and war, our study provides a baseline from which further research can readily be conducted into other cases of news media and war, thereby enabling the analysis of changes over time. But it is also important to keep in mind that this study provides a detailed assessment of one stage, albeit a crucial one, of what became a lengthy military involvement for British forces. Indeed, the withdrawal of British troops from southern Iraq took place only in spring 2009. Moreover, the need for further research has increased as the invasion has come to be seen as a disastrous foreign policy blunder, with repeated and continuing calls for enquiries into how it could have happened. These make an understanding of the performance and role of media even more significant. In order to direct further research into the case of British involvement in Iraq (2003–09), we map out a research agenda, identifying key questions and issues that it would be fruitful to pursue.

Pre-invasion coverage

Starting with the role played by news media in the pre-invasion phase, a major question to be asked of coverage during the run-up to the invasion concerns the extent to which it provided an effective evaluation of the competing arguments over the war. During the months following September 2002, when the government published the intelligence dossier on Iraq's weapons of mass destruction (Prime Minister's Office, 2002), the prospect of war generated a great deal of controversy, leading to the largest ever public demonstration in Britain and much political and news media debate. In their study of British newspapers during sections of the pre-war phase, Tumber and Palmer (2004) found a considerable quantity of what we have called negotiated and oppositional coverage (largely in the same newspapers as we have identified in this study) based on widespread scepticism toward the government's argument for war. Nevertheless, Tumber and Palmer's study raised questions about the extent to which the British news media adequately interrogated American claims of a link between Saddam Hussein and Osama Bin Laden, and about the USA's broader motives for the invasion.

A further key question, indicated by our evidence here that news media largely reinforced – implicitly or explicitly – claims that Iraq's possession of WMD justified an invasion, is the extent to which British news media questioned the government's accounts regarding the presence and threat posed by Iraqi WMD. If it is the case that most news media accepted these claims, aggressively promoted by the British and American governments, the effect may have been to constrain full and open debate because argument over war would have been confined to considering how best to respond to the Iraqi 'threat', rather than whether it existed. In other words, if British news media accepted the substance of the British and American governments' information campaign concerning WMD in Iraq, critical debate may have been restricted, for example, to assessing whether the coalition should act under the auspices of the UN or take unilateral action in order to deal with the 'threat'. Understanding more precisely the parameters of news media debate over WMD will help to determine the extent to which UK news media provided an effective platform for evaluating the case for war. Another important area warranting further inquiry concerns the influence of the humanitarian narrative on coverage during the pre-war phase. Once war got underway, we found that news media coverage overwhelmingly reinforced the humanitarian argument for invading Iraq, but the extent to which this idea shaped pre-war coverage remains unclear and, as such, warrants further research.

It would be worthwhile, then, to extend the analytical framework and methodology employed in this study to the pre-war period, paying particular attention to analyses of the extent to which news media interrogated the WMD and humanitarian arguments for war adequately, and what boundaries there were to such debates.

Post-invasion coverage

Of equal importance is the period following the invasion phase. As even the short span of this study revealed, the news media rapidly adopted a more critical stance towards events in Iraq as immediate post-war law and order problems emerged. Within months, the insurgency dominated reporting of the situation in Iraq and controversy raged on both sides of the Atlantic over the absence of Iraqi WMD and the scandal of American abuse and torture at Abu Ghraib prison. Meanwhile, the levels of conflict and violence in the country were unprecedented and sustained. Altogether, there are many issues and angles that research into news media coverage of Iraq after the invasion could fruitfully give attention to. From the perspective of this study, with its focus on the British political and military dimensions of the Iraq conflict, two issues stand out in particular for further exploration: the failure to find WMD and the way in which the conflict and British involvement in it continued to be represented.

Taking the WMD issue first, we have shown in this study that the British news media largely reinforced the WMD rationale for war during the invasion phase. Yet subsequently, the absence of WMD finds and associated concern over the legal case for war generated significant news media attention and political debate. An exceptional feature of this was the Gilligan/Kelly affair and the ensuing Hutton Inquiry, described in Chapter 4. Of great significance here was the public reporting during the inquiry itself of testimonies of witnesses from the government, security services and news media, and of the paper trail that was created in the process of compiling and editing the September 2002 dossier. While the inquiry was sitting in August and September 2003 and for months afterwards, the news media were able to subject the government's WMD case for war to unprecedented scrutiny, and a great deal of critical reporting emerged as a consequence.

The Gilligan/Kelly affair was just one of a number of media controversies over the government's decision to invade Iraq in the years that followed. Among other issues were criticisms of the preparedness of British troops, the absence of a robust post-war plan for Iraq, the degree to which British forces were able to operate independently of overall US strategic command and the legality of the war. In the latter case, in the face of long-standing criticism that the invasion had breached international law, the government persistently refused to reveal the legal advice given by the Attorney-General, which had been used to justify British participation. Finally, in April 2005, the text was leaked and the government was forced to break with tradition and publish it in full (Goldsmith, 2003). Here, as in the other cases, the story generated much reporting that was critical of the government's case for war. Taken together, these events led to repeated media challenges to the government over the WMD rationale for war, the legality of its actions and broader questions of strategy and geo-politics, suggesting the emergence of a strongly independent and oppositional news media during this period, which effectively held the British government to account. In order to establish the extent to which this occurred, detailed research along the lines conducted in this study would enable a full and accurate evaluation of just how critical parts of the British news media became in this period. In addition, the Gilligan/Kelly affair provides a fascinating insight into the ability of the BBC to remain independent of extreme political pressure and offers the opportunity for an illuminating case study.

As well as the post-war debate over the legitimacy of the original decision to go to war, research also needs to be conducted into the contours of coverage of the continued conflict in Iraq, during which the British military operation centred around Basra in Southern Iraq while US forces led military operations in Baghdad and the remainder of the country. For most of the six years following the invasion, Iraq witnessed low intensity conflict with insurgent action against coalition forces as well as sustained conflict between members of the Sunni and Shia sectarian groups. Estimates of civilian deaths range between 100,000 and 900,000 (Iraq Body Count; Burnham et al., 2006), while over 4,000 US and close to 200 British service personnel were killed. Undoubtedly, this time span is as important as the invasion itself for what it can tell us about the dynamics of news media coverage, and it demands detailed scholarly analysis.

A prima facie case could be made for news media coverage having become increasingly critical and independent during this period: no matter how deferential news media may have been during the 'major combat' phase, the failure to find WMD, the increasing number of casualties and the seemingly endless flow of bad news events, such as uprisings and suicide bombings, may well have generated high levels of negotiated and oppositional coverage. Certainly, politicians supporting the war were quick to blame news media negativity for declining public support for the war, and military officials accused news media reports of fuelling conflict within Iraq itself. Without mentioning Iraq, Tony Blair described the British news media as a 'feral beast' in a speech delivered shortly before his departure from office (Blair, 2007). Notably, he singled out the *Independent* as 'avowedly a viewspaper not merely a newspaper'. In 2004, British Chief of Defence Staff General Sir Michael Walker said 'the media's coverage may have prompted Iraqi insurgents to attack the soldiers'.[5] Debate within academic circles has also suggested that news media coverage of the post-invasion phase has been more adversarial.[6] But there are also grounds for questioning the idea that post-invasion news media coverage would have adopted a less supportive mode. For one thing, there seems to have been a distinction between the way in which US military operations in and around Baghdad and British military activities in the South were represented by British news media. While coverage of US activities continued to involve high levels of combat and conflict, coverage of British operations, according to one British journalist, became far more limited as time passed. Commenting on the withdrawal of British forces from the centre of Basra, Richard Beeston of *The Times* noted that:

> the Brits reduced the numbers [of soldiers], peddling the line that the situation was very calm in the South and we can now hand over to the Iraqis . . . A sort of fiction arose that it is fine now in Basra, we can pull out, and they left 700 soldiers in a city of two million . . . And they were the forgotten soldiers.[7]

The question raised by this suggestion concerns the extent to which the post-invasion news media narrative might have reinforced official British claims – focusing on US military difficulties while presenting a benign image of calm and military control in British-controlled Southern Iraq. Another suggestion – that once a military situation becomes more difficult, a strategy emerges to limit the access of journalists – has also been presented by Channel 4 News' Alex Thomson. Speaking of the Afghanistan conflict, and noting the lack of access for journalists in 2006 when British forces had become involved in high levels of combat activity in Helmand province, Thomson commented: 'The politicians appear to have concluded that the media are welcome to come along for the ride when things are fine, and effectively put out good PR videos – but if it all goes a bit rum then we can just get lost' (Thomson, 2006).

Other journalists have also noted how difficult reporting became for Western correspondents in Iraq, owing to the threat posed by violence. The result, according to Channel 4 News anchor Jon Snow, was a failure properly to report the violent reality of the situation in Iraq.[8] Finally, assessing US news media coverage of Iraq in the post-invasion phase from a scholarly perspective,

Entman et al. (2009) argue that an accountability gap has emerged in which the rising costs of the war are not mirrored in US news media reporting. This, they suggest, is a product of news media deference to the White House, coupled with the declining newsworthiness of casualties. The result has been that 'official good news frames tended to dominate news narratives' (Entman et al., 2009: 689).

Clearly, there is no consensus on the shape and form of news coverage during the post-invasion and low intensity conflict period and further research is necessary here. The analytical framework and methodology established in this study has proved sufficiently sensitive to detect varying degrees of supportive, negotiated and oppositional coverage across time, news media outlets and subject areas. Modifying it and applying it to news media coverage of the post-invasion phase of the war would help to reconcile these competing views. For now, such matters of description and explanation, relating both to the Iraq war and to media–state relations in war more generally, must be left for future discussion and research.

To conclude this study, we return to the normative issues identified in Chapter 3. An important finding from our study is that different modes of news media performance during war, including negotiated and oppositional coverage, are not only possible but actually do occur in practice. These findings are significant because they suggest that factors such as patriotism, reliance on official sources and ideology do not inevitably structure and determine how journalists report war; under certain circumstances, journalists can overcome these pressures. Along with this possibility comes the normative question of what journalists should do. With this in mind, we conclude by drawing on our interviews with journalists in order to outline some of the tensions and possibilities that exist for contemporary war reporting.

The normative debate: realist, liberal or critical news media?

As set out in Chapter 3, the differing modes of news media performance during war (supportive, independent, oppositional) can be legitimated by reference to three normative positions. Distrust of public opinion and an elitist attitude toward foreign policy means that realism, and realists, admonish anything but a highly supportive and, preferably, patriotic news media in wartime. In contrast, faith in public rationality and commitment to democracy even in the realm of international affairs leads liberals to uphold the notion of objective or independent news media in wartime. Critical approaches advocate news media opposition to government in wartime, partly as a consequence of a more fundamental political opposition to the state (i.e. the critical theory position) but also because of a belief in the value of a questioning news media keeping government under perpetual scrutiny.

If realism provides a rationale for the supportive mode of war reporting, we found few journalists who would willingly subscribe to this position. As documented in Chapter 5, journalists regularly refuted the idea that journalists should engage in patriotic journalism, Alex Thomson dismissing such reporting as 'advertising not journalism'. At the same time, the journalists interviewed also recognised the tendency of reporting to be pulled toward the perspective of British troops, ultimately reinforcing a sense of nationalism in the manner of Billig's (1998) banal nationalism. Ultimately, the problem confronting journalists is what Zandberg and Neiger (2005), in analysing Israeli war correspondents, describe as a conflict between two 'contradicting communities' – a national community that demands loyalty and support and the ideals of journalism that demand objectivity and neutrality. Zandberg and Neiger see these positions as inherently contradictory and, especially under conditions of war, suggest that loyalty to the nation is likely to overpower adherence to journalistic norms.

However, although there was ample evidence of the importance journalists attached to the need to report, at times positively, on British troops, they also showed a persistent commitment to journalistic norms of objectivity and balance, defined more broadly than on a national basis. For most of the journalists interviewed, war reporting should be about more than simply relaying the progress of 'our troops'. As members of the community of journalists, attempting to maintain balance, to show all sides and to be 'objective' were also important aspirations. Significantly, some journalists noted their responsibility towards 'other' communities, especially to Iraqi civilians. With respect to objectivity and balance, Bill Neely noted that, even in war, there were 'things that we as journalists hold fast to . . . to try to see the other point of view',[9] while others noted the importance of 'having an independent mind and a determination to tell the truth'[10] and the need to 'cover this thing as objectively as possible . . . [not to] take sides'.[11] With respect to the perspective of ordinary Iraqis, the *Guardian*'s Ed Pilkington indicated that 'good' war reporting should include covering 'the fall-out for civilians'[12] and Richard Sambrook explained the importance that the BBC attached to maintaining reporters in Baghdad:

> We tried to report . . . estimates of civilian casualties . . . We kept teams on in Baghdad in the face of significant danger to themselves and significant political pressure, in order to provide an independent view of how the conflict was affecting at least the capital . . . You do as much as you can, having to operate within parameters of risk and so on.[13]

Indeed, the perceived importance of placing journalists in Baghdad and other locations, so as to ensure that all sides were being covered, was noted by many journalists.[14]

Finally, reporters' sense of a responsibility beyond the community was illustrated in comments about the difficult decisions to be made in determining the extent and scope of coverage of 'distant' conflicts. For example, Alex Thomson stated: 'it troubles you – you know, we had huge debates – when, for instance, we think that . . . the Russell Brand and Jonathan Ross row at the BBC is more important than several hundred people being killed at Goma'.[15] Describing editorial discussions at *The Times* about the use of graphic images at a time of war, Richard Beeston told us:

> There were debates over dead bodies and should we run pictures of PoWs, which I think under the Geneva convention you're not really supposed to. But I also remember saying 'Well, we did it when it was the Iraqis . . . we should run the Americans as well'. . . . There was a bit of pressure on that sort of stuff: 'Is it seemly? Is it tasteful? Is it. . .?' . . . My view is always, 'That's war, you should show it.' Particularly on something that your country is responsible for, you have a duty to show people what is being done in their name.[16]

Tumber and Webster's (2006) interviews with frontline correspondents also highlight the obligation felt by journalists to people beyond their own nation. Indeed, they argue that: 'The prioritisation of the moral and ethical duties of the journalist towards the public and the world in general is part of the professional values framework within which contemporary journalism operates' (Tumber and Webster, 2006: 67). In sum, as much as journalists might accept the pre-eminence of the national perspective, there was also an awareness of a responsibility toward objective reporting and presenting war from all sides.

Overall, it seems indisputable that a tension between 'nation' and 'profession' exists for many, although not all, correspondents in wartime. At the same time, journalists and editors also show a commitment to people beyond the country they live in and to that of their profession, towards what might be described as the 'world community' or, in this case, the 'Iraqi community'. Of course, most of the time, journalists fall short of such independent, negotiated reporting. But the examples where this does occur demonstrate the potential of news media to do more than simply tell the story of 'our boys', at least when enabling conditions exist, such as particular media system characteristics and professional autonomy. By treating official sources with scepticism and being detached from competing views (as seen often with Channel 4 News), by devoting a larger share of the news agenda to civilian casualties and the consequences of war (as amply demonstrated by the anti-war newspapers) and by providing space to non-coalition sources (Channel 4 News in particular), journalists can deliver negotiated and oppositional reporting, even under the difficult circumstances of war.

In the final analysis, the tension that exists between the realities of news media reporting (as shown in this study), the self-perception of journalists that they are striving for objectivity, and the pressures to support 'our boys', need to be more clearly addressed by those working in the news media. This could mean a greater recognition and acknowledgement of those news outlets that subscribe unproblematically to the realist position that war reporting *should* be about our troops. This would require these outlets to be frank about their approach and suspend any notion that they are engaging in 'objective' or balanced journalism. But this would also involve accepting the legitimacy of the realist rationale, which sees little place for informed and open debate in the realm of foreign policy and war.

For those outlets that aspire to higher standards, believing that openness and active scrutiny are beneficial (as argued by the liberal and critical positions), there is ample evidence in this study that a more independent and balanced mode of reporting can indeed be enabled. The central focus for future research should be to understand better those conditions (e.g. professional autonomy or media system characteristics) that facilitate greater levels of independence, and to develop ways to strengthen them. Ultimately, progress in this area might enable those journalists who are committed to the liberal and critical positions to better meet both the expectations of their professional community and the concerns of communities beyond, most importantly those who are at the receiving end of 'our' firepower.

Notes

1 At the time of writing, initial efforts at research of this kind are being conducted by Scott Althaus and colleagues (e.g. Althaus et al., 2008) and we hope that our study will provide a fruitful basis for the development of a fully comparative research agenda.

2 See Robinson (2002) for a detailed evaluation of the CNN effect and intervention during humanitarian crises in the 1990s.

3 For Channel 4 News, despite a large proportion of negotiated and oppositional reports, just over half (57%) were supportive of the humanitarian rationale.

4 Indeed, the damage done to the concept of humanitarian intervention was noted at the time of the Iraq invasion by David Clark (a former Foreign Office special adviser). He argued that the aggressive unilateralism displayed by the USA, and its sidelining of the UN, created a lack of trust in the USA, which, in turn, compromised attempts to create an international consensus on humanitarian intervention (Clark, 2003). Although, subsequently, some success has been achieved in generating an international consensus on intervention (UN World Summit Agreement, 2005; Pattison, 2010), the future of humanitarian intervention remains uncertain.

5 Speaking on *Newsnight*, BBC2, broadcast 9 December 2004 (see http://news.bbc.co.uk/2/hi/uk_news/4083939.stm – accessed 5 January 2009).

6 For example, at the 'Spinning Hutton: In search of the big picture' conference,

sponsored by the *ESRC New Challenges to Security Research Programme*, European Research Institute, University of Birmingham, 20 February 2004.

7 Telephone interview with Richard Beeston, 9 December 2008

8 Speaking in the Zenith/Channel 4 documentary *Iraq: The Hidden Story*, broadcast 8 May 2006.

9 Telephone interview with Bill Neely (ITV News), 12 December 2008.

10 Telephone interview with Patrick Cockburn (*Independent*), 18 December 2008.

11 Telephone interview with Richard Beeston (*Times*), 9 December 2008.

12 Telephone interview with Ed Pilkington, 9 December 2008.

13 Telephone interview with Richard Sambrook (BBC News), 12 December 2008.

14 Telephone interviews with Richard Beeston (*The Times*), 9 December 2008, Ed Pilkington (*Guardian*), 9 December 2008, Alex Thomson (Channel 4 News), 10 December 2008, and Tim Butcher (*Daily Telegraph*), 11 December 2008.

15 Telephone interview with Alex Thomson (Channel 4 News), 10 December 2008. Brand and Ross are broadcasters whose prank telephone calls, made for a late-night BBC radio programme in October 2008, were condemned by elements of the media. As a result, their behaviour became an enormous news story in Britain, overshadowing most other events happening in the same week.

16 Telephone interview with Richard Beeston, 9 December 2008.

Appendix A: Further information about the content and framing analysis

Chapter 3 details the measures devised for our content and framing analysis. Examples of the detailed criteria provided to coders for assessing thematic frames can be found in Appendix B. For those interested in further details, the codebooks devised for the television and press analysis are available at the Economic and Social Data Service (www.esds.ac.uk), entitled 'Content and Framing Study of United Kingdom Media Coverage of the Iraq War, 2003' (catalogue code SN 5534). The databases, detailing all the results, are also available at this site. All of these documents are also available from the authors: piers.robinson@manchester.ac.uk, p.goddard@ liverpool.ac.uk.

How we did it

Coding was performed using a Microsoft Access database, allowing the handling of both text and alpha-numeric data, enabling flexible sorting and interrogation of data, and offering the facility for the export of data to Microsoft Word or Excel for the production of tables and spreadsheets. The database was adapted from earlier ESRC-supported election studies, which developed this approach to analyse sensitive and detailed data from election news content (see Semetko et al., 1991; Goddard et al., 1998). Two coders were trained over a period of five months and spent approximately six months coding, testing and analysing the results.

The sample

All stories related to the Iraq War were coded from the main evening news broadcasts of the two major terrestrial channels, BBC and ITV, and from the 'alternative' Channel 4. We also included a segment from a non-terrestrial 24-hour news channel, Sky News (10.00 p.m.–10.30 p.m.), in our analysis, although we were unable to obtain weekend coverage for this channel. Our unit of analysis was the story and, as Althaus (2003) advocates, we analysed the 'entire population of relevant news stories' rather than sampling within bulletins. In total, our sample contained 1,063 stories from television news.

With respect to newspapers, we coded all editorials, and all major news articles (n = 4449) appearing on the Iraq War pages of seven national newspapers – *Sun, Daily Mirror, Daily Mail, Independent, Guardian, The Times and Daily Telegraph*, and their Sunday equivalents. Owing to the large number of news articles, coders selected the three major news articles from each page of the Iraq War sections of the newspapers. In practice, this ensured that all significant articles were analysed and only brief articles excluded from the analysis. Articles written by experts, 'news in brief' and political sketches were omitted. The occurrence and subject description of the excluded stories (n = 444) were noted in the database.

The coding period was from 17 March to 18 April 2003, beginning three days before the invasion, continuing through the 'major combat' phase of the war, and ending four days after the fall of Tikrit. In addition to the 'major combat' phase, our survey period enabled us to examine pre-war coverage during the controversial Commons vote on military action as well as events following the fall of Baghdad when the issue of post-war law and order rapidly moved onto the news agenda. However, the principal findings presented in Chapters 5 and 6 are for the invasion period itself (defined as 20 March to 14 April) when military action was ongoing.

Reliability

Particular attention was paid to reliability issues in relation to the thematic frames (our main framing measure). One hundred stories were selected at random and subjected to inter-coder reliability tests. As well as testing aggregate reliability with respect to framing, we also monitored coders' identification of the subjects to which these framing codings were applied to ensure that there was agreement over their use. Monitoring at this level of detail was considered useful because it allowed examination of the precise criteria coders used to arrive at their judgement, thus rendering the process of making framing judgements more transparent than is often the case. For example, studies often require coders to decide whether an article is, say, critical or supportive. Even if both agree that an article is critical, 'this still leaves the precise criteria by which each coder decided that the article was critical undisclosed to outside observers' (Robinson, 2002: 138–9). The method employed here, however, sets out the precise criteria (coding frames) by which the coder should assess a story and allows an outside observer to see, for any given story, the precise rationale used by the coder in judging the story. So this method provides an 'explicit, codified and public' (King et al., 1994: 8) approach.

Reliability coefficients, using Holsti (1969), of 0.98 (television news) and

0.93 (newspapers) were reached for coding frames. To eliminate the possibility of chance agreement in the use of a three-point scale, Scott's pi was calculated for the television results and we achieved a reliability coefficient here of 0.95. The rarely-used subject framing and overall story framing measures were subjected to simple reliability testing (i.e. Holsti, 1969). Coding of the other variables (story subjects, story actors, etc.) was subjected to reliability testing also using Holsti's method. Here, owing to the large number of variables (e.g. 18 different story subjects), there was little likelihood of chance agreements and, consequently, Holsti's method is an appropriate indicator of reliability (Neuendorf, 2002). With respect to these variables, a reliability coefficient of over 0.90 was achieved.

Appendix B: Examples of the detailed criteria provided to coders for assessing thematic frames

Coding criteria for the framing of the humanitarian justification theme

Supportive coverage (elite-driven model): Pro-coalition: Reports that include reference to the official moral justifications for the war (democracy and freedom for the Iraqi people) and presented in a reinforcing manner by journalists or without any counter-arguments seriously addressed (i.e. US imperialism, economic (incl. oil) gain, regional influence, US domestic political considerations). Reports may contain unproblematic acceptance of coalition language/ claims (freedom, democracy, liberation, regional stability, world peace). Focus on the past crimes of Saddam might be used to reinforce the official rationale for a moral war.

Subjects likely to be present	Regime change: Humanitarian argument for change
	Humanitarian consequences of war: positive.
Rationale/justification	Humanitarian argument: Saddam continues to repress the people of Iraq/malnutrition and disease (straight or reinforcing).
	Use of sanctions only hurts the Iraqi people; need for military action (straight or reinforcing).
	Outcomes: Democracy in Iraq (straight or reinforcing)
	Moral: War is necessary to prevent further suffering and threat to the world.
	Passing reference to humanitarian argument for war (democracy, freedom [from tyranny]) (reinforcing).

Reporter approach	Straight or reinforcing UK
	Straight or reinforcing US
	Straight or reinforcing COALITION

Humanitarian prognosis	Optimistic

Negotiated coverage (Independent model): Reports dealing with the issue of the humanitarian rationale for war which include coalition viewpoints (see above) and which are balanced against counter-arguments (see below).

Subjects likely to be	Rationale: humanitarian general
present	Humanitarian other
	Humanitarian consequences of war: general
Reporter approach	Mixed, evaluative, straight.
Humanitarian prognosis	Neutral/none or mixed

Or otherwise subjects, reporter approach and prognosis may reflect a mixture of pro- and anti-coalition subjects/ reporter approach/ prognoses as set out above and below.

Oppositional coverage (oppositional model): Reports may include reference to the official moral justifications for the war (democracy and freedom for the Iraqi people) but these will be challenged through deflating commentary/ disdain and/ or sourcing anti-war commentators who provide counter-narrative to coalition narrative. Alternative explanations for the war (US imperialism, economic (incl. oil) gain, regional influence, US domestic political considerations) will be presented in a straight or reinforcing manner. Focus on the inhumane consequences of the war might be used to reinforce the anti-humanitarian war analysis.

Subjects likely to	Regime change: war will worsen situation.
be present	Humanitarian consequences of war: negative
	Imperialist aims UK
	Imperialist aims US
	Oil rights as reason for war
Rationale/justification	Humanitarian argument: The war will worsen
	the situation and create a humanitarian crisis
	(assumed or reinforcing).
	Use of sanctions only hurts the Iraqi people; need
	to reassess but not attack (assumed or reinforcing).

Moral: War is wrong, even if threat is proven (assumed or reinforcing).
To secure oil fields for the West (assumed or reinforcing)
War as beneficial to Bush/rallying for president (assumed or reinforcing)

Reporter approach

Deflating or straight US
Deflating or straight UK
Deflating or straight COALITION

Humanitarian prognosis

Pessimistic

Coding criteria for the framing of the battle theme

Supportive coverage (elite-driven model): Reports dealing with the military situation that are positive for the coalition and emphasizing implicitly or explicitly military *success* (in terms of the coalition winning the war). Reports might include coalition battle successes, presented in a reinforcing manner by journalist (optimistic prognosis) and unproblematic acceptance of coalition language (i.e. liberation).

Subjects likely to be present

Coalition battle gains
Iraqi battle losses
Coalition attack: effective
Coalition attack
Iraqi resistance: ineffective/lack of
Coalition troops morale (pro-coalition tone)
Iraqi troops morale (anti-Iraq tone)
Coalition troops' expertise

Rationale/justifications

Regime change: Humanitarian argument for change
WMD as justification/threat to UK/
45 minutes
Legal basis: Iraq's failure to comply with UN resolutions
Regional stability as outcome of war
Oil in trust fund for Iraqi people
Reference to Iraqi WMD capability (assumed or reinforcing)

	Reference to humanitarian argument for war (democracy, freedom [from tyranny]) (assumed or reinforcing)
	Reference to regional security argument ('safer world') (assumed or reinforcing)
	Reference to Iraq War and 'war on terror' (assumed or reinforcing)

Reporter approach	Reinforcing UK
	Reinforcing US
	Reinforcing COALITION
	Deflating IRAQ

| *Progn* | Optimistic |

*Negotiated coverage (*independent model): Reports dealing with progress of combat that might include problems but which do not offer any clear assessment of *success* or *failure* of coalition. Coalition views might be balanced against evaluative reporting by journalists and or other commentators about the uncertainty of the war.

Subjects likely to be present	Battle: Ground combat/ongoing battle/military situation
	Iraqi troop movements
	Coalition troop movements
	Logistics/supplies
	Other: battle: no appropriate code

| *Reporter approach* | Mixed, evaluative, straight. |

| *Likely prognosis* | Neutral/ none or mixed |

Or otherwise subjects, sources used and reporter approach and prognosis may reflect a mixture of pro- and anti-coalition subjects, sources, reporter approach and prognoses as set out above and below.

Oppositional coverage (oppositional model): Reports dealing with military *failures* (in terms of the coalition losing the war) with clear disdain/critical distance in reporter approach. Coalition language is not adopted, or at least not uncritically, and a pessimistic prognosis is given by journalists/commentators re. the likelihood of coalition success. Anti-war views will be drawn upon and given priority over coalition views.

Subjects likely to be present	Coalition battle losses Iraqi battle gains Coalition attack: ineffective Iraqi resistance: effective Iraqi resistance Coalition troops morale (anti-coalition tone) Iraqi troops' morale (pro-Iraq tone) Iraqi troops' expertise
Rationale/justification	Regime change: war will worsen situation WMD threat does not exist Legal basis: no UN or legal mandate Imperialist aims UK Imperialist aims US Oil rights as reason for war Regional instability as outcome of war Reference to self-interested US power projection (i.e. influence in Middle East) (assumed or reinforcing) Reference to US economic interests in Iraq (oil and reconstruction) (assumed or reinforcing) Reference to domestic sources of US policy in Iraq (assumed or reinforcing) Reference to any other non-coalition/ anti-war explanation for the war (assumed or reinforcing)
Reporter approach	Reinforcing IRAQ Deflating US Deflating UK Deflating COALITION
Likely prognosis (re. battle)	Pessimistic

Bibliography

Aday, S., J. Cluverius and S. Livingston (2005), 'As goes the statue, so goes the war: The emergence of the victory frame in television coverage of the Iraq War', *Journal of Broadcasting and Electronic Media*, 49 (3): 314–31.

Aday, S., S. Livingston and M. Hebert (2005), 'Embedding the truth: A cross-cultural analysis of objectivity and television coverage of the Iraq War', *Harvard International Journal of Press/Politics*, 10 (1): 3–21.

Addley, E. (2003), 'Ali's Story', *Guardian*, 1 August: www.guardian.co.uk/media/2003/aug/01/Iraqandthemedia.iraq (accessed 6 January 2009).

Allan, S. (2004), 'The culture of distance: Online reporting of the Iraq War', in S. Allan and B. Zelizer (eds), *Reporting War: Journalism in Wartime*. Abingdon: Routledge.

Allan, S. and B. Zelizer (eds) (2004), *Reporting War: Journalism in Wartime*. Abingdon: Routledge.

Allen, T. and J. Seaton (eds) (1999), *The Media of Conflict: War Reporting and Representations of Ethnic Violence*. London: Zed Books.

Althaus, S. L. (2003), 'When news norms collide, follow the lead: New evidence for press independence', *Political Communication*, 20 (4): 381–414.

Althaus, S. L., N. Swigger, C. Tiwald, S. Chernykh, D. Hendry and S. Wals (2008), 'Marking success, criticizing failure, and rooting for 'our' side: The tone of war news from Verdun to Baghdad' (paper presented at the 2008 Chicago-Area Social and Behavior Workshop, Evanston, IL, 9 May).

Andersen, R. (2006), *A Century of Media, A Century of War*. New York: Peter Lang.

Anderson, B. (1991), *Imagined Communities: Reflections on the Origin and Spread of Nationalism* (2nd edn). London and New York: Verso.

Anderson, F. (2009), '"Mosquitoes dancing on the surface of the pond": Australian conflict reporting and technology', *Journalism Practice*, 3 (4): 404–20.

Annis, S. (1991), 'Giving voice to the poor', *Foreign Policy*, 84: 93–106.

Badsey, S. (forthcoming), *The News Media and the Art of War – Since Napoleonic Times*.

Bahador, B. (2007), *The CNN Effect in Action: How the News Media Pushed the West Toward War in Kosovo*. New York: Palgrave Macmillan.

Barabantseva, E. (2010), *Overseas Chinese, Ethnic Minorities and Nationalism: De-Centering China*. New York: Routledge.

Baudrillard, J. (1991), 'La guerre de golfe n'a pas eu lieu', *Libération*, 29 March.

Baum, M. A. (2004), *Soft News Goes to War: Public Opinion and American Foreign Policy in the New Media Age*. Princeton: Princeton University Press.

Baum, M. A. and Potter, P. B. K. (2008), 'The relationships between mass media, public opinion and foreign policy: Toward a theoretical synthesis', *Annual Review of Political Science*, 11: 39–65.

BBC News (2007), 'My Iraq: Ali Abbas' (transcript of interview, posted 19 March): http://news.bbc.co.uk/1/hi/talking_point/6458145.stm (accessed 6 January 2009).

Beers, R. and P. Egglestone (2007), 'UK television news', in P. J. Anderson and G. Ward (eds), *The Future of Journalism in the Advanced Democracies*. Aldershot: Ashgate.

Benedetto, R. (2003), 'Poll: Most back war, but want U.N. support', *USA Today*, 16 March: www.usatoday.com/news/world/iraq/2003-03-16-poll-iraq_x.htm (accessed 5 October 2009).

Bennett, W. L. (1990), 'Toward a theory of press-state relations in the United States', *Journal of Communication*, 40 (2): 103–27.

Bennett, W. L., R. G. Lawrence and S. Livingston (2006), 'None dare call it torture: Indexing and the limits of press independence in the Abu Ghraib scandal', *Journal of Communication*, 56 (3): 467–85.

Bennett, W. L., R. G. Lawrence and S. Livingston (2007), *When the Press Fails: Political Power and the News Media from Iraq to Katrina*. Chicago: University of Chicago Press.

Bennett, W. L. and S. Livingston (2003), 'Editors' introduction: A semi-independent press: Government control and journalistic autonomy in the political construction of news', *Political Communication*, 20 (4): 359–62.

Bennett, W. L. and D. L. Paletz (eds) (1994), *Taken by Storm: The Media, Public Opinion, and US Foreign Policy in the Gulf War*. Chicago: University of Chicago Press.

Benson, R. (2004), 'Bringing the sociology of media back in', *Political Communication*, 21 (3): 275–92.

Benson, R. (2006), 'News media as a "journalistic field": What Bourdieu adds to new institutionalism, and vice versa', *Political Communication*, 23 (2): 187–202.

Benson, R. and E. Neveu (eds) (2004), *Bourdieu and the Journalistic Field*. Cambridge: Polity.

Billig, M. (1995), *Banal Nationalism*. London: Sage.

Blair, T. (1999), 'Doctrine of the International Community' (speech to the Economic Club of Chicago, Hilton Hotel, Chicago, USA, 22 April): www.fco.gov.uk/en/newsroom/latest-news/?view=Speech&id=2149376 (accessed 8 April 2009).

Blair, T. (2007), 'Full text: Blair on the media' (BBC News), 12 June: http://news.bbc.co.uk/1/hi/uk_politics/6744581.stm (accessed 30 October 2009).

Blix, H. (2003), 'Hans Blix's briefing to the security council', *Guardian*, 14 February: www.guardian.co.uk/world/2003/feb/14/iraq.unitednations1 (accessed 5 October 2009).

Bluth, C. (2005), '"Iraq: Blair's mission impossible": A rejoinder to Paul Hoggett', *British Journal of Politics and International Relations*, 7 (4): 598–602.

Boorstin, D. J. (1962), *The Image: A Guide to Pseudo-Events in America*. New York: Atheneum.

Bourdieu, P. (1998), *On Television*. New York: New Press.

Boyd-Barrett, O. (2004), 'Understanding: The second casualty', in S. Allen and B. Zelizer (eds), *Reporting War: Journalism in Wartime*. Abingdon: Routledge.

Bragg, R. (2003), *I Am a Soldier, Too: The Jessica Lynch Story*. New York: Random House.

Broadcasting Act 1990 (c. 42). London: HMSO.

Brody, R. A. (1994), 'Crisis, war and public opinion: The media and public support for the President', in W. L. Bennett and D. L. Paletz (eds), *Taken by Storm: The Media, Public Opinion, and US Foreign Policy in the Gulf War*. Chicago: University of Chicago Press.

Brown, R. (2003), 'Spinning the war: Political communications, information operations and public diplomacy in the War on Terrorism', in D. Thussu and D. Freedman (eds), *War and the Media: Reporting Conflict 24/7*. London: Sage.

Burnham, G., R. Lafta, S. Doocy and L. Roberts (2006), 'Mortality after the 2003 invasion of Iraq: A cross-sectional cluster sample survey', *The Lancet*, 368 (9545): 1421–8.

Bush, G. W. (2003), 'Full text: Bush speech aboard the USS Abraham Lincoln', 1 May: www.washingtonpost.com/ac2/wp-dyn/A2627–2003May1 (accessed 18 April 2009).

Carruthers, S. L. (2000), *The Media at War: Communication and Conflict in the Twentieth Century*. Basingstoke: Macmillan.

Castells, M. (2009), *Communication Power*. Oxford: Oxford University Press.

Chandler, D. (2005), *From Kosovo to Kabul and Beyond: Human Rights and International Intervention* (2nd edn). London: Pluto Press.

Chinni, D. (2003), 'Jessica Lynch: Media myth-making in the Iraq War', *Project for Excellence in Journalism* (posted 23 June): www.journalism.org/node/223 (accessed 6 November 2008.)

Chomsky, N. (1999), *The New Military Humanism: Lessons from Kosovo*. Monroe, ME: Common Courage Press.

Chouliaraki, L. (2006), *The Spectatorship of Suffering*. London: Sage.

Clark, D. (2003), 'Iraq has wrecked our case for humanitarian wars', *Guardian*, 12 August: www.guardian.co.uk/politics/2003/aug/12/iraq.iraq1 (accessed 1 November 2009).

Cloud, D. L. (2004), '"To veil the threat of terror": Afghan women and the <clash of civilisations> in the imagery of the US war on terrorism', *Quarterly Journal of Speech*, 90 (3): 285–306.

Cook, T. E. (1998), *Governing with the News: The News Media as a Political Institution*. Chicago: University of Chicago Press.

Cook, T. E. (2006), 'The news media as a political institution: Looking backward and looking forward', *Political Communication*, 23 (2): 159–71.

Cordesman, A. H. (2003) *The Iraq War: A Working Chronology*, Center for Strategic and International Studies: www.csis.org/index.php?option=com_csis_pubs&task=view&id=1770 (accessed 7 April 2009).

Cortell, A.P, R.M. Eisinger and S.L. Althaus (2009), 'Why embed? Explaining the Bush administration's decision to embed reporters in the 2003 invasion of Iraq', *American Behavioral Scientist*, 52 (5): 657–77.

Cottle, S. (2006), *Mediatized Conflict: Developments in Media and Conflict Studies.* Maidenhead: Open University Press.

Cottle, S. (2008), 'Reporting demonstrations: The changing media politics of dissent', *Media, Culture and Society*, 30 (6): 853–72.

Cox, R. W. (1981), 'Social forces, states and world orders: Beyond International Relations theory', *Millennium Journal of International Studies*, 10 (2): 126–55.

Cozens, C. (2003a), '4m in Europe sign up for al-Jazeera', *Guardian*, 26 March: www.guardian.co.uk/media/2003/mar/26/iraq.iraqandthemedia (accessed 6 September 2009).

Cozens, C. (2003b), '*Daily Mirror* sales fall below 2m', *Guardian*, 11 April: www.guardian.co.uk/media/2003/apr/11/pressandpublishing.mirror (accessed 6 September 2009).

Cozens, C. (2003c), 'Sky war news left big impression', *Guardian*, 23 May: www.guardian.co.uk/media/2003/may/23/Iraqandthemedia.broadcasting (accessed 17 June 2008).

Curran, J. and J. Seaton (2003), *Power Without Responsibility: The Press, Broadcasting, and New Media in Britain* (6th edn). London: Routledge.

Cushion, S. (2007), 'Protesting their apathy? An analysis of British press coverage of young anti-Iraq War protesters', *Journal of Youth Studies*, 10 (4): 419–37.

Deacon, D. (2004), 'Politicians, privacy and media intrusion', *Parliamentary Affairs* 57 (1): 9–24.

Deibert, R. (2000), 'International plug 'n play: Citizen activism, the Internet and global public policy', *International Studies Perspectives*, 1 (3): 255–72.

Department of National Heritage (1996), 'Broadcasting: Agreement dated the 25th day of January 1996 between Her Majesty's Secretary of State for National Heritage and the British Broadcasting Corporation': www.bbcgovernorsarchive.co.uk/about/agreement.pdf (accessed 20 December 2008).

Der Derian, J. (2009), *Virtuous War: Mapping the Military-Industrial-Media-Entertainment Network* (2nd edn). New York: Routledge.

Dimitrova, D. V. and J. Strömbäck (2005), 'Mission accomplished? Framing of the Iraq war in the elite newspapers in Sweden and the United States', *Gazette*, 67 (5): 399–417.

Dimitrova, D. V., L. L. Kaid, A. P. Williams and K. D. Trammell (2005), 'War on the web: The immediate news framing of Gulf War II', *Harvard International Journal of Press/Politics*, 10 (1): 22–44.

Dimitrova, D. V. and M. Neznanski (2006), 'Online journalism and the war in cyberspace: A comparison between U.S. and international newspapers', *Journal of Computer-Mediated Communication*, 12 (1): article 13.

Domke, D. (2004), *God Willing?: Political Fundamentalism in the White House, the 'War on Terror' and the Echoing Press.* London: Pluto Press.

Dyke, G. (2005), *Greg Dyke: Inside Story.* London: HarperCollins.

Entman, R. M. (1991), 'Framing US coverage of international news: Contrasts in narratives of the KAL and Iran Air incidents', *Journal of Communication*, 41 (4): 6–27.

Entman, R. M. (2000), 'Declarations of independence: The growth of media power after the Cold War', in B. L. Nacos, R. Y. Shapiro and P. Isernia (eds), *Decision Making in a Glass House: Mass Media, Public Opinion and American and European Foreign Policy in the 21st Century*. Lanham, MD: Rowman and Littlefield.

Entman, R. M. (2003), 'Cascading activation: Contesting the White House's frame after 9/11', *Political Communication*, 20 (4): 415–32.

Entman, R. M. (2004), *Projections of Power: Framing News, Public Opinion and US Foreign Policy*. Chicago: University of Chicago Press.

Entman, R. M. and B. I. Page (1994), 'The news before the Storm: The Iraq War debate and the limits to media independence', in W. L. Bennett and D. L. Paletz (eds), *Taken by Storm: The Media, Public Opinion, and US Foreign Policy in the Gulf War*. Chicago: University of Chicago Press.

Entman, R. M., S. Livingston and J. Kim (2009), 'Doomed to repeat: Iraq news, 2002–2007', *American Behavioral Scientist*, 52 (5): 689–708.

Fahmy, S. (2007), '"They took it down": Exploring determinants of visual reporting in the toppling of the Saddam statue in national and international newspapers', *Mass Communication and Society*, 10 (2): 143–70.

Fahmy, S. and D. Kim (2008), 'Picturing the Iraq War: Constructing the image of war in the British and U.S. press', *International Communication Gazette*, 70 (6): 443–62.

Flyvbjerg, B. (2006), 'Five misunderstandings about case-study research', *Qualitative Inquiry*, 12 (2): 219–45.

Friel, H. and R. A. Falk (2007), *The Record of the Paper: How the New York Times Misreports US Foreign Policy*. London and New York: Verso.

Gans, H. (1979), *Deciding What's News: A Study of CBS Evening News, NBC Nightly News, Newsweek and Time*. New York: Pantheon.

Gavin, N. T. (2007), *Press and Television in British Politics: Media, Money and Mediated Democracy*. Basingstoke: Palgrave Macmillan.

Gellner, E. (1983), *Nations and Nationalism*. Oxford: Basil Blackwell.

Gillan, K., J. Pickerill and F. Webster (2008), *Anti-War Activism: New Media and Protest in the Information Age*. Basingstoke: Palgrave Macmillan.

Gitlin, T. (1980), *The Whole World is Watching: Mass Media in the Making and Unmaking of the Left*. Berkeley: University of California Press.

Glasgow University Media Group (1985), *War and Peace News*. Milton Keynes: Open University Press.

Goddard, P., P. Robinson and K. Parry (2008), 'Patriotism meets plurality: Reporting the 2003 Iraq War in the British press', *Media, War and Conflict*, 1 (1): 7–27.

Goddard, P., M. Scammell and H. Semetko (1998), 'Too much of a good thing: Television in the 1997 election campaign', in I. Crewe, B. Gosschalk and J. Bartle (eds), *Political Communications: The General Election Campaign of 1997*. London: Frank Cass.

Goldsmith, Baron P. (2003), 'Iraq: Resolution 1441' (Legal advice to the Prime Minister prior to the invasion of Iraq, 7 March): http://news.bbc.co.uk/1/shared/bsp/hi/pdfs/28_04_05_attorney_general.pdf (accessed 20 April 2009).

Golumbia, D. (2009), *The Cultural Logic of Computation*. Cambridge, Mass.: Harvard University Press.

Gordon, M. and B. Trainor (2007), *Cobra II: The Inside Story of the Invasion and Occupation of Iraq*. London: Atlantic.

Gowing, N. (1994), 'Real time television coverage of armed conflicts and diplomatic crises: Does it pressure or distort foreign policy decisions', The Joan Shorenstein Center on the Press, Politics and Public Policy at Harvard University, Working Paper Series.

Greenslade, R. (2003), 'Their master's voice', *Guardian*, 17 February: www.guardian. co.uk/media/2003/feb/17/mondaymediasection.iraq (accessed 3 September 2009).

Greenspan, A. (2007), *The Age of Turbulence: Adventures in a New World*. New York: Penguin.

Griffin, M. (2004), 'Picturing America's "War on Terrorism" in Afghanistan and Iraq: Photographic motifs as news frames', *Journalism*, 5 (4): 381–402.

Groeling, T. and M. A. Baum (2008), 'Crossing the water's edge: Elite rhetoric, media coverage, and the rally-round-the-flag phenomenon', *Journal of Politics*, 70 (4): 1065–85.

Habermas, J. (1989), *The Structural Transformation of the Public Sphere: An Inquiry into a Category of Bourgeois Society* (trans. T. Burger). Cambridge, Mass: MIT Press.

Haigh, M.M., M. Pfau, J. Danesi, R. Tallmon, T. Bunko, S. Nyberg, B. Thompson, C. Babin, S. Cardella, M. Mink and B. Temple (2006), 'A comparison of embedded and nonembedded print coverage of the US invasion and occupation of Iraq', *Harvard International Journal of Press/Politics* 11 (2): 139–53.

Hall, S. (1973), 'A world at one with itself', in S. Cohen and J. Young (eds), *The Manufacture of News: Social Problems, Deviance and the Mass Media*. London: Constable.

Hallin, D. C. (1984), 'The media, the war in Vietnam and political support: A critique of the thesis of an oppositional media', *Journal of Politics*, 46 (1): 2–24.

Hallin, D. C. (1986), *The Uncensored War: The Media and Vietnam*. Berkeley: University of California Press.

Hallin, D. C. (1994), *We Keep America on Top of the World: Television Journalism and the Public Sphere*. New York: Routledge.

Hallin, D. C. (2000), 'Commercialism and professionalism in the American news media', in J. Curran & M. Gurevitch (eds), *Mass Media and Society* (3rd edn). London: Arnold.

Hallin, D. C. and P. Mancini (2004), *Comparing Media Systems: Three Models of Media and Politics*. Cambridge: Cambridge University Press.

Hammond, P. (2007a), *Framing Post-Cold War Conflicts: The Media and International Intervention*. Manchester: Manchester University Press.

Hammond, P. (2007b), *Media, War and Postmodernity*. Abingdon: Routledge.

Hansard (2003a), HC (series 5) vol. 401, cols. 726–8 (17 March): www.publications. parliament.uk/pa/cm200203/cmhansrd/vo030317/debtext/30317–33.htm#30317–33_spnew0 (accessed 5 October 2009).

Hansard (2003b), 'Ali Ismaeel Abbas of Baghdad', HC EDM 1046 (2002–03): http:// edmi.parliament.uk/EDMi/EDMDetails.aspx?EDMID=23221&SESSION=681 (accessed 7 January 2009).

Hansard (2003c), HC (series 5) vol. 403, cols. 618, 620 (14 April): www.publications.parliament.uk/pa/cm200203/cmhansrd/vo030414/debtext/30414-06.htm#30414-06_spnew0 (accessed 7 January 2009).

Hansen, A., S. Cottle, R. Negrine and C. Newbold (1998), *Mass Communication Research Methods*. New York: New York University Press.

Hardy, J. (2008), *Western Media Systems*. Abingdon: Routledge.

Hargreaves, I. and J. Thomas (2002), *New News, Old News*. London: Independent Television Commission/Broadcasting Standards Commission.

Herman, E. and N. Chomsky (1988), *Manufacturing Consent: The Political Economy of the Mass Media*. New York: Pantheon.

Herrera, G. L. (2002), 'The politics of bandwidth: International political implications of a global digital information network', *Review of International Studies*, 28 (1): 93–122.

Herring, E and P. Robinson (2003), 'Too polemical or too critical?: Chomsky on the study of news media and US foreign policy', *Review of International Studies*, 29 (4): 553–68.

Hoge Jr., J. F. (1994), 'Media pervasiveness', *Foreign Affairs*, 73 (4): 136–44.

Holland, P. (2004), 'Little Ali and other rescued children', in D. Miller (ed), *Tell Me Lies: Propaganda and Media Distortion in the Attack on Iraq*. London: Pluto.

Holsti, O. R. (1969), *Content Analysis for the Social Sciences and Humanities*. Reading, MA: Addison-Wesley.

Holsti, O. R. (1992), 'Public opinion and foreign policy: Challenges to the Almond-Lippman consensus', *International Studies Quarterly*, 36 (4): 439–66.

Hoskins, A. (2004), *Televising War: From Vietnam to Iraq*. London: Continuum.

Hoskins, A. and B. O'Loughlin (2010), *War and Media: The Emergence of Diffused War*. Cambridge: Polity.

Hoskins, A., B. Richards and P. Seib (2008), 'Editorial', *Media, War and Conflict*, 1 (1): 5–7.

ICISS (2001), *The Responsibility to Protect* (Report of the International Commission on Intervention and State Sovereignty): www.iciss.ca/pdf/Commission-Report.pdf (accessed 20 April 2009).

Ignatieff, M. (2000), *Virtual War: Kosovo and Beyond*. London: Chatto and Windus.

Iraq Body Count: www.iraqbodycount.org/ (accessed 20 December 2008).

Iyengar, S. and A. Simon (1994), 'News coverage of the Gulf crisis and public opinion: A study of agenda-setting, priming and framing', in W. L. Bennett and D. L. Paletz (eds), *Taken by Storm: The Media, Public Opinion, and US Foreign Policy in the Gulf War*. Chicago: University of Chicago Press.

Jackson, R. (2005), *Writing the War on Terrorism: Language, Politics and Counter-Terrorism*. Manchester: Manchester University Press.

Johnson, T. J. and Fahmy, S. (2009), 'Embeds' perceptions of censorship: Can you criticise a soldier then have breakfast with him in the morning?', *Mass Communication and Society*, 12 (1): 52–77.

Kalb, M. (1994), 'Provocations: A view from the press', in W. L. Bennett and D. L. Paletz (eds), *Taken by Storm: The Media, Public Opinion, and US Foreign Policy in the Gulf War*. Chicago: University of Chicago Press.

Kampfner, J. (2003), *Blair's Wars*. London: Free Press.

Katovsky, B. and T. Carlson (2003), *Embedded: The Media at War in Iraq*. Guilford, CT: Lyons Press.

Keane, J. (1998), *Civil Society: Old Images, New Visions*. Cambridge: Polity.

Kellner, D. (1998), 'Intellectuals, the new public spheres, and techno-politics', in C. Toulouse and T. W. Luke (eds), *The Politics of Cyberspace: A New Political Science Reader*. New York: Routledge.

Kelly, T. W. (1994), 'Provocations: A view from the military', in W. L. Bennett and D. L. Paletz (eds), *Taken by Storm: The Media, Public Opinion, and US Foreign Policy in the Gulf War*. Chicago: University of Chicago Press.

King, C. and P. M. Lester (2005), 'Photographic coverage during the Persian Gulf and Iraqi wars in three US newspapers', *Journalism & Mass Communication Quarterly*, 82 (3): 623–37.

King, G., R. O. Keohane and S. Verba (1994), *Designing Social Inquiry: Scientific Inference in Qualitative Research*. Princeton, NJ: Princeton University Press.

Knightley, P. (2003), *The First Casualty: The War Correspondent as Hero, Propagandist and Myth-Maker from the Crimea to Iraq* (updated edn). London: André Deutsch.

Kolmer, C. and H. A. Semetko (2009), 'Framing the Iraq War: Perspectives from American, U.K., Czech, German, South African, and Al-Jazeera news', *American Behavioral Scientist*, 52 (5): 643–56.

Konstantinidou, C. (2008), 'The spectacle of suffering and death: The photographic representation of war in Greek newspapers', *Visual Communication*, 7 (2): 143–69.

Kuhn, R. (2007), *Politics and the Media in Britain*. Basingstoke: Palgrave Macmillan.

Kumar, D. (2004), 'War propaganda and the (ab)uses of women: Media constructions of the Jessica Lynch story', *Feminist Media Studies*, 4 (3): 297–313.

Lawrence, R. G. (2000), *The Politics of Force: Media and the Construction of Police Brutality*. Berkeley: University of California Press.

Lewis, J., R. Brookes, N. Mosdell and T. Threadgold (2003), 'Embeds or in-beds?' BBC/Cardiff School of Journalism.

Lewis, J., R. Brookes, N. Mosdell and T. Threadgold (2006), *Shoot First and Ask Questions Later: Media Coverage of the 2003 Iraq War*. New York: Peter Lang.

Lewis, J., S. Inthorn and K. Wahl-Jorgensen (2005), *Citizens or Consumers? What the Media Tell Us About Political Participation*. Buckingham: Open University Press.

Liebes, T. (1997), *Reporting the Arab-Israeli Conflict: How Hegemony Works*. London and New York: Routledge.

Lindner, A. M. (2009), 'Among the troops: Seeing the Iraq war through three journalistic vantage points', *Social Problems*, 56 (1): 21–48.

Lippmann, W. (1955), *Essays in the Public Philosophy*. Boston: Little, Brown.

Livingston, S. and W. L. Bennett (2003), 'Gatekeeping, indexing and live-event news: Is technology altering the construction of news?', *Political Communication*, 20 (4): 363–80.

Luther, C. A. and M. M. Miller (2005), 'Framing of the 2003 US-Iraq War demonstrations: An analysis of news and partisan texts', *Journalism & Mass Communication Quarterly*, 82 (1): 78–96.

Lynch J. (2007), Statement at hearing by Committee on Oversight and Government

Reform, US House of Representatives, 24 April: http://oversight.house.gov/documents/20070424110022.pdf (accessed 3 October 2008).

Mandelbaum, M. (1994), 'The Reluctance to Intervene', *Foreign Policy*, 95: 3–18.

Major, L. H. and D. D. Perlmutter (2005), 'The fall of a pseudo-icon: The toppling of Saddam Hussein's statue as image management', *Visual Communication Quarterly*, 12 (1): 38–45.

Maltby, S. (2007), 'Communicating war: Strategies and implications', in S. Maltby and R. Keeble (eds), *Communicating War: Memory, Media and Military*. Bury St Edmunds: Arima.

Matheson, D. and S. Allan (2009), *Digital War Reporting*. Cambridge: Polity.

McClellan, S. (2008), *What Happened: Inside the Bush White House and Washington's Culture of Deception*. New York: PublicAffairs.

McLeod, D. M. and B. H. Detenber (1999) 'Framing effects of television news coverage of social protest', *Journal of Communication*, 49 (3): 3–23.

McQuail, D. (2006), 'On the Mediatization of War', *International Communication Gazette*, 68 (2): 107–118.

Mermin, J. (1999), *Debating War and Peace: Media Coverage of US Intervention in the Post-Vietnam Era*. Princeton: Princeton University Press.

Meyer, C. (2005), *DC Confidential: The Controversial Memoirs of Britain's Ambassador to the US at the Time of 9/11 and the Iraq War*. London: Weidenfeld & Nicolson.

Michalski, M. and J. Gow (2007), *War, Image and Legitimacy: Viewing Contemporary Conflict*. New York and London: Routledge.

Milbank, D. and C. Deane (2003), 'Hussein link to 9/11 lingers in many minds', *Washington Post*, 6 September: A01.

Miller, D. (ed.) (2004), *Tell Me Lies: Propaganda and Media Distortion in the Attack on Iraq*. London: Pluto.

Minear, L., C. Scott and R. Weiss (1996), *The News Media, Civil Wars and Humanitarian Action*. Boulder, CO: Lynne Rienner.

Ministry of Justice (2004), 'Investigation into the Circumstances Surrounding the Death of Dr David Kelly, conducted by the Right Honourable Lord Hutton' (The Hutton Inquiry): www.the-hutton-inquiry.org.uk/index.htm (accessed 19 July 2005).

Mirzoeff, N. (2005), *Watching Babylon: The War in Iraq and Global Visual Culture*. New York: Routledge.

Mitchell, W. J. T. (1994), *Picture Theory: Essays on Verbal and Visual Communication*. Chicago: University of Chicago Press.

Mitchell, W. J. T. (2002). 'Showing seeing: A critique of visual culture', *Journal of Visual Culture*, 1 (2): 165–81.

Moeller, S. D. (1999), *Compassion Fatigue: How the Media Sell Disease, Famine, War and Death*. New York: Routledge.

Moorcroft, P. L. and P. M. Taylor (2008), *Shooting the Messenger: The Political Impact of War Reporting*. Dulles, VA: Potomac.

Morgan, P. (2005), *The Insider: The Private Diaries of a Scandalous Decade*. London: Ebury Press.

Morrison, D. E. (1992), *Television and the Gulf War*. London: John Libbey.

Morrison, D. (2004), '45 minutes from doom', *Labour and Trade Union Review*, 132: http://ltureview.com/user/story.php?id=106 (accessed 5 October 2009).

Morrison, D. E. and H. Tumber (1988), *Journalists at War: The Dynamics of News Reporting During the Falklands Conflict*. London: Sage.

Mueller, J. E. (1973), *War, Presidents and Public Opinion*. New York: John Wiley.

Murdock, G. (1973), 'Political deviance: The press presentation of a militant mass demonstration', in S. Cohen and J. Young (eds), *The Manufacture of News: Social Problems, Deviance and the Mass Media*. London: Constable.

Murray, A. and German, L. (2005), *Stop the War: The Story of Britain's Biggest Mass Movement*. London: Bookmarks.

Murray, C., K. Parry, P. Robinson and P. Goddard (2008), 'Reporting dissent in wartime: British press, the anti-war movement and the 2003 Iraq War', *European Journal of Communication*, 23 (1): 7–27.

Nacos, B. L. (1990), *The Press, Presidents and Crises*. New York: Columbia University Press.

Neuendorf, K. A. (2002), *The Content Analysis Guidebook*. Thousand Oaks, CA.: Sage.

Nixon, R. M. (1978), *Memoirs*. New York: Grossett and Dunlap.

Nye Jr, J. S. (1999), 'Redefining the National Interest', *Foreign Affairs*, 78 (4): 22–35.

Palmer, J. (2005), 'Review article: Media performance and war efforts', *European Journal of Communication*, 20 (3): 379–86.

Parry, K. (2009), '"Our disgust will make us stronger": UK press representations of PoWs in the 2003 Iraq war', in C. Alvares (ed), *Representing Culture: Essays on Identity, Visuality and Technology*. Newcastle-upon-Tyne: Cambridge Scholars.

Pattison, J. (2010), *Humanitarian Intervention and the Responsibility to Protect: Who Should Intervene?* Oxford: Oxford University Press.

Pfau, M., M. M. Haigh, M. Gettle, M. Donnelly, G. Scott, D. Warr and E. Wittenberg (2004), 'Embedding journalists in military combat units: Impact on newspaper story frames and tone', *Journalism and Mass Communication Quarterly*, 81 (1), 74–88.

Pincus, W. (2008), 'Records could shed light on Iraq Group', *Washington Post*, June 9, p. A15: www.washingtonpost.com/wp-dyn/content/article/2008/06/08/AR2008060801819.html (accessed 24 November 2008).

Pin-Fat, V. and M. Stern (2005), 'The scripting of Private Jessica Lynch: Biopolitics, gender and the "feminization" of the US military', *Alternatives*, 30 (1): 25–53.

Potter, M. (2003), 'The real "Saving Pte. Lynch"', *Toronto Star*, 5 May: A.01.

Priest, D., W. Booth and S. Schmidt (2003), 'A broken body, a broken story, pieced together', *Washington Post*, 17 June: A01.

Prime Minister's Office (2002), *Iraq's Weapons of Mass Destruction: The Assessment of the British Government*, 24 September: www.number-10.gov.uk/output/Page281.asp (accessed 5 October 2009).

Prime Minister's Office (2003), *Iraq – Its Infrastructure of Concealment, Deception and Intimidation*, 3 February: www.number10.gov.uk/Page1470 (accessed 18 April 2009).

Ramsbotham, O. and T. Woodhouse (1996), *Humanitarian Intervention in Contemporary Conflict*. Cambridge: Polity.

Ricks, T. E. (2006), *Fiasco: The American Military Adventure in Iraq*. London: Penguin.

Robertson, J. W. (2004), 'People's watchdogs or government poodles? Scotland's national broadsheets and the second Iraq war', *European Journal of Communication*, 19 (4): 457–82.

Robinson, J. (2007), Statement at hearing by Committee on Oversight and Government Reform, US House of Representatives, 24 April: http://oversight.house.gov/documents/20070424110022.pdf (accessed 3 October 2008).

Robinson, P. (2001), 'Theorising the influence of media on world politics: Models of media influence on foreign policy', *European Journal of Communication*, 16 (4): 523–44.

Robinson, P. (2002), *The CNN Effect: The Myth of News, Foreign Policy and Intervention*. London: Routledge.

Robinson, P. (2004), 'Researching US media-state relations and twenty-first century wars', in S. Allan and B. Zelizer (eds), *Reporting War: Journalism in Wartime*. Abingdon: Routledge.

Robinson, P., R. Brown, P. Goddard and K. Parry (2005), 'War and Media', *Media, Culture and Society*, 27 (6): 951–59.

Robinson, P., P. Goddard and K. Parry (2009), 'UK media and media management during the 2003 invasion of Iraq', *American Behavioral Scientist*, 52 (5): 678–88.

Robinson, P., P. Goddard, K. Parry and C. Murray (2009), 'Testing Models of Media Performance in Wartime: U.K. TV News and the 2003 Invasion of Iraq', *Journal of Communication*, 59 (3): 534–63.

Rogers, P. (2002), *Losing Control: Global Security in the Twenty-first Century* (2nd edn). London: Pluto Press.

Rojecki, A. (2008), 'Rhetorical alchemy: American exceptionalism and the War on Terror', *Political Communication*, 25 (1): 67–88.

Rothkopf, D. J. (1999), 'The disinformation age', *Foreign Policy*, 114: 82–96.

Ryan, S. (2003), 'Charities must stop rattling the tin over poor wounded Ali', *Daily Telegraph*, 16 April: 20.

Ryfe, D. M. (2006), 'Guest editor's introduction: New institutionalism and the news', *Political Communication*, 23 (2): 135–144.

Said, E. (1997), *Covering Islam: How the Media and the Experts Determine How We See the Rest of the World* (rev. edn). London: Vintage.

Sands, P. (2006), *Lawless World: America and the Making and Breaking of Global Rules*. London: Penguin.

Scarry, E. (1985), *The Body in Pain: The Making and Unmaking of the World*. New York: Oxford University Press.

Schlesinger, P. and H. Tumber (1994), *Reporting Crime: The Media Politics of Criminal Justice*. Oxford: Oxford University Press.

Schmidt, S. and V. Loeb, 'She was fighting to the death', *Washington Post*, 3 April 2003.

Schwalbe, C. B. (2006), 'Remembering our shared past: Visually framing the Iraq war on U.S. news websites', *Journal of Computer-Mediated Communication*, 12 (1): article 14.

Schwalbe, C. B. (2008), 'Visually framing the invasion and occupation of Iraq in *Time*, *Newsweek*, and *U.S. News & World Report*' (paper presented at the annual meeting of the Association for Education in Journalism and Mass Communication, Chicago, 6 August).

Seib, P. (2004), *Beyond the Front Lines: How the News Media Cover a World Shaped by War*. New York: Palgrave Macmillan.

Semetko, H. A., J. Blumler, M. Gurevitch and D. Weaver (1991), *The Formation of Campaign Agendas*. Hillsdale, NJ: Erlbaum.

Shapiro, A. (1999), 'The Internet', *Foreign Policy*, 115: 14–27.

Shaw, M. (1996) *Civil Society and Media in Global Crises*. London: Pinter.

Shaw, M. (2000), 'Media and public sphere without borders?: News coverage and power from Kurdistan to Kosovo', in B. L. Nacos, R. Y. Shapiro and P. Isernia (eds), *Decisionmaking in a Glass House: Mass Media, Public Opinion, and American and European Foreign Policy in the 21st Century*. Lanham, MD: Rowman and Littlefield.

Sigal, L. V. (1973), *Reporters and Officials*. Lexington, MA: D. C. Heath.

Silcock, B. W., C. B. Schwalbe and S. Keith (2008), '"Secret" casualties: Images of injury and death in the Iraq War across media platforms', *Journal of Mass Media Ethics*, 23 (1): 36–50.

Smith, A. (1986), *The Ethnic Origins of Nations*. Oxford: Basil Blackwell.

Smith, J., J. D. McCarthy, C. McPhail and B. Augustyn (2001), 'From protest to agenda building: Description bias in media coverage of protest events in Washington, DC', *Social Forces*, 79 (4): 1397–1423.

Sparrow, B. H. (1999), *Uncertain Guardians: The News Media as a Political Institution*. Baltimore: Johns Hopkins University Press.

Starkey, G. (2007), *Balance and Bias in Journalism: Representation, Regulation and Democracy*. Basingstoke: Palgrave Macmillan.

Taylor, P. M. (1997), *Global Communications, International Affairs and the Media Since 1945*. London: Routledge.

Thomson, A. (2006), 'The untold story from the battlefields of Afghanistan: A reporting ban from London is damaging the morale of our soldiers on the ground', *Guardian*, 25 September: www.guardian.co.uk/media/2006/sep/25/mondaymediasection.afghanistan (accessed 29 October 2009).

Thrall, A.T. (2000), *War in the Media Age*. Cresskill, NJ: Hampton Press.

Thussu, D. K. (2009), *News as Entertainment: The Rise of Global Infotainment* (2nd edn). London: Sage.

Thussu, D. K. and D. Freedman (eds) (2003), *War and the Media: Reporting Conflict 24/7*. London: Sage.

Timms, D. (2003), 'ITV news gets record ratings', *Guardian*, 25 March: www.guardian.co.uk/media/2003/mar/25/broadcasting.overnights (accessed 22 December 2008).

Travis, A. (2003), 'Support for war surges', *Guardian*, 25 March: www.guardian.co.uk/uk/2003/mar/25/politics.iraq (accessed 12 February 2009).

Tumber, H. (2001), '10pm and all that: The battle over UK TV news', in M. Bromley (ed.), *No News is Bad News: Radio, Television and the Public*. Harlow: Longman.

Tumber, H. and J. Palmer (2004), *Media at War: The Iraq Crisis*. London: Sage.

Tumber, H. and F. Webster (2006), *Journalists Under Fire: Information War and Journalistic Practices*. London: Sage.

Tunstall, J. (1996), *Newspaper Power: The New National Press in Britain*. Oxford: Oxford University Press.

UN Security Council (2002), 'Meeting 4644': www.undemocracy.com/securitycouncil/meeting_4644 (accessed 5 October 2009).

UN World Summit Agreement (2005), 14–16 September: www.un.org/summit2005/ (accessed 30 October 2009).

US Army (2003), 'Special report: Attack on 507th Maintenance Company' (posted July 18): www.army.mil/features/507thMaintCmpy/AttackOn507MaintCmpy.pdf (accessed 5 November 2008).

US House of Representatives (2008), 'Misleading information from the battlefield: Tillman and Lynch episodes', Committee on Oversight and Government Reform Report, July 17: http://oversight.house.gov/documents/20080714111050.pdf (accessed 3 October 2008).

Volkmer, I. (1999), *News in the Global Sphere: A Study Of CNN and its Impact on Global Communications*. Luton: University of Luton Press.

Wall, M. (2005), '"Blogs of war": Weblogs as news'. *Journalism*, 6 (2): 153–72.

Warren, J. (2004), *The Ali Abbas Story: The Moving Story of One Boy's Struggle for Life*. London: HarperCollins.

Wells, K. (2007), 'Narratives of liberation and narratives of innocent suffering: The rhetorical uses of images of Iraqi children in the British press', *Visual Communication*, 6 (1): 55–71.

Wells, M. (2003), 'Start of television war brings big ratings rise', *Guardian*, 28 March: www.guardian.co.uk/media/2003/mar/28/iraqandthemedia.tvnews (accessed 17 June 2008).

Wheeler, N. (2000), *Saving Strangers: Humanitarian Intervention in International Society*. Oxford: Oxford University Press.

White House (2003), 'Operation Iraqi Freedom: Coalition members': http://georgewbush-whitehouse.archives.gov/news/releases/2003/03/20030327–10.html (accessed 28 April 2009).

Whittle, S. (2002), 'War Guidelines: Editorial Policy Guidelines' (BBC internal document, BG (02) 146).

Wilson, W. (1918), 'Fourteen points', Address to Congress, 8 January: http://web.jjay.cuny.edu/jobrien/reference/ob34.html (accessed 14 April 2009).

Wolfsfeld, G. (1997), *Media and Political Conflict: News from the Middle East*. Cambridge: Cambridge University Press.

Wolfsfeld, G. (2008), 'Book Review: When the Press Fails: Political Power and the News Media from Iraq to Katrina – by W. Lance Bennett, Regina G. Lawrence & Steven Livingston', *Journal of Communication*, 58 (1): 198–9.

Wolfsfeld, G., P. Frosh and M. T. Awabdy (2008), 'Covering death in conflicts: Coverage of the Second Intifada on Israeli and Palestinian television', *Journal of Peace Research*, 45 (3): 401–17.

Young, P. and P. Jesser (1997), *The Media and the Military: From Crimea to Desert Strike*. London: Palgrave Macmillan.

Zaller, J. and D. Chiu (1999), 'Government's little helper: US press coverage of foreign policy crises, 1945–1999': www.sscnet.ucla.edu/polisci/faculty/zaller/Gov's%20 Little%20Helper/GovHelper.PDF (accessed 10 April 2009).

Zandberg, E. and M. Neiger (2005), 'Between the nation and the profession: Journalists as members of contradicting communities', *Media, Culture and Society*, 27 (1): 131–41.

Zeger, S. and E. Johnson (2007), 'Estimating excess deaths in Iraq since the US-British-led invasion', *Significance*, 4 (2): 54–9.

Index